THE COMPLETE BOOK OF SEX MAGIC

THE OTHER BOOKS IN THIS SERIES
BY LEONARD R. N. ASHLEY

The Complete Book Of The Devil's Disciples

The Complete Book Of Devils And Demons

The Complete Book Of Dreams And What They Mean

The Complete Book Of Ghosts And Poltergeists

The Complete Book Of Magic And Witchcraft

The Complete Book Of Spells, Curses, And Magical Recipes

The Complete Book Of Superstition, Prophecy, And Luck

The Complete Book Of Vampires

The Complete Book Of Werewolves

THE COMPLETE BOOK OF
SEX MAGIC

The characters should be graven on the inner side of the Ring

Leonard R. N. Ashley

BARRICADE BOOKS / NEW JERSEY

Published by Barricade Books Inc.
185 Bridge Plaza North
Suite 308-A
Fort Lee, NJ 07024
www.barricadebooks.com

Library of Congress Cataloging-in-Publication Data

Ashley, Leonard R. N.
    The complete book of sex magic / by Leonard R. N. Ashley
        p. cm.
    Contains text of Carmilla by J.S. Le Fanu.
    Includes bibliographical references and index.
    ISBN: 1-56980-226-2 (pbk. : alk. paper)
    1. Magic. 2. Sex--Miscellanea. I. Le Fanu, Joseph Sheridan, 1814-1873.
Carmilla. II. Title.

BF1623.S4 A 85 2002
133.4'3--dc21

                                                            2002016488

Manufactured in the United States of America

First Printing

FOR RAY LEWIS
whose suggestion it was
to end the series with this subject

Here then we shall write,

Here then we shall begin,
the words of old,

The beginnings

And the taproots.

So this then is what we shall collect,

The decipherment,

The clarification,

The explanation

Of the mysteries,

Of the illumination. . . .

We shall save it

Because there is no longer

A sight of the Book of Counsel,

Any sight of the things that come

from beside the ocean,

The description of our shadows. . . .

—*The Popul Vuh*,
The Book of Counsel of the
Quiché Maya of Guatemala

Table of Contents

Witches, using "broomsticks" annointed with hallucinogens, got high indeed, and the story went around that by magical means they flew to the sabbat. The person who made this old woodcut didn't know the tradition: because witches did everything in reverse, they flew on their broomsticks facing backward.

Read This First

In the tenth book of this occult series of mine, I express my thanks to a devoted public whose kind acceptance of my earlier volumes made this one possible. This time I'm concentrating on a subject that has naturally evolved in the course of discussing magic and witchcraft, spells, curses and magical recipes, vampires, werewolves, ghosts and poltergeists as well as the more sensible though no less complex interpretation of dreams, which are occult in the sense that they contain a hidden knowledge of ourselves. The subject I examine in this book is sex magic.

Magic is the urge to power. In *Ash Wednesday*, T. S. Eliot prays, "Teach us to sit still." Montaigne, in one of his essays, says that all the trouble of mankind comes from an inability to sit quietly in one's room. Some religions call on people to bear without emotion, to rise above mundane concerns and passing troubles, to detach, surrender, accept. But people devoted to magic are unwilling to take things as they come. They are rebels and, to use an awkward word just now popular, "pro-active." "To Hell," they say, with resignation or even contentment. They defy society. They defy God. They want change. And they're willing to fight others, society, God Himself, to effect that change.

The most sought after changes are in love and money, or perhaps money that buys love and acts as a substitute for it. Sex magic holds out the promise of wishes granted or achieved. It has been a big part of magic in all countries and all eras. I believe you will find it as fascinating a topic as I have, rummaging for you in dusty old books, encountering a crowd of crazies and some wonderfully interesting people.

I have no hesitation in telling you any secrets I have discovered. As the Abbot Johannes Heidenberg (1462–1516), a Benedictine, said: "In magic it is the practice that is dangerous, not the knowledge. . . ." I give you information but my advice is not to try these things for yourself. Knowledge is power. With power we must learn when to use it, how to use it, and when to leave it alone. We must understand its cost. The good abbot went on to say, as quoted in one of my earlier books:

> Every science is good in itself, but its operation is good or evil according to the end to which it is directed. . . . Magic is neither forbidden nor evil, since through the knowledge of it, one can avoid evil and do good. . . . Magic . . . is useful knowledge, but very dangerous when one gets to know nature in depth.

Witches confessed that they had to kiss the rear end of The Devil and the industrious Francesco Guazzo illustrated this in his *Compendium maleficarum* as late as the seventeenth century.

So read and enjoy but do not lose your common sense. For heaven's sake, literally, do not engage in practices that your own religion forbids, for guilt is a heavy burden to bear. Even if, unlike me, you happen to be one of the many people who practice witchcraft in the modern world, I hope you work your craft in the spirit of Gerald Gardner's *Modern Witchcraft* (1954), unconnected entirely with Satanism and the black arts, as happily and healthily as Wicca or the worship of the pagan Goddess. We professed Christians, who, as I write are responding to an attack on our country not by turning the other cheek but by rallying to "get the bastards," are not permitted to use magic. You witches and wizards, who suffer your own problems and grudges, ought to at least try to understand and tolerate each other. I hope we have evolved beyond the "Thou shalt not suffer a witch to live" idea. We can turn our homicidal rages or "dedication to justice" toward those outside our society, not those in it. It may serve somewhat to grout the cracks in the "glorious mosaic" of our fractured society.

Read about the history of sex magic, marvel at the recipes (but don't try them), and be entertained by the fascinating facts and colorful characters you will encounter.

As ever, if you wish to offer comments or corrections, do not hesitate to write to me in care of my publisher. Over the life of this series, the books have, I believe, improved with the suggestions of readers, *i.e.* the addition of stories and inclusions of bibliographies for those who wish to investigate further. I cannot undertake to answer all letters; but I assure you I read and appreciate them all. Like any teacher, I am always ready to learn.

Brooklyn, New York
The Feast of St. Jerome, 2002

1
Sex with Demons

SEX MAGIC

Since the time of earliest man, magic has involved both the real, like shamans and witch doctors, and the imaginary, such as demons and phantasms. It has had a wide variety of practitioners in every culture. There were oracles and fortune-tellers, rainmakers and sorcerers, devil worshippers and exorcists, and practitioners of a variety of occult sciences or pseudosciences. There were people who took the Left-Hand Path of transgressive (prohibited) magic—who worked for personal gain. Others performed magical rites as honored priests; they served the society as a whole and enjoyed the support of rulers and state religions. Both kinds of magicians served, and sacrificed to, higher forces in the search for protection and power.

I don't presume to know whether leaders first became aware of a positive creating power and practiced religion in the tribe's best interest before sinking into black arts, or simply organized religions to allay superstitious fear when magic failed them. Indeed, I find it virtually impossible to divorce magic from religion or religion from magical belief. Dr. Margaret Murray, a debated historian, said she would not, in fact could not, distinguish between religion and magic. A less controversial scholar, Max Weber, wrote a *Sociology of Religion*, which is to my mind essentially indistinguishable from a sociology of magic.

In a way, I do not care whether magic is the genesis of religion or a degenerate product of it. I happen to be more interested in the extent and the manner in which the occult sciences became the hard sciences: how alchemy led to chemistry, astrology led to astronomy, how we discovered that disease is due to the presence of germs and not possession by demons. To me, the significance

1

Demons at the mouth of Hell from an old French *Book of Demonology*.

of magic and religion is that the two are almost inextricably linked and have shaped both individuals and the cultures in which they have operated. Both are crucial components of human history.

This book will not attempt to discuss a history or a philosophy of magic and religion, but will demonstrate how human sexuality and magic have been and remain closely connected. I venture to say that any book with the words *Sex* and *Magic* in its title will appeal to a large readership. Whether a person believes in it or not, he or she cannot deny that staunch believers have existed through generations of mankind. That is a matter of great interest—some would say great concern. Here I propose to present a difficult subject in as accurate but also as entertaining a fashion as I can, creating short entries suited to modern attention spans.

I believe that anyone curious enough to pick up this book and dip into it anywhere will find enough material of interest to read the whole thing, for amazement and amusement.

And now let's get down to business. I'll not begin with an appetizer of colorful facts, which has been my method in the past, but with a substantial and nourishing minestrone. The first chapter deals with the sexually charged archetype of demons that attack us while we sleep: *incubi* and *succubi*. Like much else in magic,

the *incubi* and *succubi* can be considered symbols. Like the symbols of our dreams, they point to waking realities.

DEMONS AND THE JEWS

It was the Jews principally who turned the *daimones* (spirits) into demons. Among the Jews the demons of sex were about the worst. Here is what the authoritative *Encyclopedia of Judaism* (edited by Geoffrey Wigoder, 1989) says about magic and sorcery, and why it was officially abandoned under the new dispensation of the One God:

> Since the ancient Israelites lived in a civilization in which magic was commonplace, many biblical provisions are directed to opposing sorcery of any type. Any belief in the ability of magic to attain certain ends is seen to contradict the omnipotence of God, who cannot be influenced by any human device. Even the Bible requires the death penalty for certain types of individuals who practice magic (Ex. 22: 17; Lev. 20: 27). Witchcraft and divination by the *teraphim* (household idols) are identified with rebellion (I Sam. 15: 23). Sorcerers and astrologers are the personification of delusion (Isa. 47: 12–15; Jer. 10: 2–3). . . . The Mishnah (*Sanh[edrin]*. 7: 7) equates magic with idolatry. The biblical commandment to execute witches (Ex. 22: 17) is widened to include male sorcerers as well (*Sanh*. 67a). According to the Talmud the practitioner of magic was to be put to death only when a magical act was performed, not when there was mere delusion.

Thus in the sacred Torah (in which Moses performs magic), and in Jewish commentaries that interpret and modify the basic religion, magic and sorcery were recognized but deemed punishable if and when successful. Actually the most religious of Jews not only continued some of the superstitions of the Assyrians, Babylonians, Chaldeans and others down the alphabet, but borrowed the magic performed by the High Priest, *i.e.* foretelling the future using dice concealed behind the breastplate of that highest office. Later there were to be *ba'alé shem* (wonder workers) among the rabbis of seventeenth- and eighteenth-century Eastern Europe. Were they performing miracles or magic? Was Rabbi Loew of Prague defying Jewish prescriptions against magic when he created the *golem*, or could sorcery be allowed conditionally, as when the Witch of Endor called up the dead for King Saul?

In Jewish religion there is always a tension between the dogmatic and the practical. There is also, if I may say so, an admirable openness to reason. Among the rabbis, reason and logic are honored but always, always, questions are asked. Let me ask a question. Is the *mezuzah* not essentially an amulet such as earlier peoples used and Jews tried to forbid?

Every Orthodox Jewish household has one; a little box nailed to the doorpost. Inside of it is a pious prayer for protection. This looks like religion to me, but many would rank it (and the Hand of Fatima, and the St. Christopher medal) as gross superstition or witchcraft. Is it realistic to expect religion to be without contradiction?

From the beginning of the Judeo-Christian world, the Jews gave us good reasons for condemning the witch and sorcerer as enemies of human society and divine law. From that was to come the bloody history of witchcraft in the west as well as, perversely, the oppression of the Jews themselves by the Christians.

THE DOCTOR IS IN

Although this book will offer, as promised, brief and easy approaches to complex matters, we must begin with a rather extended medical consultation involving a certain German physician, John Weirius, to address the issue of the incubus

MEDICE, CURA TEIPSUM.

"Doctor, cure thyself."

and succubus. Stay with us, because this discussion is a starting point that will put all the rest into perspective. If you must skip it for the more accessible bits of the book, come back later when the subject as a whole entrances you.

In 1991 George Mora, M.D., and a group of editors published the first English translation of a book called *De Præstigiis dæmonum*, making available to a much wider scholarly audience an obscure work written by a sixteenth-century Belgian physician known by the Latin name Johannes Wierus. In his

Witches, Devils, and Doctors in the Renaissance Wierus is listed as Johann Weyer, a name by which he became popularly known. It is a milestone work containing the early history of psychology and medicine, a compendium of superstition and folklore.

The work is in the Germanic style of the medieval disputation, the arguments meticulously marshaled and supported by copious classical documentation. As a serious medical book it brought recognition to many physicians who wrote in Arabic, for the Moors brought a great deal of medical knowledge to Europe, and directed attention to some big names in Arab science (names that were westernized in Weyer's text).

His writing is profoundly erudite and, for its time, pioneering. It antedates even Reginald Scot's *Discouerie of Witchcraft* (1595) in its assertion that magical beliefs are purely delusional yet unquestionably dangerous.

The Jews had said witchcraft could be either delusional or real. The Christian Weyer says it is all delusion, that one cannot really break the laws of God and Nature and perform magic. Others disagreed. In fact, German dissertations on magic continued until about the end of the eighteenth century. Afterwards there were German secret societies devoted to magic; they exist to this day. Dr. Weyer favored traditional religion. He was also extraordinarily versed in medical science rather than steeped in the dogma and politics of his new age.

The existence of his writings emphasizes how extensive our history of sex magic is, one not without importance in the context of world history. A careful study and rejection of its impostures is not something that began with modern thinking. It is not only connected to religious history but to medicine and psychology. Today, many people turn to psychiatrists as they turned to priests in the past. To a great extent psychology is the new theology. Sex magic is a crucial area of interest where these two disciplines intersect.

Dr. Weyer was a thorough student of both. By Book III he has worked his way to the following passage. It is worth quoting in full for its history of psychology as well as medicine, and to demonstrate that neither Freud nor any of his contemporaries were first to see the central importance of human sexuality or the connections between psychosis and magical thinking. Additionally they were the first to notice that delusions could cause psychosomatic illness.

Now let us approach the subject of spectral *incubi* and *succubi*, carefully investigating the broad question of whether there is any truth involved therein, so that this image of false belief may be banished once and for all from the minds of not only the common people but also persons of some judgment. And so I shall prove by the clearest argumentation that although old women, deluded and maddened by the evildoing and trickery of this heresy [witchcraft], think that they are pressed by a demon and that they are subject to *incubi*, this sexual mingling, like almost all their other experiences, is purely imaginary, the result of an impaired mind, or else it is simply the case that they are tit-

IOANNIS VVIERI

DE PRAE-
STIGIIS DAEMO-
num, & incantationibus ac ue-
neficiis Libri fex, poftrema
editione fexta aucti &
recogniti.

ACCESSIT
LIBER APOLOGE-
TICVS,
ET
PSEVDOMONARCHIA
DAEMONVM.

Cum Rerum ac uerborum copiofo
INDICE.

Cum Cæf.Maieft.Regiſq; Galliarum gratia
& priuilegio.

BASILEAE, EX OFFICINA
Oporiniana. 1583.

Title page of the 1583 edition of *De praestigiis daemonum*. Courtesy, Vassar
College Library.

Title page of Johann Weyer's book of 1583.

illated by some sort of friction, helped on by their imaginings. And I shall show that intercourse does not truly occur, after I have *first* pointed out that our medical men do refer to a certain disease as *Incubus*, from *incubare*, "to lie upon," because we think that a weight is lying upon us and is on top of us as we sleep, stopping our breathing and therefore impeding our voice; so that if we wish to cry out, we cannot do so, and we have many horrible dreams and imaginings, thinking that we are being attacked by others. It usually occurs by night and at the beginning of sleep, and what epileptics experience by day and when waking, persons subject to nightmare experience at night and while asleep. Pliny sometimes called it "suppressions," sometimes "nocturnal illusions," and sometimes "the illusions caused by Fauns during our repose." The Arabs called it *albedilon* and *alcratum* according to Avicenna, and *Elgadum* according to Averroes, and *alcaibum* according to Azaravius. Our own people commonly call it "heaviness," as though a weight were crushing us by "riding upon us," as they say. And so in their own tongue our countrymen say *"Die mar rydet uns"* [the mare is riding us]. Some think it to be a mild form of epilepsy, which occurs during dreams, and Aristotle was familiar with it—see his book *On Sleep and Wakefulness*. It is called *ephialtes* or "the pouncer" by the Greeks, as though someone forcefully leaps upon another and presses him down so that he cannot move until delivered from his assailant. Themison names it *pnignalion*, from the Greek word for suffocating. These symptoms proceed from the lessening of heat, and they occur when the vital spirits in the brain are darkened by phlegm and melancholia because of ascending vapors, so that their strength is overwhelmed and something heavy seems to be weighing upon them, although it does not really exist. Incubus or nightmare occurs when one is lying supine, and usually when the mouth of the stomach is oppressed with thick and viscous phlegm or an abundance of hard-to-digest food. Now, since *sagæ* or witches are for the most part "phlegmatic" by virtue of their sex and age and "melancholic" because of the state of their mind, why should they not be vulnerable to this malady when lying supine? And when we add to this the corruption of their common sense by the constant promptings of an unclean spirit, they will then think and admit that they have truly that which has become known to them only through sleep or through an overactive imagination. I have seen fit to include at this point a pertinent story from the writings of Jason of Prato. It concerns an idle priest and it goes as follows.

Quite recently a priest met up with me. He said, "Sir, unless you help a wretched and afflicted man, it is all over for me and I am done for—because I am wasting away. Do you see how emaciated I am, how feeble? My thin skin barely covers me, whereas I am usually plump and rather good-looking and in good health. Now I seem a gruesome specter, the empty image of a man" "What is tormenting you," I said. "And what do you suppose to be the cause of your affliction?" "I will tell you frankly," he said, "and you will

Artemis as Selene, Goddess of the Moon.

be amazed. Almost every night a woman, not unknown to me, slides onto my breast and presses me with great force, and constricts my air passages so that I can hardly breathe. Indeed, when I wish to cry out, she stops up the channel for my voice, and though I try to raise my voice, I cannot. Nor can I free my hands, to ward off the attack, or my feet, to take flight. She keeps me bound and chained." "Well, now, there is nothing remarkable in what you say," I replied with a gentle laugh (for I knew from his description that it was a case of Incubus). "It is pure imagination, simple illusion." Without further delay, he said, "Imagination and illusion it assuredly is not! So help me God, what I describe I have seen with my own eyes, encountered with my own hands. While awake and in full possession of my faculties, I see her before me, I receive her assault, and I attempt to struggle against her. But because of my weakness, my fear, my distress, and the force that she brings to bear against me, I accomplish nothing. Therefore, I have run madly hither and thither, asking everyone whether he can help a person who is perishing wretchedly. I consulted a Franciscan Friar, who was said to be a shrewd and wily fellow, and I hoped for some immediate help, but I was frustrated totally, and he provided no salvation. He merely advised me to pray earnestly to Almighty God (Whom I had already wearied with prayers) that He deign to avert this troublesome vexation. Then I went to an old woman who was popularly reported to be a 'cunning wise woman' or witch. She told me how, at daybreak, right after urinating, I should stop up the chamber pot with my right boot, and on that very day the woman that was working the evil—the *maleficia*—would visit me. Although the scheme seemed pointless to me and I was not a little deterred from trying it by my religious beliefs, nevertheless, overcome by my powerlessness and the weariness that resulted from my long struggles, I did make the attempt. And, by Jove, the predictions came true. Coming to my house, the *maleficia* complained of terrible bladder pains; but neither

by threats nor entreaties could I get her to agree not to visit me repeatedly at night in frightful form. She has continued her long-standing
habits implacably, and has decided to finish me off for good with gruesome torment." Scarce any line of reasoning enabled me to recall this
man from his madness, but after our second or third meeting, he
became more cheerful and began to acknowledge his illness and to
conceive a hope of regaining his health.

THE DOCTOR AND THE HUMOURS

Dr. Weyer is off-track because he is, like the physicians of his time and for
some time afterwards, relying on the doctrine of humours advanced by the
Greek physician Galen, connecting illness to the imbalance in the system of
the four elements (earth, fire, air, water). The theory proposes that too much
water in the system causes "black melancholy." Greek medicine of this sort
was long in vogue, as were the prescriptions of Discorides, which lasted well
into the modern age, during which the treatment for humours entailed bleeding the patient. Aristotle was wrong in his belief that the brain was not used
for thinking but for cooling the blood, any excess heat bringing disorder to
the system. In the seventeenth century, Charles II was literally bled to death;
neither bleeding nor plasters of pigeon dung saved him.

SUFFERING THE SUCCUBUS

The patient needed treatment for gastric reflux, perhaps, which could be
treated by diet, and the real trouble was a stoppage that caused him occasionally
and briefly to cease breathing when asleep but was ameliorated automatically
when he woke and sat up. Today his sleep apnea might send him to a dentist
for an oral device that would keep his air coming regularly while sleeping. In
those days tooth-pullers knew of no such thing.

The patient should have been advised to sleep sitting up, supported by
pillows. Had the physician convinced him that would work, the patient's psychology would likewise assist in the cure, for a medical diploma is as powerful as a witch doctor's staff in inducing belief in authority.

In this case, the patient was a priest, and a celibate one, because this incident, reported by Jason of Prato, is pre-Reformation. For centuries, though
not at first, the clergy of the Roman Catholic Church were called upon by
tradition (though not by doctrine) to take vows of celibacy.

This priest's sexual urges rather than those of any *malificia* should be taken
into account, as well as his guilt over nocturnal visitations. Despite the fact
that he was a priest, he turned to a "wily" friar, which belies a touch of the
anti-friar sentiment found even in the Roman Catholic Church in the Middle Ages, let alone exacerbated by the Protestant Reformation. When that did

The *Succubus* from Mathias de Giraldo, OP's *Histoire curieuse et pittoresque des sorciers, augmentée par M. Fornari,* 1854.

not work he, like many of his less religious coreligionists, reverted to forbidden, pagan superstition. He went to consult a witch.

Presumably this produced more guilt and no relief, although he does report that the "predictions" came true! Did the witch send the woman to him? That seems the most obvious explanation.

By God (or by Jove)! What he needed was both medical and psychological treatment. As with magic, belief in the operation has solved his problem.

This is an interesting example of alleged nocturnal sexual visitations suffered by the innocent, against whom witchcraft is accused, rather than wizards or witches who performed magical rites in order to enjoy sexual release.

SEX FOR FUN

Some practitioners of magic indulged in orgies at the sabbat or during rites in which mind-blowing drugs were rubbed on the skin, which is better than injecting, breathing or swallowing. Drugs were also burned in braziers, purportedly as incense pleasing to diabolical entities. Some witches claimed to

Lilith Bound for a Mesopotamian spell.

have sex with the Devil and some actively sought to induce the sexual visits of demons.

After all, the church had assured them they would not get pregnant, an important matter for the unmarried woman in an age when there was no such thing as a single-parent family. Some charitable clergy encouraged women who gave birth to illegitimate children just to leave them on the steps of the church. They were taken in and raised as servants of the church, including monks and nuns. That is where such Italian surnames as Esposito (Exposed), De Angelis (Of the Angels) and della Chiesa (of the Church) came from. Poor and isolated women—and witches were usually these—could not afford to bring up bastards. Old women, another group that comprised the witch population, could not conceive anyway. The church decried that all such women as well as unmarried men ought to do without sex. No way, said some renegades.

Here is the early Christian theologian John Cassian in his *Collations* 2: 8 on the subject of whether sex with demons (which he was certain could happen) could make one pregnant:

> We must in no way believe that spiritual natures can naturally have intercourse with women, because if this could have happened once, in a literal sense, how would it not be the case that the same thing happens now also—whether frequently or rarely—and that some persons are born without the seed or the sexual act of a man? Similarly we would observe demons to be conceived by women.

A demon has sex with a sleeping woman in this fourteenth-century illumination from a manuscript.

Let us leave aside what John Cassian should have known. That "it happened once, in a literal sense" that a spirit caused Mary to conceive with no assistance from man. That is how Jesus was born. That is why, as a matter of fact, many early opponents of Christianity, quite apart from the miracles he performed, said He was a Magician and not a Messiah. See what early objections to Jesus the pious Christians permitted to survive and read M. Smith's *Jesus the Magician* (1978) or, better, E. V. Gallagher's *Divine Man or Magician: Celsus and Origen on Jesus* (1982). Note that in documents recently unearthed in the east dating from about the time of the *Dead Sea Scrolls* Jesus is flatly accused of being a magician: it is alleged that Mary bore him illegitimately, was forced out of or fled Judea and went to Egypt with the child. There Jesus was brought up and taught the same kind of magic that the Egyptian named Moses is recording as using in competition with the magicians of the pharaohs.

Christ tempted by demons.

Christians do not believe that Jesus was a mere magician. The Immaculate Conception, avoiding thereby the sin of Adam, makes it difficult for us merely human Christians, guilty of Original Sin, to achieve what St. Thomas à Kempis beautifully calls *The Imitation of Christ*. However, it was in fact that virgin birth that was to give our Savior his singular power. "Not of woman born" was supposed to give one the power to perform miracles.

Think of Banquo, who fulfilled the requirement described by the witches, defeating Macbeth in Shakespeare's play. Banquo was born merely by Caesarian operation. True, that is cheating on "not of woman born," because of course he was born of a woman though not in the usual way, but witches cheat. You knew that. Macbeth knew that, but like everyone dabbling in witchcraft or seeking to profit from it, he didn't get his thoughts together about these "fiends who lie like truth," and always cheat.

Much later than John Cassian, the church disagreed with his conviction regarding demonic parents. The Catholic Church started the rumor that Martin Luther was sired by a demon. How else, they asked, could you explain The Reformation?

Johann Klein's 1731 report on Satan copulating with humans.

Wizards and witches, especially, believed that demons could be deliberately summoned for sex as well as sent to trouble others with it, or to prevent others from enjoying sex. Selfishness and a resistance to the natural order of things—born, breed, die—lie at the very heart of magic.

Some rites of magic are devoted to getting sexual partners. Dr. Weyer said the women who claimed to be having sex with demons were lying or deluded: examine their hymens and see that they still are virginal! Of course men did have what later were politely called "nocturnal emissions" but these were to be explained by physics, not demons extracting semen.

Men are notably interested in using the semen the body produces. When Dr. Faustus sells his soul to Lucifer, Mephistopheles summons up for him the beautiful Helen of Troy (played, wordlessly, in the movie by Elizabeth Taylor). Faustus was looking for fun with the Seven Deadly Sins and with Helen (whose very name means Trouble), not for an heir.

He claimed he was seeking knowledge but to say he was after carnal knowledge is not inaccurate. He was to waste the magical powers given to him—and the magical powers of his God-given seed, not to mention his God-given reason. His very body rebels against this hideous sale of a soul. When he stabs his arm to sign the deed of gift with his own blood, it refuses to run until heated up. Symbolically it signals passion overcoming nature. A message, in Latin, of course, appears on his arm the import of which might be rendered, "Man, beat it out of here!" After his soul is sold, he has no restraint.

No pregnancies when sex magic is used are ever involved. Pregnancies were God's reason for sex, said the church. Sex as recreation was The Devil's idea.

IS MAGIC ALL-BAD?

The fathers of the Christian church apparently did not condemn magic out of hand, though at that time magic was certainly everywhere. Origen notes that there are various kinds of magic and seems to approve of the occult insofar as that means delving into the secrets of nature. Origen says that magic for healing is good. Some opponents of Christianity faulted it for its own magical beliefs. Celsus, you will hear, went after Jesus as a magician. In the next century after Celsus a man called Hierocles (as Eusebius records) attacked Jesus, calling Him a mere magician.

DOES THIS SOUND LIKE ANYONE YOU KNOW?

Dom Thomas Malvenda, OP in *Antichrist* (1604) describes the devilish offspring of an incubus as "from a natural cause . . . tall, very hard and bloodily bold, arrogant beyond words, and desperately wicked."

ST. JOHN CHRYSOSTOM'S NARROW ESCAPE

The father of the early Christian church I happen to favor is Tertullian. He has his faults, some of which might be excused if we had all of what he wrote. But there is another one whose work has come down to us mostly complete; 13 huge folios in the Benedictine edition, written by Suidas, indicate that this man preached and wrote so much that only God Almighty could construct his bibliography. This highly prolific holy man was John, called Chrysostom— Golden Mouth—for he was a superb preacher in the Bible-thumping tradition. Let me tell you a little about him.

John (b. 347) came along in the fourth century of our era and did not get his epithet of Chrysostom until the fifth, by which time his writings were part of the cornerstone of a burgeoning religion that had survived persecution and spread with great rapidity, significantly assisted by preaching and writing such as his own.

John was born of a good family. His father was a successful soldier, but John became a man of peace. He was converted to Christianity in his native city of Antioch, where St. Paul had preached, and at one point tried to become a monk. Many sincere early Christians became monks, hermits and anchorites, removing themselves from the sinful world. But John, one biographer tells us, returned to public life "not being able to extirpate the instincts of human nature." I do not know if that means sex or not, but it was often a problem for such men, as we see in the temptations of St. Anthony and the sex scandals involving priests today.

Having been a monk (AD 370–381), John returned to Antioch as a deacon and a preacher (AD 381–398). He attempted to avoid being consecrated a bishop, though he tricked his best friend into that. In AD 398 be was made bishop of Constantinople. He remained in that see until he was exiled (AD 404–407). He devoted much of his adult life to God.

He saw the magicians of Antioch as enemies and pressed to have them driven out or executed. It got to be that if you were found in Antioch with what the French were much later to call a *grimoire* (a book of magical rites and recipes) you would be killed. He claimed to have one day happened upon some leaves of a book floating in the river Orontes and gathered them up. They appear to be, if not a Devil-spawned temptation, from a book that some frightened magician had discarded. He was almost caught with this material but, seeing a soldier approaching, threw the damned leaves back into the river. He remained a foe of magic all his life, afraid of what it could do to both body and soul.

SÉANCES

The nineteenth century saw the rise of the séance, but mediumship did not really take off until millions of people were killed in World War I. On occasion, mediums would offer more than jangling tambourines and airborne trumpets or "apports" such as roses. Customers swore human beings would materialize. On 25 September 1877, for instance, a medium—for once a male, a Mr. Monck—brought "exquisite womanhood" to the séance room by his black magic. Archdeacon Colley, who reported being touched in more ways than one by this apparition, commented that it was "damp and stone cold." Sex demons are said to be like that.

DISRUPTIVE FORCES

Now let's consider a bit about body and soul and the perils of magic. Magic has always been considered a disruptive force. No sooner had societies got what they wanted from the sorcerers on whom they utterly relied to propitiate angry gods and defend humanity against disaster and disease, than they began to worry about how wise women might overcome men and magicians might topple kings. According to the *Encyclopedia of Early Christianity* (1997), magic was regarded as "threatening, anti-social, immoral, and criminal." After all, magicians, as we cannot overstate, are out for themselves and to Hell with other people.

Beelzebub, The Lord of the Flies from
Colin de Plancy's *Dictionnaire infernal*.

The Ship of Religion from *The Pilgrimage of Man.*

Then Jesus arrived, along with a number of self-declared Messiahs, as prophesied by Isaiah. The Romans regarded Jesus as a threat to the body politic. Herod, governing Judæa for the Romans, did his best to kill Him soon after His birth. His parents took him to Egypt, a country famous for its magic (as the Egyptian called Moses would demonstrate against the Egyptians themselves and in favor of the Jews). Jesus grew up to claim He was the Son of God, a term frequently applied to magicians.

By his goodness and charisma He drew apostles to him. Celsus, in the second century, deemed Christianity a popular religion infected by the magic of the Chaldeans and the Persians (whose Magi gave us the word *magic* and the term *magus* for magician). Celsus also denounced Jesus Christ as a mountebank who had "won over only ten sailors and tax collectors of the most abominable character"—and come to no good end.

Celsus and other opponents of the disturbing new Jewish religion declared that the baptism of Jesus by John the Baptist launched a political campaign, not a religious movement, and that Christ had been rejected by the Jews simply because he was a magician rather than a politician. He could offer them miracles and the promise of life eternal but refused to be their king and offer them revolution, or a Jewish state of their own.

"Render therefore unto Cæsar the things which are Cæsar's" may have been a clever rabbinical response to a difficult question but it did not go down well with what we may call Early Zionists. The Romans eventually destroyed the Jewish temple and scattered the Jews in a diaspora, which modern Zionism aimed to correct. That did not require magic. The founder of modern

Zionism knew what he was up against but said that it would succeed not only because Jews would see it was good but because, "anti-Semites will help us," if only for the wrong motives.

Even Christians had to admit there was some magic in their religion, not just vestigial superstitions from early Judaism. Christian baptism, for instance, is a magical act of transformation. The pagan becomes a Christian and, as Tertullian and other early fathers of the church said, it takes us out of the grip of innumerable demons and puts us under the protection of the One True God. Magically. The transubstantiation of the Mass is magic, effected by the incantation of *hoc est corpus*, or hocus-pocus.

Three of the gospels report the miracles performed by Jesus. John's is more Greek and philosophical than the others, but famously begins with the magic "word that creates"—the Greek *logos*. However, Jesus did not attribute his miracles to magic but to God. He or God in the Person of the Holy Spirit did equip the apostles with magical powers. Simon Magus, the famous magician from whom we get the word *simony* for the despicable act of selling church benefices, offered to buy the magic tricks of St. Peter.

The public was converted not only on the basis of Christ's good ideas and fine promises but also to some extent by the confidence apostles showed in the power of God and His miracles (the "armor of righteousness"). They were also swayed, frankly, by miracles performed in the earliest days of the establishment of Christianity and down through the centuries by its saints. You cannot get to be canonized, you cannot get to be a saint, without some miracles.

Every single saint created by the pope in recent years—and there have been more than the earlier church would ever have contemplated—have performed, to the satisfaction of very cautious ecclesiastics, what they declare to be unquestionable miracles.

Christ performed magic, the holiest humans of all performed magic, the *Acts of the Apostles* records early Christian magic and apostles' battles against rival magicians from the ranks of the pagans. As we shall see in a subsequent chapter, later Christianity was burdened by Christians' tenacious faith in Jewish and pagan magical beliefs and practices.

Now, where does sex magic come into this? Jesus performed no sex magic. The closest he ever came to a miracle with the slightest connection to sex involved catering a wedding. If you will bear with me I think I can say something inspirational about that.

To please His holy mother and the guests when the wine ran short, Jesus turned water into wine. I like his motives in this (as in the miracle of the loaves and fishes) but I have to admit that water-to-wine was one of the standard magical tricks of his day. As children we watched chemical experiments in class wherein a clear liquid transformation to red liquid was indeed impressive. Of course we did not taste the result and the friends of Jesus and His holy mother must have been called upon to test His. Or, and this is simply my idea, could it be that the miracle of water-into-wine was something other than a color change?

Could it be that Jesus' power was to change people? Consider this: Jesus' power was such that He made ordinary people better in His presence. When the wine was running out, perhaps He influenced people to be more *Christian* and to say to their brothers and sisters, "Well, there isn't much wine, so I'll just drink water and pretend it is wine. You take the wine. Go ahead." I suggest the same thing might have occurred with the miracle of the loaves and fishes: a little can go a very long way and satisfy all if each person has learned unselfishness and charity, "No, you have it. Your need is greater than mine. I'm OK."

I believe that Jesus' sermons and example were able to perform *those* miracles, which are, in my view, stupendous. He taught us to conquer our selfish nature, a great gift, for man does not live by wine or loaves and fishes alone.

As for sex magic, sex can be healthful or make us sick in mind and body, like wine. "Take a little wine fir thy stomach's sake," is the biblical injunction. Use sex for its proper purposes, and it is another great gift. If you prostitute sex in sex magic, you disrupt society, pervert yourself, and go against the God that gave you the things you misuse. There is the disruption.

THE POPE AND HIS *SUCCUBUS*

Walter Mape (or Mapes) in his collection of anecdotes, some scurrilous or satiric, tells in his *De Nugis curialium* (On the Trifles of Courtiers, c. 1185) with a straight face and expects to be believed that one of the popes had a *succubus*. He meant Gerbert d'Aurillac, who reigned as Sylvester II (999–1003).

Gerbert as a young man fell in love with the daughter of the provost of Rheims. She rejected him and he moped. One day he came upon a gorgeous maiden, seated on silks, surrounded by money. She said her name was Meridiana and volunteered to be his faithful lover and teach him black magic so he could become rich and famous. Who could turn down a deal like that?

Gerbert immediately forgot about the provost's daughter. He used black magic to become archbishop of Rheims, then cardinal archbishop of Ravenna, finally pope. He and Meridiana had sex every night throughout this rapid rise and so attractive did Gerbert become that once, when he was drunk, the daughter of the provost of Rheims seduced him. But he remained basically faithful to his *succubus*, though not to his priestly vows of chastity.

At last Meridiana told him his death was coming: he would die in Jerusalem. Though he had been planning a pilgrimage to the Holy City, the pope decided to cancel the trip. His caution did him no good. He fell ill and was taken to a church called Jerusalem (because it boasted a relic of the True Cross, which St. Helena, the mother of Constantine the Great, had found). At the very end, Pope Sylvester is said to have confessed his sins and begged forgiveness.

Mape adds that the tomb of Pope Sylvester II "weeps" moisture every time a pope is about to die. Those *papabile* now, with an aged pontiff, must be keeping an eye on it.

SOME OTHER MEDIEVAL SEX ESCAPADES

The hagiography of St. Bernard (*Sancti Bernardi vita*) says that when the saint was in Nantes in 1135 a woman came to him in the confessional and said she had been having an affair with an *incubus* for years but eventually her husband discovered it and left her. The *incubus* kept coming. What should she do? The saint gave her "his staff" to take to bed with her, which seems to have driven

Artemis Tauropolos

Artemis Tauropolos

off the demon. St. Bernard then preached a sermon against demons, exorcized this one, and, when the members of the congregation blew out their candles, the demon was snuffed.

Cæsarius of Heisterbach in his *Dialogus* (*c.* 1230) repeated the experience of St. Bernard and told another tale. A father learned that his daughter was being visited by a sexy demon and sent her away. The demon was so angry he struck the father in the chest with such force that the father died three days later. The demon presumably had to find another bed partner, or maybe he discovered where the girl had been sent and took up with her again.

There are many other such tales from the Middle Ages. At Toulouse in 1275, Angela de la Barthe was put to death for having sexual relations with a demon and giving birth to a monster that had the head of a wolf and the tail of a serpent. She had the dubious distinction of being the first woman burned alive in France for witchcraft. With that monstrous baby, she had no defense. In medieval times, any monstrous births (and many were rumored if not seen) were blamed on diabolical forces.

St. Bonaventura (Fra Giovanni di Fidanza, 1221–1274) explained how sex demons obtain semen from men and use it to impregnate women (useful in explaining pregnancy to a husband away on a crusade):

> Devils in the form of women yield to males and receive their semen; by cunning skill the demons preserve its potency and later, with the permission of God, they become incubi and pour it into female repositories.

I don't like that "with the permission of God," but I guess all sin is "with the permission of God," for in the religious view how could we do anything that God did not permit?

The husbands also had to worry that the demons' performance surpassed their own. In some cases women complained that sex with demons was unpleasant but medieval men tended to judge women as lustful, and seductive toward the demons. Demons were said to be tireless lovers and their ministrations many times better than an ordinary erotic dream.

The official church doctrine (in the *Canon epsicopi* for the instruction of bishops) at first judged it all as dirty dreams and mere delusions, but at the height of witchcraft persecutions sex with demons was not only considered possible but terribly widespread.

Sex was given as one of the main reasons weak women were drawn into the world of witchcraft. This position was maintained, with only a few dissenters, until about the Age of Reason and, in some places, beyond it.

SEX WITH DEMONS IN THE FIFTEENTH CENTURY

The Inquisition did not start out as a campaign against *incubi* and *succubi*; it went after witches and sorcerers for other reasons. But, from about 1430 onwards, prosecutions on charges of sex with demons became a reality. In time they were the highlight of any really good trial for witchcraft. Salacious details were in curious demand as the Inquisition progressed. According to the American historian of witchcraft, Henry C. Lea, "The curiosity of the judges was insatiable to learn all the possible details as to sexual intercourse [with The Devil or demons], and their industry in pushing the examinations was rewarded by an abundance of foul imaginations."

After the accusation and the tortures the trial would be held, the witnesses heard, the verdict arrived at, the sentence passed, the chairs in the hall upended, the procession formed, and the witch burned. She was taken to the pyre accompanied by officials and townsfolk. In Germany, one source says, the proces-

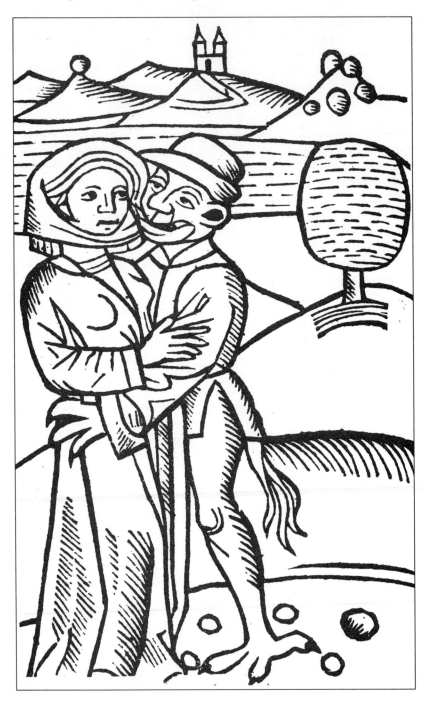

A Devil gets very friendly with a woman. From Ulrich Molitor's *De Lamiis* (*Of Lamias*, 1489).

sion would be headed by a choir of schoolchildren singing *Gott der Vater wohn uns bei* (God the Father Abide with Us). If you were lucky, you were strangled or beheaded before your body was burned.

SEX WITH A DEMON IN THE SIXTEENTH CENTURY

In 1594 a young woman was tried by the *parlément* (court) of Aquitaine. She related how her Italian boyfriend took her to a witches' sabbat:

> Afterwards the Italian boy took her again to the same place and then the goat [a demon in goat form] asked the girl for a tress or lock of her hair, which the Italian boy cut and gave to it. By this token the goat took her aside as his mate into the nearby woods and, pressing her down on the ground, entered her. But the girl reported that she found this completely lacking in any pleasant sensation but rather experienced a very sharp pain and a sense of horror at the goat's semen, which was as cold as ice.

She may have been lucky, at that. It seems that at some sabbats persons wearing strap-ons of leather or horn may have treated witches roughly. Some reported objects, either smaller than the usual phallus, "like a finger," or large, "like a horse's," "like a mule's," that were incredibly hard.

Henri Boguet, Chief Judge of St.-Claude in the Jura region of France, burned some 600 witches in the Burgundy area alone and his *Discours des sorciers* (Discourse of Sorcerers, 1602 in Lyons, 1605 in Paris) enjoyed twelve editions in twenty years. However, when "the Devil in the form of a dog," was accused (Cologne, 1566) of sexually attacking a group of nuns, Bouget gave his considered opinion that it was "just an ordinary dog." The Devil was credited with sexual relations with—you'll love the name if you know *The Wizard of Oz*—one Margaret Hamilton of Scotland, in the form of a man. Then the Devil changed into a big black dog and ran away.

About this time it was said that the Devil had intercourse with pretty women from the front and ugly ones from the rear but the rumor was going around that demons had double phalluses which enabled them to have vaginal and anal sex at the same time. By 1608, Henri IV, the French king, dispatched Pierre de Lancre (1553–1631) to the Basque

region to root out the notorious witchcraft. There it was reported to him that the double phallus was not true. No, it was triple, and the third went into the mouth. He told all in his *Tableau de l'inconstance des mauvais anges* (Picture of the Inconstancy of the Bad Angels, 1612), adding details about rampant were-wolves and the upwards of 600 witches he personally sent to be burned. Lancre's score may not have approached that of the French jurist Nicolas Rémy (who sent 900 or more witches to their deaths) but he considered he had done a good job and wrote several books boasting his knowledge of lustful hags and their diabolic paramours. The public ate up those reports. "Enquiring minds want to know."

SEVENTEENTH-CENTURY CASES

These include one woman to whom (I hope) I am not related: Anne Ashley. According to *A Prodigious and Tragical History* . . . (1652), she and five others were on trial at Maidstone (Kent) when they claimed to be pregnant with fetuses created by demons.

In Würtzburg in January of 1628 a number of females were tried for sex with The Devil. Anna Rausch confessed she had had sex half a dozen times with *Meister Hämerlein*, Sybille Lutz confessed she had had sex with *Meister Federlein*, and a younger female named Mürchin is recorded, in Latin, as stating in German that she had *coitus con demone* (sex with demons). Seven others were also questioned. They were all found guilty. Anna and Sybille, ages 12 and 11, were put to death and Mürchin and the others were remanded to their parents, because, after all, they were only between the ages of 8 and 13.

From de Lassus (*Les Incubes*, The Incubi), also quoted in a modern encyclopedia:

In 1643 I was ordered by my ecclesiastical superiors to exorcize a young girl of twenty years of age, who was pursued by an incubus. She acknowledged without evasion everything this impure devil had done with her. But after what she told me, I came to the opinion that in spite of her denials she had given the demon some indirect encouragement. Indeed, she was always forewarned by a violent over-excitation of the sexual organs, and then, instead of having recourse to prayer, she ran straight to her room and threw herself on her bed. I tried to rouse in her some feeling of trust in God, but I did not succeed, and she seemed almost to be afraid of being delivered from the devil.

Persons offered exorcism often try to refuse it (or the demon inside did). Today exorcism is comparatively rare, even in the Roman Catholic Church, where the permission of the bishop is usually required and, although any priest has the power of exorcism, an expert is chosen by him to officiate. Assuming you have seen *The Exorcist*, you're aware that the procedure is a dangerous one at best. When sex is involved demons can be violent. The present pope, old and feeble, was brave to conduct a recent, much-publicized exorcism himself.

"Sin with a succubus or incubus," wrote St. Alphonsus Ligouri in *Theologia moralis* (The Theology of Morality), a Carmelite manual, "is called bestiality [sex by a human with a non-human]; to which sin is added also malice against religion, sodomy, adultery, and incest." I do not see how bestiality and incest can be united, but I am not a theologian.

THE EIGHTEENTH CENTURY

By this time the witch craze had pretty much died down (meanwhile the vampire craze had begun in Transylvania). Still, in 1747 the twentieth edition of the encyclopedia on magic and witchcraft by the Jesuit "expert" Martin Antoine del Río (1551–1608) was published in France. He was broad-minded for his time and training in that he suggested that witches ought to get legal representation in capital prosecutions. He did not know about vampires and denied the existence of werewolves but on the subject of *incubi* he was absolutely certain that they presented a huge threat to the human race.

THE NINETEENTH CENTURY

The writings of the "Rev." Montague Summers deal with a number of alleged cases of *incubi* and *succubi*. Summers never questioned that these things existed, especially in France, but believed they were not exclusive to it. In the latter part of the century in France the Black Mass seems to have been more popular than the witches' sabbat. Of course the Black Mass involved a sexual orgy, scatology and the somewhat modern touch of drug use.

Sadism was often mingled with sex magic too. Renegade priests were sleeping around with lascivious women at a tremendous rate. Sexual perversion added the extra thrill of witchcraft's sense of the forbidden—sorcery meets sodomy. Paris was beginning to outdo Cyprus, a city notorious for its sex magic.

A woman from whom the Seven Deadly Sins
which possessed her are being driven out.
From a thirteenth century French illuminated manuscript.

FURIES

It is instructive to consider how many supernatural terrors were involved with
sex and how many creatures were considered to be female. Think of the
epiphaltes if you happen to be a real expert on the classical world and if not
think of the *erinyes* which I think you have heard of as The Furies, three vengeful women (whose names, for all you trivia buffs, were Alecto, Megæra, and
Tisiphone). The Romans called them *diræ*.

These creatures of ancient times started out as the irate dead, both sexes,
and then seem to have become female. What's up, do you think? May I suggest to those on the bandwagon of feminist history that in the subject of sex
and the supernatural we have a neglected and illuminating link in misogyny's

connection with religion and other establishments? Maybe even a hidden history of sexual politics?

BASIC EQUIPMENT

Naturally there were male rebels as well as vengeful women. William Stapleton, who had been a Benedictine monk, engaged in black magic between 1527 and 1530. He called up demons such as Oberion or assorted *incubi*. When he was arrested, authorities seized "magic books, a ring, a plate, a circle, and a sword." What they did not really get a hold of was perhaps the most significant thing of all: motive.

IS THE *SUCCUBUS* A SYLVAN NYMPH OR IS IT SATAN?

From *The Magus* (1801) by Francis Barrett (who undertook to give us mug shots of the *incubus* and other demons):

> And seeing the fauni and nymphs of the woods were preferred before the other [spirits] in beauty, they afterwards generated their offspring among themselves, and at length began wedlocks with men; feigning that, by these copulations, they should obtain an immortal soul for them and their offspring; but this happened through the persuasions and delusions [generated] of Satan to admit these monsters to carnal copulation, which the ignorant [humans] were easily persuaded to; and therefore these nymphs are called succubi; although Satan afterwards committed worse, frequently transchanging himself, by assuming the persons of both incubi and succubi in both sexes; for they conceived not a true young by the males, except the nymphs alone.

Stories of a sex demon appearing in the form of a satyr do exist but I cannot find one in which the aggressor is a fairy or a nymph.

MODERN BELIEF IN THE *INCUBUS* AND THE *SUCCUBUS*

Lest you think that the *incubus* and the *succubus* are weird beliefs to which no modern people pay attention, I suppose I could include so-called recipes for calling them up (or down). Some current practitioners of black magic claim they are fully effective. I should not, however, like to give them publicity.

What I will do is quote at some length from what one scholar of the history of magic said in his *Witchcraft and Black Magic*, considered a classic and often reprinted since its first publication in 1946. I warn you, the "Rev." Mon-

Photograph of the Rev. Montague Summers.

tague Summers is perfectly sincere when he bases his beliefs on much earlier so-called authorities and is not being at all hesitant to agree with them. He claimed to be an ordained priest and certainly was well versed in standard Christian doctrine:

> That the 'sons of God' spoken of in *Genesis* were, or at any rate became, Incubi demons is maintained by a very large number of learned men, as, for example, Archbishop Paul de Santa Maria of Burgos, Lord Chancellor of Spain (died 1435), and Francisco Valesio, a famous Spanish physician whose translations of and excursuses upon the old medical writers are highly esteemed. Hugh of St. Victor says that Incubi are spiritual beings who assume corporeity and thus com-

mit lewdness with women. Michael Psellus, the famous Byzantine scholar of the tenth century, in his treatise *On the Activities of Demons*, makes it quite clear that demons are capable of sensual passions, and he explains how they are able to perform the venereal act. 'Almost all Theologians and learned Philosophers are agreed, and it has been the experience of all times and all nations, that witches practise coition with demons, the men with Succubus devils, and the women with Incubus devils.' Thus writes the judicious [Francesco Maria] Guazzo. St. Augustine says quite positively that the fact of such uncleanness being practised is so well known and so well assured that it were brazen impudence to deny it.

The physiological and psychological bearings of these unions are treated of in detail by all demonologists, who are further unanimous in believing that Incubi can generate children. The *Malleus Maleficarum* discusses this question at great length and is entirely convincing. Guazzo proposes that a human child can be born of a witch and an Incubus devil. This is also the studied opinion of the learned Martin Delrio [Del Río], who cites a very large number of authorities to that effect.

A POSITION ON THE QUESTION

There are undoubtedly "a very large number of authorities" who have testified to the existence of these creatures, but are they really authorities? On what basis? And is it not the case that a lot of things have been testified to and stoutly defended by "authorities," particularly ecclesiastical authorities, which were not true. They were wrong about the earth being the center of the universe. So, having read this carefully compiled collection of statements by a few people about *incubi* and *succubi*, do you agree or disagree with Dom Dominic Schram, OP (*Institutes of Mystical Theology*, 1848)? Here is what he writes, "It is positively certain and proven that—whatever the incredulous may say—there actually exist such demons, incubi or succubi."

I contend that you have a right to an informed opinion, if you think you are sufficiently informed. Notice, however, that to deny the possibility of witchcraft is to deny the inerrancy of The Bible. Are you a fundamentalist? To believe in The Devil as a real person is essential for membership in some religious denominations.

For instance, are you a Roman Catholic? With religions such as that comes belief in demons. I do think that to believe in *incubi* and *succubi*, or even that demons can procreate with humans goes beyond where most of us, whatever our denomination, care to position ourselves in the twenty-first century. It is, of course, disturbing that this makes centuries of superstitious belief look ridiculous to us. Major figures in science, philosophy, and divinity of the past appear to us to have been outrageously deluded, and that has immense repercussions on modern life.

Today in advanced societies most people, albeit reluctantly, echo the pronouncement of the great English jurist Sir William Blackstone: "To deny the possibility, nay, actual existence, of witchcraft and sorcery is flatly to contradict the revealed word of God . . . the thing itself is a truth to which every nation in the world hath in its turn borne testimony."

I shall assume as we go on that in some measure most of you have some belief in "the revealed word of God," however you define that, but that extremes such as *incubi* and *succubi* are not part of your belief system. I shall also assume you have a real interest in, perhaps actually share, other superstitions to which "every nation in the world hath in its turn borne testimony." I know many people who hotly deny being superstitious at all but if you scratch their surface some form of it is found not very far below. Many relate to birth, sex and marriage as well as to fate and luck and death. Nicholas Kiessling has written on *The Incubus in English Literature* (1977) and there are plenty of other things to read if not facts to know about sex in the night with demons.

So, now we move on to other, less terrifying, superstitions—those connected with sex. Which ones do you happen to share and which reject? As always, *why*?

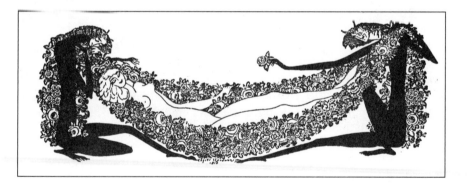

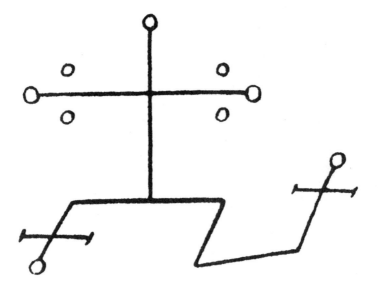

The *Sigil* of Dantalian, duke of Hell, who knows all arts and sciences, kindles love, and produces in visions anyone you wish.

THE LOVERS.

2
Superstitions

THE FACTS ON SUPERSTITION

Belief in superstition is unlucky. Lucky for you, you have me to tell you about superstitions connected with sex without pressing you to believe in them. I want to present them as history. I am your Ancient Mariner. I stoppeth one in I don't know how many but I give you a great deal of information because you are not merely an unwary passerby but a willing listener, preselected by having picked up this book. So "the Mariner hath his will."

This chapter will be longer than most but not interminable. My "glittering eye" cannot hold you indefinitely, however well I select or present my examples. I have tried to create a mix of the familiar and the strange and I hope you will enjoy what I include and not worry too much about what space or other factors compel me to omit.

If readers write in to demand that this or that superstition go in, then in the next edition (if there is one) I shall include it. We all have superstitions that we cherish, if we would admit it. We may not be having our palms or Tarot read by gypsies, and tearooms do not feature tea leaf readers as they used to when I was a child, but now people consult "psychics," and there must be 200,000 more or less "professional" astrologers at work in the U.S. today. People who have a lucky charm are legion. Let's start with the most superstitious holiday. . . .

The fourteenth-century *Ormesby Psalter* shows a virgin with a unicorn. The knight attacks virginity.

TO SEE YOUR FUTURE SPOUSE ON HALLOWEEN

Let's begin here with some superstitions you probably have heard, maybe even follow. Then we can go on to an alphabetical listing for your convenience in finding things as we range far and wide. Don't eat this box of chocolates all at once. You'll get intellectual indigestion. Sample. Try the soft centers. Taste. Think about each one, where it may have come from, what it tells you about the real subject of *Sex Magic*: the nature of human nature.

On Halloween, peel an apple in one piece and throw the long peel over your left shoulder. It will show you the initial of the forename of your wife or husband to be. On Halloween a young woman can select several apple seeds and give each one the name of a potential mate. Placed before the fire, the seeds will pop, and the first one will give her the name of her future husband. On Halloween a young woman can catch a snail and put it under a dish for the whole night. In the morning the slimy trail the snail has left will give her the initial of her future husband's forename. On Halloween a young man can crawl under a blackberry bush and see the shadow of his future wife. On Halloween a young woman can, on going to bed, hang her chemise on a chair and if she can stay awake long enough her future husband will seem to come into the room and turn the chemise.

On Halloween even before going to bed a young woman can get to see who will bed her in the future: all she has to do is to take a willow switch and run three times (that magic number again!) around her house. On the third round the future husband will appear to take hold of the other end of the willow switch. On Halloween a young woman can stand before her mirror and eat an apple while combing or brushing her hair. Her future husband's face will appear in the mirror.

HOW DO YOU LIKE THEM APPLES?

More apple tricks for Halloween. Give each apple a name and, hands behind your back, bob for apples. The one you manage to get (push the apple to the bottom of the container full of water and bite it firmly before coming back to the surface) will tell you whom you will marry. Or a group of you can tie apples

A German woodcut of the late fifteenth century shows a man collecting a magical stone from the head of a toad.

to strings and whirl them around your head. The first apple to fly off the string will identify the first of the group to be married.

Not just on Halloween but any time you have an apple you can count the seeds in "she loves me, she loves me not" fashion. As you count the seeds in your apple, recite:

> One I love, two I love, three I love, I say.
> Four I love with all my heart, five I'll cast away.
> Six he loves, seven he loves, and eight they both love.
> Nine he comes, ten he tarries,
> Eleven he courts and twelve he marries.

Do you know how many seeds are regularly found in the variety of apples you habitually eat? Does it usually have a dozen seeds? You might consider shifting to another variety.

If you don't want to marry anyone, here is what you do (courtesy of Thomas Cogan's *The Haven of Health*):

> He that will not a wife wed,
> Must eat a cold apple when he goeth to bed.

An apple a day, apparently, keeps more than the doctor away. An old saying is:

"To eat an apple without rubbing it first is to challenge The Devil."

If your apple tree blossoms in the Fall, a wedding will soon follow.

APRON

When an unmarried woman's apron falls off, she is thinking of her sweetheart. When a married woman's apron falls off, something is coming to vex her. When she wears her apron high, she's probably pregnant.

Some fishermen would not go to work if on their way they met a woman wearing a white apron, and women on ships were always bad luck, aprons or not.

In Germany, if a man wipes his face on a woman's apron he will fall in love with her. That's traditional. In the U.S., if a man insists on wearing an apron at the barbeque with a male chauvinist remark printed on it his wife may fall out of love with him. I made that one up.

ASPARAGUS

Recommends itself to superstition by the magical theory that what a plant looks like will tell you what pharmaceutical use it will have. This was called the Doctrine of Signs, as if the Creator had given us clues to the medicinal use of plants (say, heart-shaped leaves on digitalis, which turned out to be right). Asparagus spears look phallic and strongly affect the smell of urine when you eat them, so they must be up to something, right?

Add to that the ancient Greek tradition that wove wild asparagus into wedding garlands. Surely the Greeks would know.

BUT ABSOLUTELY NUTS

Maimonides is usually right on the money but he does report in one of his medical studies that if a man's right testicle is bigger than his left one his first child will be a male. I trace this to the old-fashioned belief that the right (or better) kind of an offspring to have is a son, not a daughter.

BABY TEETH

Babies born with teeth, or bastards of what was supposed to be a celibate priest, may turn out to be vampires. If they are born without teeth but the first tooth appears in the upper jaw the baby will probably die in infancy.

According to the Azande of Africa, a baby whose first tooth appears in the upper jaw is said to be unlucky, and if that baby eats of the first fruits of the harvest, the crops will be scant or ruined. In what used to be Dahomey (when I was a kid and collected stamps), now Benin, a baby born with a full set of teeth was immediately drowned. In Central Asia, such babies were regularly exposed and left to die.

If you want to participate in your own superstition, take the first baby tooth that falls out and give it to the squirrels, the request being for new teeth as strong as that rodent's. Baby teeth when they fall out ought to be put under the pillow for the Tooth Fairy. Take note that since the days you received a coin from the Tooth Fairy inflation has set in. Kids expect folding money now.

BABY SUPERSTITIONS

There are thousands upon thousands of superstitions, many about sex. I have attempted to select samples that will interest you and have steered clear of almost all of those from truly foreign climes so as to better relate to my readers' lives. In my books on witchcraft, demonology, vampires, werewolves and such, I offered worldwide coverage: the English-speaking world and the rest of the world. Here with superstitions and sex, and the occult in general I address a large topic, which requires greater selection.

A book such as this could be written in and of every one of hundreds of cultures and countries in thousands of languages, each with its peculiarities. But when all those books were written certain basic themes would emerge. They are, amid all the examples, what I hope you take away from this book. A line comes into my head from a Christmas carol I have always loved and which I think you must know: ". . . The hopes and fears of all the years. . . ."

Just to give you some indication that this book could be on the topic of this chapter alone, I shall cite quite a few under the rubric of babies. How many of these did you know? Write down all the related superstitions you know that I left out.

Jews used to say that when a boy is born the world welcomes him but when a girl is born the walls weep. Don't want your walls weeping? Eat no sweets when pregnant.

The first child is going to be luckiest and an only child is the luckiest of all. If you are going to have two children, the boy should come first:

First a son
Then a daughter
You've begun
As you oughta.

First a daughter, then a son,
The world is well begun.
First a son, then a daughter
Trouble follows after.

For a boy, put a knife under the mattress of the bed in which he is to be conceived. For a girl, put a frying pan under the mattress. Or you can follow the custom of the Bohemians (people in Bohemia, not gypsies) and put poppy seeds on the outside windowsill to conceive a boy; if you want a girl, use sugar. Girls are "sugar and spice."

As you are trying for a baby, to keep demons from lurking, put something iron under the pillows.

If you want the baby to look like its father be sure to look the dad-to-be right in the eye as you orgasm. No orgasm? Try again.

To cut the pain of childbirth put a knife or (in extreme cases) an ax under the bed.

While pregnant, women should be kept happy and given whatever they want to eat or the child may bear a birthmark shaped like the withheld food. Pregnant women should also be kept away from all danger of fright. A big shock could damage the baby more than smoking or alcohol.

Pregnancy.

A baby carried low would be a boy and if high a girl.
Babies are best born when the tide is coming in.

Babies born at night, they say in Ireland, will be able to see ghosts. In Germany they say that babies born at sermon time (one hopes not in church) will have the same ability.

A shooting star may mean that a baby is being born somewhere or it may just be God firing missiles at evil angels (demons) who are trying to get back into Heaven. Or wait for the last item in this chapter.

In Sweden they say the stork was so called because at the Crucifixion it flew around saying "*stryrke*" (have strength). It has been silent ever since. Silent or not, if a stork flies over your house you should expect a birth.

In France, instead of being brought by storks babies are found under a cabbage leaf. In Britain, it is under a gooseberry bush.

Males born when there is no moon will not live. As they say in Cornwall, "No moon, no man." A child born on the third day of a new moon will not live to grow up. A child born under a waning moon may be sickly.

Behemoth.

Babies delivered by Caesarian section have higher IQs than other children.

Children born in February are said to have the best chance of genius. Children of mature parents are said to have a better chance of higher than usual intelligence.

Twins were often feared or taken as proof of wifely infidelity but some peoples said twins had magical powers and could be rainmakers. The way to prevent twins is this: if the male spills pepper, have him throw some over the left shoulder as a sacrifice to evil spirits, as salt is thrown.

To make sure your children will not be ugly, never quarrel when pregnant.

When pregnant try to be as saintly as possible, give charity, listen to "good" music (Mozart is best, as it is also best for house plants), stay cheerful, look at beautiful things so the child will appreciate art or be beautiful itself.

Blue is for boys, pink is for girls, and if you do not know which sex is on the way yellow is lucky.

Once the sex of the infant is known, it is blue or pink all the way, never both.

As soon as the baby is delivered, spit on it. This is not to show contempt but to give it some of the strength of your own identity. Or you could rub lard all over it. Right away, to protect the infant from the evil eye, kiss it three times, spitting (not on the baby)

Asmodeus.

after each kiss.

Now that the baby has entered the world it is finally safe to decide definitely on a name. But do not use the name to or even about the infant until baptism. Call the baby simply he or she. Not it.

Don't let the husband touch the umbilical cord. Look at it carefully to see if it has any pronounced lumps; each lump means a baby this mother will have.

Pay the obstetrician and/or midwife immediately or the baby will not grow. (Here is a case from which I think you can see where the superstition arose.)

Within the first few hours of its life, rub bay leaves on the baby's legs so it will not grow up lame or have its legs injured in an accident.

Belphegor.

Make sure a newborn sees a sunrise before a sunset. That insures a happier life.

Tie a red ribbon on the infant to protect it from demons.

Mary is said in tradition to have burned ash twigs to keep the Christ Child warm, so give your baby a cradle made of ash wood, if you can. Do not buy a

Adam and Eve without genitals, on the ceiling of a church in Hildesheim, Germany.

cradle, however, until after the baby is born; a baby that sleeps in a cradle bought before its birth will die.

Cradles and bassinettes should be natural wood color or white, never any other color.

Don't rock an empty cradle. That will attract another baby, just as rocking an empty rocking chair will attract a visit from a ghost.

Babies do not need to be "born with a silver spoon" but a teething ring may have a silver mounting. Coral used to be preferred for teething. See Recipes, later, for ways to soothe painful teething. And keep it from being too loud.

Don't measure a baby with a tape measure; that will stunt its growth. Stepping over a crawling infant will stunt its growth. Letting it bite its nails will stunt its growth. Maybe a little manure in its booties will make it grow faster.

When a baby first leaves the room in which it is born it must be carried (no elevators) downstairs, never upstairs. When first picking the baby off a hospital bed, a nurse can stand on a telephone book so that she can step down.

If a married woman is the first female to see the new infant, she will have a baby.

It is bad luck for the newborn or the mother (worse for both together) to have a photograph taken. In many parts of the world people still object to being photographed lest they lose their souls to the photographer. In sex magic photographs are "the person" as much as a lock of hair or a fingernail clipping.

If you want the baby to have curly hair, place it on a fur rug or nappy material.

For the first three Sundays of its life, dress the baby in its finery. With a bonnet.

Among the Crow Indians, a baby might be named as the result of a dream, an incident at the time of birth, etc. Wild-carrot incense was burned and the baby was lifted up in the air four times, a little higher each time. This would make the baby grow up. If the baby was

The demon Andras, wise as an owl and ravenous as a wolf, from de Plancy's *Dictionnaire infernal*.

sickly, he might get a new name. This superstition is similar to one among Orthodox Jews that says if a baby is sickly his or her name may be changed so that if the Angel of Death comes he will not be able to find the infant.

Names might be changed to mark notable events in the life of a regular Indian as he grew up and males who became berdaches (transvestite shamans) might assume feminine names as well as women's dress. Their sexual practices were said to give them magical powers as adults.

The first louse you see on the baby's head should be cracked on The Bible if you want the lad to grow up to be a preacher man.

A baby baptized with water from the holy well of St. Ludgvan in Cornwall will never be hanged when adult.

A girl baby baptized in the same water with which a boy was baptized will

Nota, what I say
And bear it well away.
If it please not theologys
It is good for astrologys.

A knight named Stathum and his three wives are all buried in one tomb at Morley in Derbyshire with this monumental brass of 1481.

grow a moustache when she grows up.

Martin's *History of St. Kilda* tells us that Saturday is the only day to have a baby baptized if you want it to live. Generally Saturdays are unlucky; it is the worst day of the week to marry, as May is the worst month. But children born on Saturday can see ghosts. Do you want your child born with that talent?

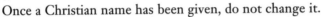

Give bread and cheese or a silver coin to the first stranger you meet as you take the baby to church for baptism.

It is a good sign if a baby cries at baptism. It may signal a good singing voice.

Once a Christian name has been given, do not change it.

As soon after the baby is baptized as possible call it by its name for the first time.

Make sure yours is not the first child christened in a new church. Like the first corpse buried in a churchyard, the child will belong to The Devil.

The baby's crying as it is christened is the lamentation of The Devil on being driven out of the child.

Or the child approves of its new name.

Kiss the bottom of baby's feet to make the baby lucky.

Never hand a baby through a window.

Never place a baby with its head at the bottom of the crib or cradle.

Never place a baby on an ironing board or windowsill.

Godparents' surnames should not begin with the same letter as the surname of the baby.

Friends coming to see a new baby should always bring something to eat.

Breast-fed babies are happier and stronger.

If your baby cries loudly, it may grow up to be a singer or an orator. To insure it will be a good singer, bury its nail clippings under an ash tree. But never cut the baby's nails until it is a year old. Bite them off.

To protect the baby from harm or disease (or to dedicate it to The Devil, some say) pass it through a natural hole in a rock or tree trunk.

Do not permit it to see itself in a mirror in the first year of life.

But take a photo of it at age one prone and naked on a fur rug to show it to the child when it grows up. (Prevent the adult from tearing up the photo.)

To prevent colic, give to the baby water that has been poured into a shoe.

Scottish midwives carried snuff to make the newborn sneeze, believing that until a baby sneezed it was in the grip of the fairies.

To keep the fairies from bothering the baby, give it a little sap from an

The Wonders of the Invisible World:

Being an Account of the

T R Y A L S

O F

Several Witches,

Lately Excuted in

NEW-ENGLAND:

And of several remarkable.Curiosities therein Occurring.

Together with,

I· Observations upon the Nature, the Number, and the Operations of the Devils·

II. A short Narrative of a late outrage committed by a knot of Witches in *Swede-Land*, very much resembling, and so far explaining, that under which *New-England* has laboured.

III. Some Councels directing a due Improvement of the Terrible things lately done by the unusual and amazing Range of *Evil-Spirits* in *New-England.*

IV. A brief Discourse upon those *Temptations* which are the more ordinary Devices of Satan.

By *COTTON MATHER.*

Published by the Special Command of his EXCELLENCY the Govencur of the Province of the *Massachusetts-Bay* in *New-England.*

Printed first, at *Boston* in *New-England*; and Reprinted at *London,* for *John Dunton,* at the *Raven* in the *Poultry.* 1693.

ash tree. Ordinarily tree sap goes in magical recipes to replace semen if that is unavailable.

Put some iron (the fairies' bane) near the cradle, or a horseshoe (ends up, so the power will not drain out) over the door. Never hang up a horseshoe with the points down; that is inviting catastrophe. It might even fall down and brain the infant.

You can hand an infant objects belonging to various members of the fam-

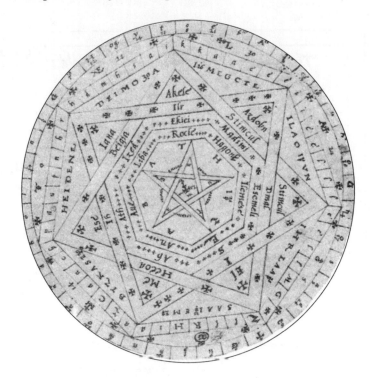

Dr. John Dee's calculations.

ily. The one it takes hold of belongs to the person it will most "take after."

You can place objects like The Bible (the baby will grow up to be a preacher), a bottle of Jack Daniels, etc. on the floor and let it crawl around them. See which of the objects he or she goes to. This is how a reincarnated Dalai Lama is chosen.

If a baby refuses to grasp a coin, it will not be good with money when it grows up.

Do not wash a baby's hands until it is a year old. Otherwise it will not be able to hold onto money when it grows up.

Do not permit rain to fall on the baby in the first year or it will have freckles.

Do not permit a baby to walk before six months. If it does, it will always walk into trouble as it grows up.

The first time a baby leaves the house it must be given some salt (a preservative that wards off evil), an egg, a piece of bread, and some money. That way the child will grow up with the "wherewithal" of life.

In Pomerania, it was considered fatal for a newborn to be carried over a crossroads. Crossroads belonged to The Devil. That was where one went to

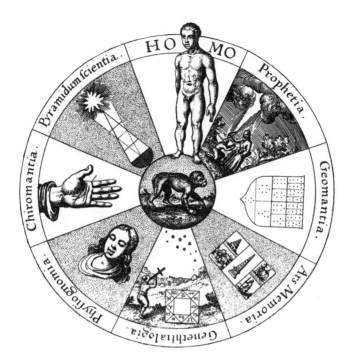

meet him at midnight, where murderers were buried, etc.

The excessive number of rituals related to the belief in magic accounts for some of the infant mortality in days gone by. Naturally, the weaker the person who was to be protected, the stronger the magic that person needed, and the less capable they were to defend themselves against terrors both visible and invisible.

After a woman has given birth to a baby, says A. Wutke in *Der deutsche Volksaberglaube* (German Superstition, 1860), she should not change her underwear for six months or she will have a baby every year. That might indeed keep men off.

BAD DAYS

For birth, marriage, or death, be careful about the first of the month. The especially bad days are the first of April, not because of April Fool's, but because that is the traditional birthday of Judas Iscariot; the first of August, the day assigned to the destruction of Sodom and Gomorrah; and the first of December, the day that Satan was expelled from Heaven. There are altogether 42 unlucky days:

January 1, 2, 6, 11, 17, 18

February 8, 16, 17 (I would add 29)
March 3, 12, 13, 15
April 1, 3, 15 (even before IRS), 17, 18
May 8, 10, 17, 30
June 1, 17
July 1, 5, 6
August 1, 3, 17, 20
September 1, 2, 15, 30
October 15, 17
November 11, 17
December 1, 7, 11

There doesn't seem to be any logic to the numbers. I can discover no reason why 17 crops up so often. As with so much in superstition, one does well to ask: "Sez who? What is the source of these ideas?" Do these dates, for example, have any correlation to crime statistics or hospital emergencies?

This seems as inexplicable as the old Illinois superstition that anyone born between the 21st and the 24th of any month is lucky every time 13 rolls around. As you know, most people say the number 13 is unlucky. Don't be born on any 13th, superstition says, or you'll die on one. On which day(s) do more Americans die than on any other? Did you know that, over a long period of time, there are more Fridays the 13th than any other day? In my view, the only really unlucky day to be born is 25 December because you get fewer birthday presents.

The two unluckiest days to meet a new mate are Friday or your birthday.

BALDNESS

The popular notion is that baldness is inherited from the mother's side of the family. It is related to testosterone, so there may be something substantial to associating it with virility. Either way,

The sixth (perfect number) of the major arcana of The Tarot is The Lovers. In the Kabalah the sixth *Sefirah* (Tifereth) is the central, harmonizing factor in the Tree of Life. Marry in a 6 year. If you marry a 6 your life will be steady if a bit dull.

remember, it's "not a chrome dome; it's a solar panel for a sex machine."

GO BANANAS

The banana is the fruit to wish on before you peel it. Some people may wish for something shaped like a banana.

GO BATS

Wash your face in the blood of a bat, an old superstition said, and you will be able to see in the dark (very useful while having sex with someone shy). Like many old ideas, this is not a good one. Think rabies.

BARN

Dream of a barn and you will marry rich. If you dream anything three times, even this, it will come true. There is a catch: dreams sometimes go by contraries, and in fact the Japanese expect the opposite of the dream every time. If you don't remember dreaming of a barn or anything else, that is lucky, though your psychoanalyst will be annoyed.

BEARDS

Witches may have moustaches but only men (excepting women in freak shows) have beards. If his beard is a different color than the hair on his head, don't marry him. The Germans say "a man with a red beard is never any good." Are they thinking of Frederick Barbarossa?

A Basque proverb:

A woman with a beard is to be feared.
A man without a beard will be weird.

If a man cuts his beard he must immediately burn the hair, or The Devil will get it and work magic on him. Women with facial hair may be witches.

BED

When you get into bed with someone, never climb in over the end of the bed. That is bad luck. Orthodox Jews say an unmarried man sleeping alone will be bothered by demons. Demons are especially randy on Wednesday nights. (See Wednesday, below.)

Beds should be placed in a northern-southern direction (graves are east-west, with the corpse facing east, from which the resurrection will come, like the sun). Heads at the south of the bed are the best for sex, but heads at the north are said to be (a) either properly lined up with magnetic forces and thus best for you or (b) dangerous and "you will die." We shall all die, eventually, so maybe we will be happiest sleeping in a north-south bed—with heads in the south, full of "warmer" thoughts.

A witch turns the tables and rides with The Devil in this illustration from a famous example of *incunabula*, the *Nuremberg Chronicle*, late fifteenth century.

The first person to turn over in bed on the wedding night will be the first to die. And don't sleep back to back on your "Opening Night" or your marriage will be wracked by quarrels; sleep face to face, and face life united.

The bride must not put her feet on the floor once she gets into bed on the wedding night. No, I don't know about going to the bathroom.

BIRD CALLS

From the north, it's for tragedy.
From the south, it's for good crops.
From the west, it brings good luck.
From the east, it brings good love.

BIRTHDAYS

These days deliveries can be more or less adjusted. Parents may wish to have the baby arrive according to the following epigram, which you probably have heard:

Monday's child is fair of face,
Tuesday's child is full of grace,
Wednesday's child is sorry and sad,
Thursday's child is merry and glad,
Friday's child is loving and giving,
Saturday's child must work for a living,
But the child that is born on the Sabbath Day
Is bonny and merry and glad and gay.

Not only are the beliefs an anachronism, but the concepts as well. "Gay" has taken on a new meaning, and while the Jews used to have the Sabbath on a Friday it's now on Saturday. Most Christians have moved their Sabbath from Saturday to Sunday. I suggest that in the little poem the rhymes may have dictated the details, which is the case in many spells and superstitions, by the way. But the poem did have influence. In New England in early times we developed the old ideas as follows:

Born on a Monday, fair of face,
Born on a Tuesday, full of grace,
Born on a Wednesday, merry and glad,
Born on a Thursday, sour and sad,
Born on a Friday, godly given.

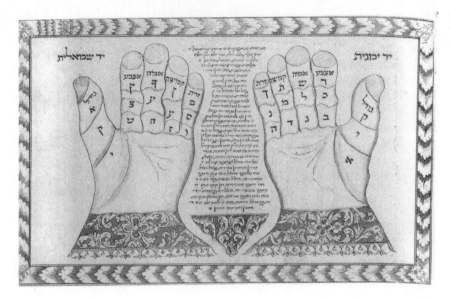

A Lithuanian manuscript on palmistry of 1754 uses Hebrew letters to indicate parts of the fingers.

Born on a Saturday, work for a living,
Born on a Sunday, never shall want,
So there's the week and the ending on't.

BIRTHDAY CAKE

We got the concept of birthday cakes from the worship of the love goddess Artemis. On her birth anniversary people ate moon cakes with a candle on top.

You blow out as many candles on the cake as the years you have lived. That puts closure to them. If anyone puts an extra "to grow on," you would be a fool to blow that one out, wouldn't you? Ask which one to avoid, before you blow. Take it off and then blow out the others.

Cheapskates use one candle.

Watch out as you eat the cake. You could choke on it. Evil fairies like to spoil birthday celebrations. If you know any malicious witches, invite them to the party and make sure they eat a nice piece of cake.

BIRTHSTONES

You know yours; don't wear anyone else's. Birthstones started as magical gems. The Jews adopted the 12-stone breastplate, a square set with 12 precious stones representing the twelve tribes of Israel, from Egyptian magicians' breastplate of the High Priest. The Christians said the 12 stones stood for the apostles. (Which one was for Judas Iscariot?) Eventually, the 12 stones stood for the 12 months of the Zodiacal year, and we had birthstones.

Put your birthstone in honey; that is said to make it more brilliant. I hope yours is not a diamond. Diamonds cause sleepwalking.

It is considered especially unlucky not only to wear someone else's birthstone but your own as well if the planetary alignment at your birth is negative. To determine that, will take a great deal more effort than buying a one-size-fits-all book by some kook on fire signs, love signs, or what-have-you. You'd need a real, detailed horoscope, which is beyond these people. It's about more than the date on which you were born. After all, haven't you met people with whom you share a birth date only to discover how very unlike you they are?

By the way, since you are so convinced you are unique—and why wouldn't you be, considering that no one has had all your experiences?—how can "you are an Aries," or whatever, describe you? Are you particularly horny? An old goat? Smell bad? Read the other horoscopes in the paper. Don't they sound like you, too? Are they ever negative? Surely *sometimes* they ought to read "nothing in particular is going to happen to you for the next 11 weeks," etc.

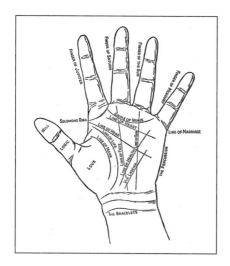

Lines of the hand (after "Cheiro").

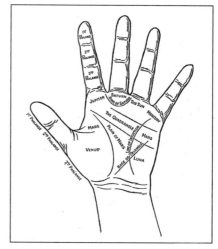

Mounts of the hand (after "Cheiro").

BLANKETS AND QUILTS

An old New England belief was that sleeping under a brand new blanket or quilt gave you dreams, including dreams about lovers, which would certainly come true, especially (as with all dreams) if the dream came three nights in a row.

Some quilt designs consciously or not were derived from love magic symbols.

BLIND HIM TO ADULTERY

In The Balkans, people actually used to disinter corpses to retrieve coins that had been placed on the eyes of the dead (so that the dead could pay Charon, the ferryman, to transport them across the river Styx to the other world). Superstition said the coins could be washed in wine and the husband who innocently drank it be made blind to any infidelities of his wife. I have known people to get "blind drunk" and still be able to tell when wives were cheating on them. You can do it, custom has it, with "half an eye."

BLUE

The superstition of blue as a lucky color can be traced to Chaldean and Egyptian magic.

Touch blue,
Good luck to you.

Blue painted around windows and doors (as in Greece to this day) keeps vampires from entering. In New York, some Puerto Ricans buy blue chalk to make marks on their bodies to prevent demons from getting at them while they sleep. Witches hate blue; it is the color of Heaven and of the mantle of the Blessed Virgin Mary.

In Ireland there is a colorful story of Biddy (Bridget) Early, the "hedge witch" of Co. Clare. She possessed a magic bottle. It was alleged that she won it from a fairy in a card game, or, in another version of the story, received it from the ghost of one of her husbands, Tom Flannery of Carrowroe. The magic bottle was blue. When Biddy died, a priest threw the bottle into Kilbarron Lake, which is blue. They say the bottle is still in there somewhere.

If your love for me is true,
Send me quick a bow of blue.
If you ever think of me

A pink bow I should see.
If you send a bow of yellow
You have got another fellow.
If I get a bow of red
I'll know love for me is dead.

WEDDINGS

Bread and butter, together as when two people walking together are parted by an object such as a lamppost.

Ritualizing two things that go together, like bread and butter, reinforces the fact that the two people are together infinitely even though for a moment something has come between them. In Welsh weddings bread and butter were given to the bride to eat before the wedding cake was cut (with a sword in the old days).

I used to think this was something like the Yorkshire custom of making a "pudding" doused in the drippings of meat, and served as filler before the main course so guests would accept smaller portions at dinner. Perhaps by filling the Welsh bride up on bread and butter the family would keep her from stuffing herself with the wedding cake that had to feed many guests. I've heard the Welsh used to believe bread and butter would make the bride eat her wedding cake less hungrily, more daintily. It was also designed to ensure that her children would have attractively small mouths.

The old shoes tied to the car in which the newlyweds depart are for fertility. If they don't want children, use tin cans.

Mirror of the Mind.

If you trip going upstairs, a wedding is on the way. If you "fall" in the bedroom, maybe the same thing is in store.

BRIDES

> Married in white, you have chosen right;
> Married in red, you'd better be dead;
> Married in blue, your fellow is true;
> Married in yellow, ashamed of the fellow;
> Married in green, ashamed to be seen;
> Married in brown, you'll live out of town;
> Married in pink, your spirits will sink;
> Married in black, you'll ride in a hack.

In earlier times, however, a woman in mourning might be married in black, forbidden to wear any other color.

> If when you marry your dress is red
> You'll wish to God that you was dead.
> If when you marry your dress is white
> Then everything will be all right.

Whatever color you wear, put a (silver) sixpence in your shoe, for luck. Today maybe 20p or a quarter will do, but it is not silver. The something borrowed, if you can manage it, should be gold. Do not let the groom see you in the bridal dress until you come down the aisle at the wedding and do not look in the mirror at yourself until you are completely decked out, with the veil in place if not down. Never lose the veil—very bad luck.

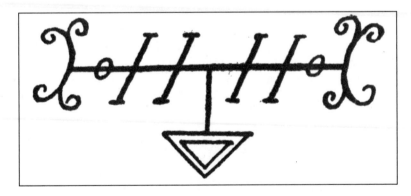

The *sigil* of the demon Furfur.

When the clergyman says "kiss the bride," if the bride does not want tears in the marriage she should cry then, "or at least pretend to" one source says. Learning to pretend can never start too early for brides.

It used to be forbidden to marry in Lent. Some people think it is still to be avoided, but perhaps a wait is ill advised for brides that are pregnant. These days most, or a lot of them, are.

Don't let them throw rice at you if you want a childless marriage, because it is supposed to create fertility. For best results rice should get into the bride's bra. Rice was also intended as food for demons hovering over the new couple, to keep them from getting mean. If you marry a military man you may get a canopy of drawn swords, and that ought to protect you. Or you could have firecrackers to drive off demons, as the Chinese do. When they invented gunpowder it was for such a use.

BRIDESMAIDS

It is luckier for all concerned not to have all bridesmaids dressed in the same color; try a selection of pastels, but no white except for the bride and never green at any wedding. The dress design can be the same for all bridesmaids, but not the color.

Make sure no bridesmaid stumbles as she goes down the aisle. That brings almost as much bad luck as the bride stumbling on the threshold of her new home (which is why the groom should carry her over). Superstition has nothing to say about what happens if *he* stumbles while doing that, but make sure he doesn't drink too much at the reception. He has other important duties to perform.

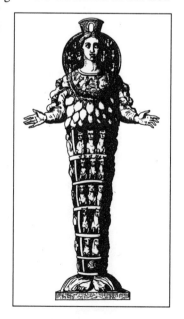

The bridesmaid who catches the bride's bouquet (in France, her garter, a custom occasionally seen in the U.S.) will be the next to marry. (A sprig of gorse in the bouquet adds to its value, for "when gorse is out of bloom, kissing is out of season," which is never.) It is in bad taste to throw the bridal bouquet right at an unlikely prospect. To help her along, the bride can give her the wedding shoes after the ceremony. For luck these are not new shoes anyway. The bridesmaid who does catch the bouquet should put a piece of wedding cake under her pillow if she wishes to dream of her future husband.

Artemis, at Ephesus (Efès).

Let the bridesmaids keep their gowns but save the wedding dress. You may need it to protect the family against fairies or wish to hand it down to a daughter if the marriage has been happy. Lend the bridal veil to other brides if your marriage is happy; it may bring them equal luck.

Three times a bridesmaid and you will never be a bride.

> Why am I always the bridesmaid,
> Never the blushing bride? . . .
> Ding-dong, wedding bells
> Always ring for someone else. . . .

BUTTERCUPS

Hold a buttercup under someone's chin and ask him or her if they love you. If the reflection does not shine, they are lying. If it does they may be telling the truth—or they just "like butter."

Sigil (seal) of Schemhamphorus.

CANDLES

Candles make sense considering that night is the traditional time for both sex and magical operations—midnight is "the witching hour." But candles are also phallic symbols, symbols of enlightenment, and symbols of prayer. Some people in both religious and superstitious contexts light votive candles to "pray," as it were.

It was rumored that the candles of witches were made of human fat. They were black for the Black Mass, black or green for the sabbat, unlike the white candles regularly used by the Roman Catholic Church. They were consecrated to evil in the way religious candles were blessed. Some magical operations absolutely require candles and some wishes, it is said, will come true if you do no more than burn the appropriate candle. Candles for sex are big business. In any big city, and some small towns, there are shops with pillar candles designed for Love and other intentions. Love is said to outsell other kinds, even those for Money or Revenge.

In sex magic where the candle wax is dropped as part of the ceremony on the naked skin, beeswax candles should not be used because the wax is hotter than the wax of other candles and bad burns will result.

CARNATIONS

Used in funeral wreathes because it was said to grow on the graves of lovers, carnations can also indicate love: pink on Mother's Day if your mother is living, white if she is not living, and green any day for homosexuality (once a year for St. Patrick's Day, when gays are not welcomed in the New York City parade).

CATS

You already know lots of superstitions relating to cats. Here's a new one. The Azande in Africa keep cropping up because their magic has been so thoroughly studied. They are relevant whenever one speaks of magic, witchcraft, and superstition in general. They swear that some women give birth to cats. This is hard to prove or disprove because if you see one produced like this, you die.

Cats have always made some people nervous. Black cats, used as familiars by witches, were supposed to become witches themselves after seven years. So if a black cat crossed your path from left to right only, you may be happy to learn, it might be a witch's familiar. You can always identify them because all such animal familiars are supposed to be imperfect in some way, like the "rat without a tail" in The Scottish Play by Shakespeare.

There are court records of nuns who kept cats, for mice in the convent, being accused of possessing familiars who turned into handsome men in private. In the case of one nun, other nuns who heard conversations and sexy noises from a nun's cell turned her in.

Cats seem to know something we do not, besides, they are standoffish compared to dogs, neither fawning nor loyal. Also, we secretly envy cats; they are so calm and collected (usually) in our hectic modern world.

In one *Mother Goose and Grim* cartoon, a headhunter offers a cat a job: "They'll pay your board and room, you sleep 18 hours a day, you eat your fill, then do whatever you want," and the cat says, "I'll have to think about it."

Cats can, however, be lucky. A black cat is lucky to have in the house, but only if it came to you not if you brought it there. A cross-eyed cat is said to improve sexual activities where it lives. I keep telling people superstition dictates that when you move you must not take your cat (or cats) with you, but cat lovers are extremely attached to their feline companions and will not listen. They probably shouldn't. If you can really care about a cat you probably are the sort of person who finds loving humans comparatively easy. And be wary of making an enemy of a cat.

Indeed, caution is required for most superstitions. People are inconsistent: they will accept this superstition and that one but put up a big fight about the other. I say take the ones you like, if you want any at all, and leave the rest for others. Walk under ladders but carry your rabbit's foot. Decide never to date anyone with a 9 in their phone number, which is a problem now with some cell phones. At least it keeps you off 900 lines. Avoid 13th floors.

But I digress. Let us return to cats, which should be tan if you live on a 13th floor, never white or black. Black cats pulled

the Norse goddess Freya's chariot; Christians said she was a witch. The Cat is also one of the animal signs of Chinese astrology. As I write, the last Cat year was 1999. The next Cat year will be 2011. They are supposed to be good news for people born under that sign.

If you dream of kittens it means children.

Keep cats out of the baby's room; a cat may sit on the baby's face and stifle it.

If you love your cat, that's great. There is too little love of any kind in the world. Love "all things great and small," even independent cats and tomcat people. You may love or hate catty people, but *catty* is an unfair term, because cats (except for the frightening one in *Tobermory* by "Saki") do not gossip the way people do.

CIGARS

Kipling was the fellow who said, "a woman is only a woman" but "a good cigar is a smoke." Not very romantic, although he was named Rudyard for a place where his father proposed to his mother, so his parents were. Or maybe he was conceived there, as Margaux Hemingway owes her name and her origin to a good bottle of French wine her parents drank one evening.

Back to cigars. If you see one in the street and you are a woman, do not step on it. Old wives' tales say that if you do you will marry the first man you meet thereafter, and you may wish to be more selective. Of course if you happen to be there when some dreamboat movie star tosses down his cigar, there's your big chance.

COBWEBS

A cobweb in the kitchen means, "there's no courting there." Fanny D. Bergen's *Current Superstitions* (1896) says if a girl finds a cobweb on a door it means "her beau calls elsewhere."

CONTRACEPTIVES

If you don't want a child, grow lettuce in the garden. Superstition says that a woman will not conceive if lettuce is grown in her vicinity. Does this have any connection at all to the most boring of all lettuces, called Iceberg?

The Greeks again. This time to contradict the superstition rather than to support it. Juno, the wife of Zeus, conceived Hebe after eating lettuce. But then, goddesses used to get pregnant in the strangest ways. In Christianity, if you will permit me to suggest that the Blessed Virgin is a kind of goddess, Mary became pregnant with an immaculate conception. That's unusual, though some non-humans accomplish it.

Dangerous superstitions still held by some people include the idea that you cannot get pregnant if you have sex standing up (the British call this a knee-trembler) or urinate immediately afterwards or jump around or throw yourself downstairs. (How much does this account for more than half a million accidents on stairs in the U.S. each year?)

Older methods before The Pill included holding a dead man's hand for two minutes or stealing the pennies off a dead man's eyes (his fare for the ferryman) and putting them under your pillow before having sex. (See Recipes for herbs said to fight conception.)

The Most Miraculous Conception from the book *The Rosary of the Blessed Virgin* (1524).

CROSS-EYED PEOPLE

To encounter a cross-eyed person of the opposite sex is lucky. To encounter a cross-eyed person of the same sex is unlucky. Spit through your fingers and stare them down.

CROWS

One means anger.
Two means mirth.
Three means wedding.
Four means birth.
Five is heaven.
Six is hell.
Seven is The Devil you know well.

CUCKOOS AND MAGPIES

These birds, accused of laying their eggs in the nest of other birds and leaving the work of hatching to be done by others, are surely not the best omens for sexual relationships. However, tradition tells us that a young girl on hearing the cry of a cuckoo can find out when she will get a spouse.

> Cuckoo, cuckoo, tell me true:
> When shall I be married?

After this she listens for how many cries the cuckoo supposedly issues in response. Each cry means one year.

Magpies are piebald, two colors, and superstition has a lot to say about that. Most of all, magpies are ornery creatures. It is said that they refused to get into Noah's Ark and insisted on perching on the roof. Like crows, we use them to foretell marriage and other events, like this:

> One for sorrow.
> Two for mirth.
> Three for wedding.
> Four for a birth.
> Five for silver.
> Six for gold.
> Seven for a secret not to be told.
> Eight for Heaven.
> Nine for Hell.
> Ten for The Devil his own sel'.

"Sel[f]" comes from the Northumberland dialect in which this version was collected.

Other versions elsewhere include:

> One for sorrow.
> Two for joy.
> Three for a girl
> And four for a boy.

These numbers are for sightings, not calls. Another version goes, in part:

> Five for rich.
> Six for poor.
> Seven for a witch—
> I can tell you no more.

And another:

> Five for rich.
> Six for poor.
> Seven for a bitch.
> Eight for a whore.
> Nine for burying.
> Ten for a dance.
> Eleven for England
> And twelve for France.

Whatever that means, it is probably just for fun, or a rhyme. Sometimes a superstition's explanation is obvious, as in "a baby born with hands open will be generous," or "do not decide a baby name before the birth." Sometimes explanation may be far, or futile, to seek. Exactly why would bees not sting a virgin, lions respect them, and unicorns eat them?

CUPID

The Roman version of Eros, Cupid is the son of Venus and Mercury, therefore a messenger of love. Those whom his arrows hit fall in love. Unfortunately, he is blind. But if he hits you, you're done. If he breaks his bow, you will never marry. It is interesting to see how a malicious creature in early mythology came to be the cuddly if corpulent little Cupid of valentines.

Valentines themselves have changed. Today they are all cute and complimentary; in Victorian times people anonymously sent comic or highly critical valentines, which is why they were never signed.

DAISIES

To see if someone loves you, pull the petals off a daisy. You know, that "loves me, loves me not" routine. There are plenty of daisies around; the seeds have been scattered, superstition says, by the spirits of children who died in infancy and want us to be happy. To dream of a lover, put not daisies but their roots under your pillow.

DATED

You are lucky if you get a kiss, or more, on the first date. Speaking of dates, if you will go back and look at old books such as Fanny D. Bergen's *Current Superstitions* (1896) you will see that a great deal of nineteenth-century superstition is still around. Moreover, if you look at the ethnic backgrounds of certain areas of the U.S. you will see that people brought (and have kept) superstitions of the Old Country here.

For examples of superstitions from the Scotch-Irish of the South, read about the Celts or get J. F. Campbell's *Superstitions of the Highlands and Islands of Scotland* (1900). Alternative medicine is not as new as it might seem: see works like W. G. Black's *Folk Medicine* (1883).

DIMPLES

Dimple in the chin,
Devil within.

This may be the best place to repeat that I think some superstitions are generated by nothing but the rhyme. Rhyme is a common mnemonic device. Superstitions were originally conveyed by oral transmission and are, to a great extent, still perpetuated that way. As such, they depend on being memorable.

DRESS MATERIAL

Yankees used to believe that dress material not made up into a dress before marriage occurred was bad luck. Part of their Yankee thrift, I think.

EAR, EAR

If your left ear tingles, someone is speaking ill of you somewhere; if your right ear tingles you are being praised. If your ears feel hot, someone is speaking of you somewhere:

> Left: your lover;
> Right: your mother.

This must be Cockney in origin, because you rhyme *luvver* and *muvver*.

From Robert Herrick:

> My ear tingles, some there be
> That are snarling now at me.

EGGS

When people think of conception the first thing that comes to mind is usually the word *semen*, or some euphemism or vulgarity for it, but that was only the fertilizer. We all came from eggs.

It is no wonder that many superstitions regarding sex should have gathered around eggs, symbols of life and of resurrection (the chick comes out of the egg as the body comes out of the "whitened sepulcher"), which is why we have eggs at Easter, a Christian holiday named for a pagan goddess.

Plenty of sex magic can be done with eggs. It ranges from removing infertility, as an egg is passed over the body to draw all evil into it and away from the victim, to little ceremonies for discovering whom one was going to marry, a subject that held far more power over a woman's destiny than it does today.

Perhaps that little bit of sex magic belongs in another section of this book but I shall tell you here how to use eggs for that purpose. You roast an egg, take out the yoke (which has too much cholesterol in it for you anyway) and fill the cavity with salt. You skip supper and eat only this before going to bed. You will, the old books assure us, dream of a future husband. As with many other divinatory devices, repeat if necessary.

EROS

We are programmed to get eggs fertilized. That's what it is all about. After you do your reproductive duty, Nature more or less has done with you. Freud called the force that drives us *eros*. The opposite tendency is called *thanatos*—the urge toward death. For the ancients, Eros was not a cute kid with a bow and arrow. You met him above, as Cupid. He could be very naughty.

Sex magic undertakes to harness him, to whip him into line, to sic him on others, to make him a slave rather than a master. But *eros* or Eros is hard to handle. Give him his head and you will be fornicating in the fields to increase the fertility of the ground, dancing wildly with "suggestive" movements, dealing in love philtres and aphrodisiacs, losing control over this or that person like they were The One and Only.

You'll go wild just "getting it on." You'll suffer from cupidity and turn to eroticism. You might also suffer from venery, derived from Cupid's mother "Venus," as in *venereal disease*.

FETISHES

Under this heading we could speak of African religions or of modern American sexual perversion; both deal in material objects invested with spiritual and sexual power. They can be traditional (blood or whips), clothing (spike heels, underwear, latex or leather), or so untraditional they foil the imagination. In fetishism (see Sacher-Masoch's *Venus in Furs*) we give a kind of magic power to fetishes. In a sense, like the fetishes of Africa, they are worshipped as idols and we look to them for power.

Relics
These were thought to have magical power. This is the skull of Lazarus kept in the Chapel of The Holy Grail at Ansbach, Germany.

There are many superstitions connected with sexual fetishes. They can be as simple as lipstick. Lipstick was originally used not to shout "over here, sailor" in sex in much the same way color decorates the posterior of baboons, but to keep away demons. So say historians of religion, but I think Egyptian beauties were using it and other cosmetics to appear more alluring. Some of the oldest writing extant in the world deals with cosmetics.

FINGER

In L. Strackerjan's *Aberglaube und Sagen aus dem Hertzogtum Oldenberg* (1867) the superstition of the county of Oldenberg says that if your joints crack when you pull your fingers somebody loves you.

FIRSTBORN MALES

In primogeniture, naturally firstborn sons are lucky. In recent years there has been a lot of scientific study about placement of siblings, but scientists have not investigated the Muslim belief that firstborn sons can be rainmakers just by stripping naked and standing on their heads. They believe that in India, where it is said firstborn sons can be dangerous to have around because if they lean against anything it will be struck by lightning.

FLOWERY SENTIMENTS—SAY IT WITH FLOWERS

This does not work as well as it used to because people don't know what the flowers are trying to say anymore. So write a sexy card. This is an excerpt of the old system:

Love: Carnation, Hawthorn, Locust, Myrtle, Rose,
Tulip, Yellow Acacia, etc.
Self-Love: Daffodil and Narcissus
Coquetry: Dandelion
Innocence: Daisy, Lily, Marguerite
Happiness in Marriage: Lily of the Valley
Souls United: Phlox

. . . And don't forget the Forget-Me-Not. It is bad luck (some say) to bring Hawthorn in bloom into the house. No ferns in bouquets. Is this kind of flower talk just a (florists') convention or does some kind of sex magic lie behind it?

FORTUNA

The Roman goddess of Fortune was portrayed as a woman (fickle) standing on a ball (suggesting instability). Women were especially connected with divination and superstitious people turned to sibyls, who worked in trance; oracles, who may have been under the influence of hallucinogenic gasses; mediums; gypsy card readers; and other "cunning women" to predict the future.

Maybe this had something to do with another sexist superstition, the superiority of woman's intuition. Certain male shamans thought it necessary to dress and live as women, as you read above.

"Luck be a lady tonight," Frank Sinatra used to sing to Las Vegas patrons. Sophie Tucker complained that Lost Vegas gamblers didn't like women around, not even ample, busty ones like her. Cleavage to gamblers, Ms. Tucker said, is "just another place to lose the dice." But gamblers prayed fervently to Lady Luck, their own version of the Roman Fortuna.

FRIDAY

Traditionally the day of The Crucifixion, The Flood, and The Fall, Friday is a terrible day to start anything, so never propose marriage on a Friday. It might be okay to ask someone to go away with you for the weekend.

In The Tyrol, they say children born on Friday will suffer. If a sick patient is visited on a Friday she or he will get worse, and if you call a doctor on a Friday the patient may die. (Call on a Wednesday and the doctor is out playing golf.)

Freya, the ancient Norse goddess of love and marriage, made Friday the favored day to marry—but where are the ancient Norse now? Prior to that, Friday came and went as the favored day for sexual connections in ancient Syria.

Orthodox Jews have sex on Friday nights.

FUNERALS

An old American belief is: "Always choose your second mate at the funeral of the first." I don't know if it is true, because he was dead long before I was born, but I was told that my maternal grandfather met and proposed to my grandmother (his second wife) at the graveside of his first wife. The two women were cousins and looked very much alike. He had courted the first wife for years. He married the second during the weeks after first seeing her. The marriage produced nine children and my grandmother (who long outlived him) was in love with him until the day she died.

GEMS

Rubies, the birthstone for people born in July under Cancer, have been highly valued since at least biblical times. Rubies were popularly believed to protect chastity, which is why celibate clerics sported them in the Middle Ages. Unfortunately, being the color of blood, they attract werewolves.

Pearls are unlucky in engagement rings. Diamonds are a girl's best friend. Don't wait until your seventy-fifth wedding anniversary to get one.

There are many books on the supposed powers of rare and common, precious and semiprecious, and ordinary stones. For love, amethyst may be best, if it is your birthstone. The assertions of this or that power made in antiquity or the Middle Ages were basically repeated in the likes of *The Secrets of Albertus Magnus of the Vertues of Herbes, Stones, and Certain Beasts* (1637) and are still being proffered today, without explanation. More on Spells and Charms, later.

GESTURES

Would you consider the act of genuflection as superstitious as crossing your fingers? A difference between religion and superstition lies in whether the gesture is considered piety or power. Sex magic means making passes.

It seems more natural for the cosmos to have been birthed by a goddess than a god and it may be that matriarchal religions came before patriarchal ones. Today many pagans serve the Moon Goddess. Nobody seems to be interested in moon gods such as Nannar and Sin. The Great Mother appeared in numerous forms. Here are two that you can read about in mythology: Cybele and Rhea.

GILGUD

The Jews believed in reincarnation but they seem to have given that up lately. *Gilgud* is what the cabalists called it, the continual reincarnation of a soul seeking its loved one across

Cybele.   Rhea.

the centuries. Lee Langley's new novel *Distant Music* is based on this idea. Emmanuel and Esperança are a Jewish sailor and a Portuguese peasant in Madeira in 1429. After various reincarnations, they appear as a rock musician and a suburban housewife in London 2000. Does this kind of thing explain Marlowe's line that Shakespeare quoted, "Whoever loved who loved not at first sight?"

GREEN

You have read elsewhere in this chapter that superstition is dead set against brides wearing green. I suppose Green deserves a special note of its own. First, the reason green clothing is unfortunate is that it is the color of the fairies, pixies and other little folk—they prefer to be called Good Companions—that resent humans wearing their color.

What they thought of Robin Hood and his Merry Men in forest green, I do not know; probably they liked Scarlet best.

Green is considered by theater people to be unlucky on the set, along with peacock feathers, real flowers onstage, wigs, and many other things, from whistling in the dressing rooms to putting a hat on a bed. Green is considered lucky by sex magicians and useful in operations involving fertility (the green of Nature).

HAIR

Hair is sexy. When a woman married, her husband might cut her hair. Mutilating property kept others from stealing it. This could go as far as tattooing, stretching the lips hideously or blackening teeth. Men in old Japan shaved off their wives' too-sexy eyebrows. Was this protective, or a gesture of dominance?

HAND

Few people like a clammy handshake but a damp hand is supposed to be the sign of an amorous nature.

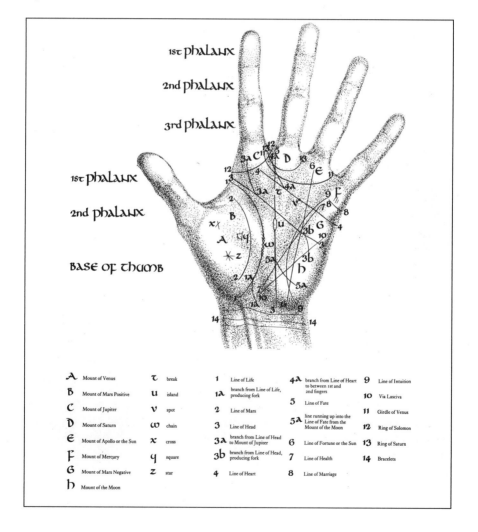

A	Mount of Venus	**τ**	break	**1**	Line of Life	**4a**	branch from Line of Heart to between 1st and 2nd fingers	**9**	Line of Intuition
B	Mount of Mars Positive	**u**	island	**1a**	branch from Line of Life, producing fork	**5**	Line of Fate	**10**	Via Lasciva
C	Mount of Jupiter	**v**	spot	**2**	Line of Mars			**11**	Girdle of Venus
D	Mount of Saturn	**ω**	chain	**3**	Line of Head	**5a**	line running up into the Line of Fate from the Mount of the Moon	**12**	Ring of Solomon
E	Mount of Apollo or the Sun	**x**	cross	**3a**	branch from Line of Head to Mount of Jupiter	**6**	Line of Fortune or the Sun	**13**	Ring of Saturn
F	Mount of Mercury	**q**	square	**3b**	branch from Line of Head, producing fork	**7**	Line of Health	**14**	Bracelets
G	Mount of Mars Negative	**z**	star	**4**	Line of Heart	**8**	Line of Marriage		
h	Mount of the Moon								

HANDKERCHIEFS

Do not give a lover a handkerchief as a present. If you do, the relationship will break up (which is nothing to sneeze at). A handkerchief says "Blow!"

HEARTS

Superstition sites love in the heart, so the hearts of animals may turn up in recipes for sex magic, as well as plants and herbs with heart-shaped leaves.

The heart was also thought to be the place from which courage came. That is why the Cowardly Lion wants a heart in *The Wizard of Oz*. Amerindians used to eat the hearts of enemies who had died bravely in battle, to obtain their courage.

No less impressive was the technique of the Aztecs. Here is a translation of a passage in what is called *The Florentine Codex*, a document dated around 1550 and taken from Mexico to Florence:

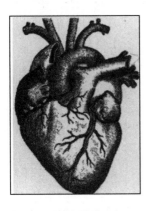

And they named the hearts of the prisoners "precious fruit of the eagle cactus." They lifted them up to the sun, the turquoise prince, the eagle that soars. They offered them to him; they fed him with them. This they called sending up "the eagle man," because whoever died in battle went unto the presence [of the sun]; he went before and he rested in the presence of the sun. He did not go to the land of the dead. Thus [by eating the heart] the valor of the prisoner would not perish in vain; thus he [the one who took the heart] took from the prisoner his renown.

One of the noblest things a brave of our own Plains Indians could do was rescue the dead body of a fallen comrade from the enemy; that way it could not be mutilated.

In Mexico, Hernán Cortés arrived with some men and horses at Vera Cruz in 1519. Among the first things he saw was evidence of cannibalism at the Isle of Sacrifices. With the aid of enemies of the Aztecs, Cortés and his men reached Tenochtitlán, the capital of an empire that had grown ever stronger since the twelfth century. They destroyed

the city and the empire and replaced the superstitious eating of captives' hearts with the eating of the body and blood of Christ. The Aztecs fed their gods; our God feeds us.

The heart was likewise important in other religions. When archeologists found the mummy of Thutmose III, who ruled Egypt in the 18th dynasty, they discovered that the grave robbers Ahmed abd er-Rassul and his brothers had cut a hole in the wrapped mummy to get the jeweled scarab placed in the heart of it. That amulet had been intended as the pharaoh's ticket, as it were, to the kingdom of death.

HORNS

Horns on a god are signs of virility, as with the Horned God of the Celts. Think of warriors with horned helmets, whether Vikings or Amerindians with buffalo horns on their headdresses. On The Devil horns are symbolic of his bestial nature. Symbolically, horns on a man mean cuckoldry. All this inspires such ingredients as powdered horn in sex magic recipes.

An unusual Horned Goddess was Hathor, whose headdress had cow horns and a sun disc by the time she was taken into Egyptian religion. She was a goddess of childbirth and fertility, Lady of Byblos, and Lady of the Heavens. As Sekhmet (Eye of Ra) she was associated with Ishtar, and as the Golden Goddess she was associated by the Greeks with Artemis. Hathor was hell on wheels and terrible in battle, but they quieted her down by tricking her into drinking beer with pomegranate juice in it. Maybe that ought to come later under Recipes, in case anyone has a horny but rambunctious girlfriend to deal with.

The horns on Moses in Michelangelo's statue, by the way, are just an amusing error: the Hebrew for "rays of light" and "horns" were confused. Like many holy people, Moses exuded radiance. Even before the Jews and before the halos of Christian saints, people said they saw light around the heads of certain people. As a matter of fact we all have auras. Christ's halo has a cross in it. Dead saints have round halos, and living saints square ones in medieval iconography.

Your health but not your holiness or lack of it can be diagnosed from the color of your aura.

HORSES

If you are pregnant, don't pass under a horse's head. Hanging around horses will prolong gestation. Step over the reins or rope by which a horse is tethered and you will be pregnant within a year.

In Texas they say, "A child who is ugly in the cradle will be beautiful in the saddle."

INVISIBILITY

Magic is rich in formulae for invisibility, but you will not see one here. I should mention invisibility, though, for the voyeurs amongst us. I might add that the Chinese, much bothered by invisible terrors, have a way to make the invisible visible: you throw dog blood at it.

ITCII

No, I'm not going to talk about the "itch" for sex. Just the old saying, "If your upper lip itches, you will be kissed by someone tall; if it's your lower, by someone short." If some more private part of your anatomy itches you may already have encountered someone unfortunate.

IVY

On your way to town, to make sure all will go well, clutch some ivy to your bosom. It lasts long and most of all it is green, the color of Venus (though also the color of envy and jealousy). Along with the ivy goes a little prayer or incantation:

> Ivy, ivy, I love you.
> In my bosom I put you.
> The first young man who speaks to me
> My future husband he shall be.

Sounds a little desperate to me. Choose your route carefully and you may be able to exercise some control over the first person you will meet.

Some say it is unlucky to have ivy (and hawthorn blossoms, and rubber plants, and more) in the house.

Ivy will grow profusely on the grave of a girl who died of unrequited love. If ivy will not grow well on a grave, the occupant is not happy where he or she has gone. As you know from Christmastide, holly is male and ivy is female, an old druidic idea.

As for poison ivy, carry an elderberry in your pocket to protect you.

KNIVES

If you give a knife as a present you will cut the relationship. If someone gives you a knife as a present, hand him or her a penny, as what you have thereby bought cannot hurt you. If a knife or other sharp object wounds you, superstition says, keep it shiny or your wound will not heal well.

Never leave a jackknife open. Never hand a person a knife; put it down and let them pick it up. These may not be superstitions, rather simply good advice, but superstitions, like the Ten Commandments, are often simple sound advice reinforced by some kind of higher authority than reason. There is "something in it."

KNOTS TO YOU

Among the famous people reported to have suffered impotence due to witches who tied cursed knots in cords, were The Prophet Mohammed and King James I and VI (of England and Scotland). James was married to a Catholic princess

from Denmark but was gay. His young boyfriends did not seem to worry about old James' problem. Mohammed found who had laid the curse and made sure the cords were destroyed. Then he was himself again.

In some cultures you must untie all knots in your clothes to get married. In others "true lovers' knots" are put in the ribbons of bridal bouquets, etc.

LADDERS

You know it is unlucky to walk under a ladder. You may not know that one reason for it has nothing to do with the possibility of something like a can of paint being dropped on your head. The real reason, people say, is that the ladder,

Aphrodite.

the wall, and the ground form a triangle. To invade the triangle is to attack The Trinity—three persons in one God. If a woman walks under a ladder it is particularly unlucky. Just as when she sits on a table, it means she will not get married in the coming year.

LAUNDRY

When doing the laundry, don't get yourself wet or you will marry a drunkard. If you get your t-shirt all wet at the laundromat maybe someone will ask you out for a drink.

LIGHTS

May attract bugs but discourage demons, especially those with sex or other possession on their minds. A virgin, you learn elsewhere in this book, can make a candle that has just about gone out flare up again. (Who else tells you these things?) Light a candle for luck.

The first person to blow out a lamp on the wedding night will be the first to die. You don't buy a suit without taking it out in the daylight to look at it, so don't marry someone you met that night in Las Vegas until at least noon the next day. For such weddings, Elvis impersonators are okay to officiate. Travel light: take half as many clothes (and twice as much money) as you were planning.

THE LIVER

Superstition used to say that the seat of the affections was the liver. Today we have "I ♥ New York" bumper stickers, and hearts are on every pop song and valentine, for the heart has stopped symbolizing the source of wisdom (haven't you heard of "learning things by heart" and "taking things to heart"?), or even courage ("he has the heart of a lion"). Now it's the site of love (*Two Hearts in Three-Quarter Time*, a lovers' waltz).

LUCKY IN LOVE

Superstition has it that those who are lucky at card games are unlucky at love. What superstitions do you know connected with gambling? What superstitions do you personally believe bring success in love? Here's one for Vegas: it is unlucky to gamble in a room with any woman present who is not gambling also.

MANDRAKE

Magic says get one and work marvels. Superstition says that if you get a hold of one, burn it immediately or disastrous things will happen to you. Later on, I'll tell you where you can find out how to use a magical mandrake, if you dare.

Mandrake.

MARRIAGE DATES

Dating may lead to marriage, and here is superstition's advice on the best dates to tie the knot:

January 2, 4, 11, 19, 21
February 1, 3, 10, 19, 21
March 3, 5, 12, 20, 23
April 2, 4, 12, 20, 22
May 2, 4, 12, 20, 23
June 1, 3, 11, 19, 21
July 1, 3, 12, 19, 21, 31
August 2, 11, 18, 20, 30
September 1, 9, 16, 18, 28
October 15, 17, 18, 27, 29
November 5, 11, 13, 22, 25
December 1, 8, 10, 19, 23, 29, 31

More superstition:

Married in January's hoar and rime,
Widowed you'll be before your time.
Married in February's sleepy weather,
Life you'll tread in time together.
Married when March winds shrill and roar,
Your home will be on a distant shore.
Married 'neath April's changeful skies,
A chequered path before you lies.
Married when bees o'er May's blooms flit,
Strangers around your board will sit.
Married in month of roses (June),
Life will be a honeymoon.
Married July with flowers ablaze,
Bittersweet memories in after days.

Married in August's heat and drowse,
Lover and friend in chosen spouse.
Married in September's golden glow,
Smooth and serene your life will go.
Married when leaves in October thin,
Toil and hardship for you begin.
Married in veils of November mist,
Fortune your wedding ring has kissed.
Married in days of December cheer,
Love shines brighter year by year.

22	47	16	41	10	35	4
5	23	48	17	42	11	29
30	6	24	49	18	36	12
13	31	7	25	43	19	37
38	14	32	1	26	44	20
21	39	8	33	2	27	45
46	15	40	9	34	3	28

It is also considered luckiest to marry in January and tactful to marry in the first month of pregnancy.

Marriage on the last day of the year has useful tax advantages. Of course you will avoid any Friday the thirteenth and April Fool's Day. If you think you are going to have trouble remembering your anniversary (or are cheap about presents), I suggest 29 February.

As for the day of the week:

Monday for wealth,
Tuesday for health,
Wednesday's the best day of all.
Thursday for crosses,
Friday for losses,
Saturday, no luck at all.

Always avoid unlucky Friday:

> Friday's moon
> Come when it will, it comes too soon.

THE MARRIAGE SERVICE

Unmarried women were advised never to read the marriage service all the way through. This may simply have been to keep the bit about "obey," from them. When entering the church to participate in the marriage service, step in right foot first. Don't have a double wedding; one couple will be unstable. These days, when half of all U.S. marriages (even those at which only one couple is wed) end in divorce, you don't want even worse odds.

MAY

Count backwards nine months from May. That is a good time to be careful about conceiving, for superstition says (in Britain): "A May baby is always sickly; you may try but you'll never rear it." Even cats born in May are failures: they won't catch any mice. In Wiltshire and Devon, one source says, the May cat will, on the contrary, bring "snakes and slow worms" into the house.

THE MAYPOLE

May be originally a tree (with a Teutonic god resident), or just a sun-worshippers' symbol (the long ribbons attached to it representing the rays of the sun), but I say it is a phallic symbol.

Pagan May Day was rather rude, even the medieval May celebrations could get very out of hand. In Britain a number of traditions converged on May celebrations. They ranged from ringing Christian bells to drive away demons and wake up the spring, to druidic fertility rites of Beltane, the fire of the god Bel, lit to honor the sun and defeat the powers of darkness. Beltane was and is one of the major holidays of the witches. To boost fertility, jump over the fires holding hands with a member of the opposite sex.

MENSTRUATION

People used to believe that touching menstrual blood would cause tuberculosis or syphilis, kill fruit trees, ruin milk or food, and worse. Even before *Leviti-*

cus, which declared that menstruating women are unclean and that having sex with them is a capital offense for both parties, men feared menstrual blood. Some still do.

Menstruation was called The Curse. It was thought to be bad for bees in the vicinity and to cloud mirrors in the house and stop butter from coming in the churn (even if you put a silver coin in), among other things. The Christians picked up the prejudices of the Jews, though after about six centuries a pope (a Gregory, in AD 579) said it was okay for menstruating women to attend church. Some Protestant sects have still not become that liberal.

Some menstruating superstitions (like you don't feel stressed enough at that time of the month!):

Menstruating women may have greasier hair but shouldn't wash it and in fact should pretty much stay away from water. If they put their feet into cold water it will cause blood to rise to the head and make them melancholy. No swimming. No water at all but I guess there is no ban on carrying plastic bottles of designer water wherever they go.

The presence of three menstruating women in a room at one time was supposed to render one of them pregnant before the year was out.

Among some Amerindian nations, menstruating women were not permitted to go near a wounded brave and they were kept away from a war party setting out lest they bring defeat upon them. They were never allowed near sacred objects (such as medicine bundles) or sacred places, lest they defile them. They might have to stay in a special teepee until their periods were over, smoke their clothes over evergreen fires, and take sweat-baths to purify themselves (as Orthodox Jewish women still do). They had to avoid long grass because snakes that could smell them lurked there and would strike.

If you want to risk the death penalty that *Leviticus* threatens (or have decided that some things in that book might not be a good idea—such as killing your children if they do not obey you or observing a ban on scarlet clothing), and you have sex during menstruation, your child may turn out to be a monster (see II *Esdras* 5: 8). Or a redhead. By the way, the commonest surnames in Italy are *Rossi*, *Russo*, etc., for redheads.

MICE

Mice seem to have active sex lives so sometimes either the tail or the whole thing is thrown into the witches' cauldrons. The rat without a tail mentioned in that unmentionable Shakespeare play is not a regular rodent: the fact that it is imperfect brands it as a familiar. The devil makes only imperfect creatures, Brand X copies of God's creations.

The worst magical use of mice I can think of is to take a needle and thread and poke the needle in one eye and out the other of a live mouse. As the mouse's vital energy drains out of it, it will be transferred to the infant, strengthening the frail little baby.

I think this is horrible, but it is a lot better than drinking the blood or eating the hearts or livers of other animals or of human sacrifices. Another unpleasant idea is to feed three roasted mice to a child to break it of the habit of wetting the bed.

To some extent, the horrific nature of magical ingredients and acts energizes the magician. It also keeps those for whom the magic is performed aware of the transgression being perpetrated.

MIDSUMMER'S EVE

This is the time for fairies to be around—and for young maidens to pluck a rose and put it carefully away. If it is found to be still (fairly) fresh on Christmas day, she must wear it to church. Her intended will take it from her. Even if one has no intended, it pays to advertise. Don't let anyone who takes the rose from you at church propose there, because a proposal made in church always leads to a bad marriage. This may be the brainchild of some parson who didn't want the congregation fooling around in those box pews when he was preaching—or to see a congregation preying instead of praying.

MISTLETOE

Everyone knows we kiss under the mistletoe but few know it comes from old superstitions of the Druids, who regarded it as part of their sun-worshipping religion and cut it with a golden knife, and the Norse goddess Frigga, goddess of love. The Romans said the white berry came from the tears of Venus when wounded by Cupid's arrow.

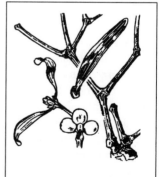

Pliny said that mistletoe was used to guarantee conception. You'll see more about this in the chapter on Recipes.

DAT OL' DEBBIL MOON

Sicilian superstition says boys will be born under a waxing moon, girls under a waning moon. Proponents of women's liberation may wish to criticize the implications here. They may prefer: "A baby conceived under a full moon will be female." If it's a full moon beware not only the Goddess, but vampires and harpies too.

Mistletoe.

"ILL MET BY MOONLIGHT"

Everyone knows that moonlight is romantic. It is said to make people fall in love—or become lunatics. If you reflect moonlight with a mirror into the eyes of a sleeping person, you can make them fall in love with you. And if you expose a pebble to moonlight for three nights and then wear it in a string around your neck, you will not have to worry about your HMO. Such a pebble will bring you good health. Or are they calling it "wellness" everywhere now?

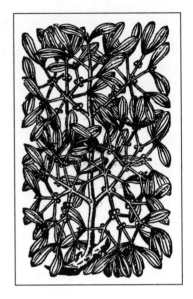

THE MOON

Lovers should never swear by the moon. As Juliet had learned, among other superstitions picked up from her nurse, the moon is "inconstant."

Mistletoe.

MOTHERS-IN-LAW

Mothers-in-law have been much maligned. Among the Apache and Navajos, a man never looked directly at his mother-in-law for fear of going blind. The Zulus spoke to the mother-in-law only through a third person, never directly.

NAME MAGIC

I have a chapter on name magic in my general survey of onomastics (the study of names and naming), *What's in a Name?* (1989, revised in paperback 1995) and more on names and the occult in my *Names in Popular Culture* (2002). Check them out (of the library if you don't want to buy them). There is much to be said here in connection with sex magic but one example will have to suffice. I choose to stress the fact that superstition likes to keep the real names of men from women because women are all suspected by primitive men of being up to no good and very likely to try witchcraft against them.

To perform witchcraft, as you know, a lock of hair, a fingernail clipping, "magic" semen and so on, are all very useful. But a name is also an integral part of a person, magic assumes, and with it sex magic can be performed.

In some societies, people will not give their real names to strangers. A census in India was difficult because some wives there are forbidden to speak the names of their husbands. In some societies, people have names so secret they do not know them themselves. They are whispered into the ears of infants (who will not remember this) and then kept secret by the witch doctor. If you don't know your secret name it is really, really secure, so you cannot let it slip and put yourself in danger.

Some primitive men will not allow the names they use between themselves to be overheard by their women. The more primitive the tribe the more names are kept secret and the more women are not trusted to handle such dangerous things as names.

NOÂNITZ

Vampires are for another book, but it's important to mention the widespread fear that blood-sucking creatures will take form and attack babies in the night. *Noânitz* is a particularly virulent Russian variety of predators that go after infants.

NEWLY-MARRIED COUPLES

These happy pairs should take care that no dog barks at them as they go to the church and that no stone rolls across their path, nor any other symbol of obstruction greets them until they go off on their honeymoon (a time when Anglo-Saxon couples celebrated by drinking wine made of honey).

It is considered extremely unlucky to trip over the threshold when making an entrance (except onstage, where actors say it is fine, perhaps because it may raise an easy laugh), and that is why it is the custom for the groom to carry the bride over the threshold of their new home or their honeymoon accommodations. I mentioned this earlier. Another reason for carrying the bride may be related to the holdovers from the days of a bride being stolen and run away with, similar to the tradition of having a best man to fight pursuers, pelting the couple with rice or flowers when they come out of the

Franz Anton Mesmer
There is nothing magical about mesmerism (hypnosis) but it was often used to seduce women and thought to be a kind of sex magic.

church, and slipping away or running away to begin the honeymoon after the reception, etc.

ONIONS

Culpepper's *Herbal* says that onions will "increase the sperm." This seems to me about as reliable as the old belief that if a man will get stark naked and collect henbane early in the morning while standing on one foot it will "bring love."

THE WISE OLD OWL

Common belief is that the owl is wise. It was the symbol of the Greek goddess of wisdom, Athena. Thus the owl becomes part of certain mythological and demonic figures to indicate wisdom. It also symbolized other things to the Greeks, such as victory, and was the symbol of Athena's city, Athens.

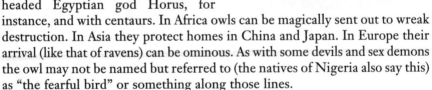

As you probably know, animal/human creatures often occur in myth, religion, iconography, and folklore to indicate bestial aspects or dual natures of men, gods, and demons. That explains why The Devil is portrayed with horns and a tail, why satyrs had the legs of randy goats, and so on.

You are familiar with the hawk-headed Egyptian god Horus, for instance, and with centaurs. In Africa owls can be magically sent out to wreak destruction. In Asia they protect homes in China and Japan. In Europe their arrival (like that of ravens) can be ominous. As with some devils and sex demons the owl may not be named but referred to (the natives of Nigeria also say this) as "the fearful bird" or something along those lines.

The owl can be an evil omen. Owls' eggs were used in magical recipes and it was said owls could reveal a woman's innermost secrets. As a night-flying bird it could be associated with witches, such as the Latin *volantica* and the Italian *strega*, the Spanish *bruja*.

From Colin de Plancy's French history of the diabolical, the figure you see here—part owl, part human, is the demon Andras, a demon of strife.

PEACOCK FEATHERS

May be the most decorative contraceptive, for superstition says that no baby will ever be born in a house where peacock feathers are kept. Nicer than a gaudily colored condom.

PHOTOGRAPHY

I do not know how many of these sex superstitions you believe but here is one you will very likely reject. Superstition says that if a couple is photographed together they will never marry. I have seen too many halves of photos to believe that one myself.

PINS AND NEEDLES, NEEDLES AND PINS

There should be neither pins in a bridesmaid's dress nor any jewelry pins worn by her. If a pin is given to a bridesmaid, even if she is the lucky one to catch the wedding bouquet, she will not be married until the next Whitsuntide, the Pentecost time (usually late May to early June).

If while she is sewing a woman's needle breaks into three pieces, a marriage is on the way.

Hungarians say if a woman takes her needle case and distaff (symbol of with woman's role) to her new husband's home, all the children will be female.

In Northern England, if a woman gives another woman a pin she must say she is not giving it, or there will be bad luck. Never lend a needle: it pricks the friendship.

Superstition says that a pin placed in the heart of a poppet will cause the person whom the poppet represents to die. So sex magic may stick pins in the genital areas, etc., but never in the heart (which otherwise would be regarded as the site of love). Witches' needles recall phallic symbols.

RIDING TO YOUR WEDDING

Back in the days before stretch limos, the man might ride horseback on his way to his wedding. He had to be careful not to ride a mare or else his children would be females.

"GATHER YE ROSES WHILE YE MAY"

But never scatter red rose petals (they represent blood) at a wedding, on a bed, etc. This brings nothing but very bad luck, however romantic it may seem. The deep red rose means "bashful shame."

If a red rose petal falls into your glass, do not drink.

Ordinarily roses speak of love but always make bouquets of an odd number—a dozen is a mistake but 13 would be worse and 11 looks like you kept one to give to someone else. White roses suggest purity. Pink roses suggest romance. Red roses suggest passion. The cabbage rose is "the ambassador of love."

The yellow rose is luckier than the white (and in Texas is particularly welcome). The dog rose means both pleasure and pain. A rose without thorns is said to mean "early attachment." There is a widespread tradition about statements that flowers can make but the most important is that one should bring only white ones when visiting a residence for the first time. They will go with any décor.

To complicate matters, some other experts say you should never bring white flowers of any kind into a house, that they are almost as likely to bring disaster as a branch of flowering hawthorn. You know how unlucky that can be—don't you? Hawthorn was, tradition says, the Crown of Thorns.

Never let a florist put fern with flower bouquets, especially bridal bouquets. Why not try baby's breath? Almost everyone says fern should never be brought into a house. (A friend of mine adds that she will not enter a restaurant, coffeehouse, or bar that has them!)

Watch out that when visiting Greeks you do not bring white flowers on any occasion. Greeks think of white flowers, especially chrysanthemums, as flowers of death. Some other Europeans do, too, while Mexicans say orange or yellow chrysanthemums are the flowers for the Day of the Dead celebrations (when they hold picnics for the departed, in cemeteries, to which all the living are invited as well).

THE RUN-AROUND

In Darjeeling (India, where the tea comes from) there is a sacred tree of Poona. I mentioned it in my book of superstition (as I mentioned many of the superstitions in this book) but it is so gee whiz a story that I feel I have to retell it for those who have not seen that book, the first in this long series on the occult.

> Some years ago an old woman called Shelibai ran around [the tree] a million times to ensure the birth of a grandson. When the boy was born, the news took three months to reach the grandmother, so she made 200,000 laps too many.

These days there are easier ways, if you want to adopt them, to make sure the baby will be a boy.

SCANDINAVIAN SUPERSTITIONS

If the couple did not refrain from intercourse for the first three days of the marriage their child might be misshapen. In a 1687 *bonespractica* (farmer's guide) from Valdres (Norway) it is noted that if you want a fair-haired child don't conceive it on a Saturday or Sunday. At that time, Saturday was the traditional day to get married, so apparently the first night (quite apart from the feudal custom of the lord taking the bride the first night!) was a no-no. The same guide warns a woman never to spin with the distaff held between the feet of a man if she does not wish him to lose the power of erection.

The three-night ban (sometimes called "the Tobias nights") is reported in the saga literature and there you will also find tales of impotence being created by *trolldom* (the evil magic of trolls). Impotence, considered an impediment to marriage and a sufficient cause for annulling marriages, was often heard of in the sagas and, for instance, in *Kormak's Saga*, we hear of a witch who sacrificed three geese to put a spell of impotence on someone.

Galder (magic) could also remove bad spells (in Norse folklore all impotence spells are blamed on women and women have to be attacked with counterspells) and even help a young man to seduce a female. Finns were especially sought out for their presumed magical powers. A Finn might be able

Näcken (Water Sprite) by Ernst Josephson (1851–1906).

to assist you to have a son even if you were unlucky enough to have been born on a Sunday yourself. If you could not hire a Finn, you could try to find a so-called "black book" (*grimoire*) brought up north from Germany. These were common in Scandinavia from medieval times right through the Age of Reason, and maybe later.

One of the "black books" from the middle of the eighteenth century in Sweden gives a magical method for making a girl fall in love with you. You take a frog and put it in a box with some perforations in it and, stopping up your ears so you will hear nothing, and speaking no words, you go to an anthill and place the box on top of the anthill, then stepping backward 9 steps and finally rushing back to your home in silence. After 9 days you return and you will find that the ants have consumed the frog but have left a tiny bone in the shape of a fork. All you have to do then is fasten the forked bone on the clothing of the girl you desire (stealthily, of course).

Ola J. Holten informs me that this was a much earlier custom, there being a sixteenth-century Norwegian law specifically forbidding this *grobein* (frog-bone business). He adds "this bone was used to capture a girl or a boy." In a medical book from Telemark (Norway) of 1520, Holten reports:

> You must take the left shoulder bone of a toad. One part looks like a fork, the other like a hook. The hook part should be used (with a formula to be recited) if you think the girl is rather willing; the fork should be used if you think she is not.

Holten also refers us to the sagas and "black books" for a number of magical ways to discover if a girl is a virgin or not. In one method, you got a feather off a hen at the time it was mating and put it under a girl's pillow. How you interpreted the result, I do not know, but there are more common methods of finding out if a female is a virgin. Folklore, you must be warned, also has its methods of faking virginity.

In Italy, it was the custom to hang blooded sheets from the window of the room in which the newly-married couple spent their (presumed) first night together, but if the sheets had not been bloodied you could always get blood, not a feather, from a hen. . . . Many societies have similar customs.

If a joint makes snapping sounds, you will have as many lovers as there are cracks. Spots on a girl's nails also number her lovers. If a toe is just as long as its neighboring one, it means you will get an evil partner. If a man treats his horse badly, he will treat his wife badly too. Pain in the big toe is a sign of love. Being ticklish means a girl is keen on boys and ticklish around the knees means she is a jealous person, so don't get romantically involved with her. If your garter gets loose, you lover has been cheating on you. If you've lost it, the lover has had an accident. If a young man has loose shoelaces, he will marry an old widow. If a woman's belt constantly slips down she will marry a faithful man and if she has a high forehead she will marry a man of higher rank.

Meet a toad on the way to a date and you're going to get lucky. Hear a fox bark in the night and you know someone in the neighborhood is pregnant and in Telemark they say that if you hear a cuckoo a bastard will soon be born nearby or maybe just a lot of pregnancies will soon occur. If the cuckoo is heard after haymaking, pregnancies will be scarcer. If a woodpecker is heard at Toten north of Oslo they expect a marriage soon.

If a girl released a butterfly, it would fly in the direction of her lover, but she could get the same information from a horsefly.

As we play loves-me/loves-me-not with the petals of flowers in Norway they have *gitt/ungitt* (married/unmarried). In northern Norway, a young man able to turn a bellflower inside out without damage to it could count on getting the woman he wanted.

Fish, eggs, and salt stimulate the sex drives, Scandinavian folklore tells us.

If you eat the head of the fish you'll marry the oldest girl in the family, if the middle of the fish the middle girl, if the tail the youngest one. When eating eggs, crush the shell, or you won't get married. Why is that girl putting too much salt on her food? In Telemark they used to pour salt on a baby girl; it was thought that when she grew up she would attract a lot of boys. That boy who loves cakes will make a faithful husband. The boy fiddling with his food is not a good marriage prospect. The boy off whom a girl brushes dust has success taken away from him by that action.

The pot hanging crooked foretells an unhappy marriage. If the servant girl made the washing-up water too warm or burned the porridge or broke the thread when spinning, well she would not get married that year and when she did eventually get married if she had trouble getting fires started her husband would be an angry one and if she splashed the washing water too much she would get a drunkard. (Those threats seem like good ways to keep her in line.) The one who makes a good porridge will get a good husband. If the porridge bubbles too violently, expect a nasty mother-in-law.

If you drop a ball of yarn accidentally, look up at the ceiling; you may see your future spouse. If you make good brooms you will get a good wife. If a girl dropped her end of a sheet she was folding with another girl she would be told, "You'll be tending a cradle first!" If a woman puts down her knitting without having finished a row, her lover will turn back halfway toward visiting her. But if she pricks herself accidentally with a needle while sewing . . .
.

SOUL MATES

If you believe in reincarnation—which we have pretty much given up on in the West, though we still have people named René, Renée and Renata—you may think love at first sight is due to their relationship in a previous life.

SPIT

A magic fluid. Theocritus wrote: "I spit thrice on my breast to guard me against fascinating charms." Exchanging spit in kissing can charm.

STILLBIRTH

Many superstitions hover around such sad disappointments in life as a still-born, whether because of natural causes or the curses of witches. Witches tried to get hold of the bodies of stillborn infants to use in hideous rites. Better-intentioned persons buried the remains in the same grave with adult dead in the belief that the innocent would help the afterlife of the grown-up. Grown-ups, as you may or may not know, must be buried lying east/west, and the south side of a graveyard is the best place to be if you have to be there at all.

A VISIT FROM THE STORK

Ancient superstition said that a stork would fly over a house where a birth was soon to happen and in time it was believed that the stork brought the baby.

SUNSHINE

If you are menstruating, keep out of the sunshine; the sun could make you pregnant, just as it breeds maggots in meat. This was Hamlet's advice to Ophelia; ironically he was the most dangerous son.

FEAR THE GREEKS EVEN WHEN BEARING GERMS

Ancient Greeks thought that any sexual intercourse gave one *keres* (little demons) so that magical means were necessary to render one clean again. For all their superstition they were given to various forms of intercourse, including pederasty. Slang still credits the derivation to Greek, as well as using the word *buggery*, referring to Bulgaria.

Touching another person sexually was as unclean as touching a corpse. Even madness was supposed to be contagious; at the sight of a madman you had to spit or you might catch his insanity. There were various magicians with cures for everything and guaranteed, money refunded if no satisfaction received magic for the impotent, the lovelorn, and the infertile. Or you could pay for a first-class curse on potency, love life, or fertility of your enemy. If you killed anyone by magic, the law would get you. If you killed anyone accidentally, you had to be fumigated in the same manner as you were after sexual intercourse. In this case fumigation treated you for having come too close to death, rather than coming too close to life—the reason for the former.

TEETH AND TOES

In the north of England, if a baby's teeth come early it is a sign that "fresh toes," another baby, will soon be on the way.

TIME AND TIDE

Some superstitions limit times to have sex to ten days or fewer a month. One comedienne says that with premenstrual syndrome, menstruation, and post-menstrual syndrome she has "one good day" a month.

Whatever your good day or days, if you want a boy, lie on your right side and sleep on that side every night for a week. Also for a boy, keep your diet such that your system is acid; alkaline systems are supposed to produce girls. Naturally check the day, hour, minute, and geographical location for ideal conception and find a stopwatch as well as an extremely talented male. Get started right away on arranging the very best instant and place for the child to be born. Avoid times of eclipses; the child conceived or born during one may be a monster. Full moons and rising tides are propitious times to conceive. Check the *Farmer's Almanac.*

If you have a great deal of time on your hands, you could read through *Who's Who* and discover the best of all 365 days to be born if you want your child to have a chance at fame. If you like, you can specialize in the best day for famous doctors, lawyers, etc. Witness one woman who said of her tots, "The doctor is three and the lawyer is two."

TUESDAY

Tuesday, on the whole is not a good day; that's what you will find in many books. Superstition says it was on a Tuesday that Eve first menstruated. But we'll come back to Tuesday somewhat later, just to show you how frequently these superstitions contradict each other

TURNOFFS

Anaphrodisiacs are fewer than aphrodisiacs in the superstitious pharmacopoeia (where salt petre leads the list) but nuns say that the best way to fight the temptations to sins of the flesh is to get on your knees—to pray or to wash the convent floor.

TWINS

Twins are not all that unusual; they're born "once in every 86 times." An old joke goes, "If that is so, how did the mother of twins ever find time to do her housework?" Superstition says that identical twins are able, like the pair in the famous old play *The Corsican Brothers* (a melodrama translated from French by Irish playwright Dion Boucicault in 1848), to feel what the other is feeling and know what the other is thinking.

It is said that if your twins are a boy and a girl they will be your last offspring.

The Guinness Book of Records accords to the wife of Feodor Vassileyev of Shuya (Russia) the record for twins: 16 pairs of them. She also had seven sets of triplets and 4 sets of quadruplets. Altogether, between 1725 and 1765, she gave birth to 69 children, only two of whom died in childbirth. Match that!

VALENTINE'S DAY

Write the names of your boyfriends on little slips of paper and put each slip into a little ball of clay. The first to float to the top of water will reveal the name of the one with whom you should get most "serious."

There were several early saints named Valentine, one of whom was said to have worn an amethyst ring with a cupid engraved on it. But 14 February, superstition said, was the day when birds sought their mates, so that might have had something to do with it.

A song by a character in *Hamlet*:

> Tomorrow is St. Valentine's Day,
> All in the morning betimes,
> And I a maid at your window
> To be your valentine.

(Later on it gets dirty. Ophelia doesn't reach those verses but the audience knew them and this helped them to realize that this sweet young thing has lost her reason.)

If you are an unmarried female and see a bird on St. Valentine's Day, a bunting or a robin redbreast (in most cases a harbinger of bad luck, even death) means you will marry a sailor. If it's a goldfinch or yellow bird, a rich man, a crossbill a cross husband. Steer clear of a sparrow (love in a cottage), a bluebird (not happiness but poverty) or a wryneck (you will remain a spinster).

Mid-February was also the time of the Roman festival of the Lupercalia, and men drew lots to see who would share the lovers' spring festival with them. The Christians may have highjacked a Roman holiday in the same way they appropriated Saturnalia, which they made Christmas. Although I must admit "shepherds abiding the fields" at the Nativity indicates some other, warmer time of year in Nazareth.

WEDDING RINGS

Do not remove them. Actors are advised to put tape and makeup over them rather than to take off a wedding ring because it is wrong for the part.

WEDNESDAY

This is the luckiest day to get married. Monday is unlucky, and of course one never ever begins any new venture on a Tuesday or a Friday. Thursday, they say in Devon, has one unlucky hour: the hour before sunrise. But nobody gets married then anyway except perhaps in Las Vegas. So make it a Wednesday, and not in Lent. Cloudy means bad luck. Rain, however, is good luck, although the dresses may be ruined.

WHIPPOORWILL

This has nothing to do with whipping poor Will, just an imitation of the bird's cry, and not a really correct one at that. However, it will be of immense interest to young women.

If one hears the first call of the bird in spring just once, it means that her lover will soon appear. If the bird is heard calling twice, all bets are off until next year. All other superstitions concerning whippoorwills tend to suggest they are unfortunate to encounter.

WHITE LIES

Lying is a sin but lies to women don't count. "The first white lie a bride tells will bring her money." Is that "I do" to "love, honor, and obey"?

WIDOWER

Do not take the chance of a widower being the first one to enter your house at the New Year. That is almost as unlucky as a redhead. You need a dark man to do what the Scots call first footing, so station one at the front door to run in as soon as he hears cheering and champagne corks popping—the noise we make to drive away the demons, of course. Have him get in before the old redhead next door comes over to wish you a Happy New Year.

WIDOWS' PEAK

Widows used to wear a mourning headdress that came to a point on the forehead. It was said that if a married woman's hairline came to a peak she was certain to become a widow. Men's hairlines were not involved (and often receded anyway).

WITEKIND ON SUPERSTITION

In 1585, when witch persecutions were rife, a professor at Heidelberg named Herman Witekind (pseudonym "Lercheimer") published his *Christlich Bedencken und Errinerung von Zauberey*, an attempt to introduce some rationality and moderation into the discussion of *Zauberei* [Witchcraft].

He attacked the blind superstition of the time just as Reginald Scot, horrified by the witchcraft trials, would later do in his *Discoucrie of Witchcraft*.

James I, who saw any questioning of superstition as a threat to his most cherished beliefs, including his belief in the Divine Right of Kings, ordered Scot's book burned and would have burned Scot too had he been able to lay hands on him. At that time it was a very brave thing to oppose the excesses of "the burning time" and to denounce superstition.

WITH THE STARS TO PLAN IT

One of the reasons, among many, that I so admire the works of Maimonides is that he was one of the few learned men of his time who considered astrology bunk. Edward VI thought so, too: he banned astrological books in England in 1552. There is something to astrology, I admit, but the general public is simply not up to understanding what that is, and they become the dupes of charlatans.

I am Sagittarius with Scorpio rising if that means anything to you. It doesn't to me, because I cannot believe there are only a dozen basic personalities, a limited number of variations within them, and that they derive (in some way nobody ever explains precisely) from when you were born.

My mother was on vacation in Florida and I arrived almost three months early. Does that mean I was not intended to be a Sagittarius? What did I accomplish by my haste to get started that changed all my life? Had I been born as planned in Boston, what might have *been*?

See what I mean?

When the superstitions of astrology get connected to herbal medicines, alternative medicine seems to take on the guise of magical recipes. I admit that a great deal of the pseudoscience of sex magic is connected to the pseudo-science of astrology. I see something in that, as did Carl Jung.

The astronomy of Ptolemy, Erhard Schön, Nuremberg 1515.

I'm reminded of the big dinner table in Trimalchio's *nouveau riche* palace in the first novel, *The Golden Ass* of Petronius Arbiter. That heavily laden table had painted around the edges the signs of the Zodiac and at each place the food that "went" there, astrologically (beef at Taurus).

I always ask: Who *says* this? What do they know? Don't tell me what someone told you to believe. Tell me what someone proved to you to be true. What proof is there that Geminis are as you say? Or Leos? That "Paris is Virgo" (as one "metaphysician" told me when someone rescued her from the coffee shop where she works an occult gig and invited her to a Thanksgiving dinner I attended).

I know, as people are tired of hearing me say, that I had a different very early childhood than if I had come when expected three months later. Yes, I would have been born under a different sign, but because of our holidays the air is charged with anticipation in December that is absent in September.

Also, I defy anyone to show me how that affects whether I should trust a dark person I will meet next Tuesday. (If the person turns out to be a blonde people might say, "well, dark in *character*.") Let alone how I should live the rest of my days or which day I shall go, as Rabelais put it, "to meet the great Perhaps."

The Zodia according to medieval Arabs.

Just note, so I can get off this touchy topic (touchy because of my know-it-all attitude—or perhaps my nobody-knows-very-much attitude) that probably more Americans sneak a look at the horoscopes in the daily paper than check current events. That doesn't make it right. Just because almost everyone, whether they will admit to being superstitious or vehemently deny the accusation, believes that if you break a mirror you will have seven years of bad luck. That doesn't make it a fact.

Sex magic, as I have said, often calls on astrology to add potency or pertinence to its operations. I have never seen a convincing explanation of how sex magic astrology works comparable to, for instance, the best time for planting or harvesting, details traditionally published in the farmers' almanacs.

VENUS

I really cannot address astrology very sensibly here, but lest I be faulted for not saying anything, I shall attempt a brief discussion of the planet said to govern love, Venus.

Venus is associated with love, emotion, the lumbar region, the throat, the kidneys, the feminine (in both sexes), major arts such as poetry and drama and minor arts such as decorating and fashion design, but always there is an urge toward beauty. Those whom Venus controls may well be beautiful themselves and vain about their own appearance. The vanity may include those with whom they create relationships.

Those controlled by Venus may have many affairs, be gentle and refined, socially and artistically gifted. They can also be weak-willed, clinging, and impractical, romantic to their detriment or, strangely, uncertain about their desires and less than forthcoming about expressing love. Conversely, back in Mesopotamia, where this stuff seems to have started, Venus was associated with Ishtar, who had more to do with flat-out lust than anything romantic.

Venus works as follows in the twelve Houses of the Zodiac:

In the first House people can be pretty but spoiled. In the Second House they may tend toward the arts but be financially irresponsible. In the Third House they may be very sociable. In the Fourth House they may be into the minor arts. In the Fifth House they are even more likely to be in the arts (especially the theater) and somewhat dramatic, especially as regards love. In the

The conjunction of the planets at birth.

Sixth House their dislike of dirty or hard work comes to the fore. In the Seventh House they may be lucky in marriage. In the Eighth House they may be sexually unfulfilled but could get rich. In the Ninth House they will love travel and perhaps be a trifle difficult to hold onto (or more than a trifle so). In the Tenth House they will get along famously with others, perhaps more so in nonsexual relationships, but will take any setbacks too much to heart. In the Eleventh House their social skills are predominant. In the Twelfth House they will be attracted to the occult and possibly withdrawn. In all cases, astrology impels but does not compel. These generalizations are to be taken as regarding general tendencies and not applicable to all persons.

If you are an Aries with Venus significantly affecting you, you may be impulsive in love. If you are a Taurus, you will be perhaps too possessive. If you are a Gemini, you will be flirty and somewhat unreliable. If you are a Cancer, you will be domestic and overprotective. If you are a Leo, you will be domineering and over-possessive and somewhat extravagant in an attempt to buy love. If you are a Virgo, you may be overly critical of your partner. You are perhaps as cool as a Gemini but more outspoken. If you are a Libra, you may rush into affairs but generally will be happy in them. If you are a Scorpio, you will be passionate and probably well partnered. If you are a Sagittarius, you may be too independent or ego-driven to be a first-rate mate unless you choose someone very giving and tolerant, and even to them you will perhaps be slow to commit. If you are a Capricorn, you will be too cool for a Scorpio and need a partner who seeks independence or knows how to be independent without you noticing it very much. You will also be detached, independent, and overcautious in relationships if you are an Aquarius. If you are a Pisces, someone may walk all over

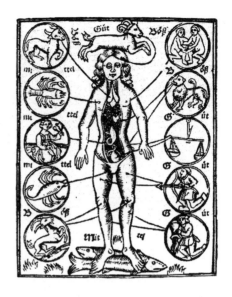

you. And if you show these remarks to any astrologers you will likely be told that they are all wrong, and be given completely different information by each one you consult.

Jeff Mayo in *The Planets and Human Behavior* (1972, reprinted 1985), says Venus means "cooperation, harmony, sympathy, compromise, creativeness, artistry, idealism, aestheticism." Traditional associations are "love and romance, marriage, sociability, love affairs, sensuality, sexual intercourse, beauty, pleasures, entertainment, social functions, festivities, the arts, dancing, rhythm, money, beautiful possessions, females generally, sugars and spices, the signifier of victory in war, trades and industries catering mainly for women (such as cosmetics and jewelry)."

Venus with Jupiter is exceptionally favorable; anything good in Venus will be helped by the power of Jupiter, they say. Venus mitigates the influence of "stronger" planets such as Mars. There your charm will help, but Mars almost always brings out the worst in weaknesses in those ruled by other planets (and Venus as the Morning Star was the goddess of war, as Mars was the god of war). With Leo or Libra you will overdo the charm. Saturn will dampen your Venus love of life. To mention three planets discovered after traditional astrology got its so-called rules together, look at Uranus, Neptune, and Pluto. Uranus will make you a distant and stubborn partner. Neptune will increase your artistic drive but if you do not succeed extravagantly you may be extravagantly negative in love and in career. Pluto will cause sexual repression and/or self-indulgence. Those "new" planets, it seems to me, rather throw into confusion all the comments made about the Sun, Moon, etc.—Mercury had a 17-year heyday but that ended in July 2000—before the "new" planets were

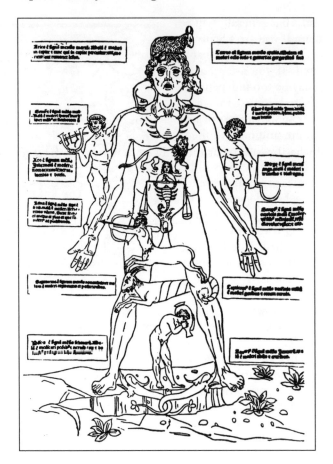

discovered. Now astrologers are awaiting the discovery of still another new planet and will probably make that dominate Libra, currently ruled by Venus. I hasten to confess I do not know how to fit in the new ones we have now, but there is plenty of information in books about Sun Signs, and Venus is never more than two Zodiac signs away from the Sun. Naturally the Moon must have a big effect on lovers and lunatics.

I readily admit that I don't know all about the conjunctions, hard aspects and the trines, degrees and minutes and other complexities. I do know that casting a horoscope is an exceptionally complex business and that for exactness you must know precisely the moment of your birth, latitude and longitude of the place, and exactly where all the planets were in relation to each other at that very minute.

There are computer programs that do just that, but I guess my sign militates against coping well with computer programs.

Given that, you still may find that if three different astrologers work with the same personal details they will give you three distinctly different readings. If you really are greatly influenced by Venus you may well be too lazy to go and get a horoscope anyway; you'll probably just read the newspaper horoscopes. I do that. But I read them all and pick the one I like that day with no compulsion to worry about my sign.

It seems to work fine. But I may be doing the wrong thing altogether. In fact, when you get right down to it, astrologers will as often tell you the exact opposite of what I say or what the daily communiqué says rather than agree with my brief characterizations or the newspapers'.

With Venus in the ascendant you may succeed too easily and be incautious, impractical, and afraid to get too involved. But you'll be attractive and creative and successful if not financially successful. With Venus in mid-heaven you may have difficulty expressing affection or, on the other hand, other factors may grant you a wonderful love life—and a hell of a lot more variety than most of us enjoy.

I wish that wonderful love life for you. I think who you are and how you turn out has more to do with you and your genes and your environment and your outlook and your unique experiences than with your stars.

I would think that, if Venus is important in your chart, you should imitate the Venus Flytrap: be sweet, lure rather than pursue, and when your Significant Other comes along snatch them and close out any escape or seductive others. But of course my horoscope says that's just what Sagittarius with Scorpio rising, etc., etc., *would* think.

PETTICOAT

This Friday night, while going to bed,
I put my petticoat under my head
To dream of the living and not of the dead,
To dream of the man I am to wed,
The color of his eyes, the color of his hair,
The color of his clothes that he will wear,
And the night the wedding is to be.

POISONS

The witches condemned in The Bible seem to have been poisoners and their sin was really murder. In later times, such as in the reign of Louis XIV in France, a French fascination with the occult reached a point that was not to be equaled there until the latter nineteenth century. In the latter seventeenth

century, Catherine de Montvoisin ("La Voisin") assisted at Black Masses conducted by a hideous old rake of an abbé who used her nude body as the altar and made sex magic and poisons for Mme. de Montespan, the mistress of the king. La Voisin was involved with many ambitious and unscrupulous persons very high at court.

They got away with it. She was burned alive at the stake as a witch in 1680.

The French were not only extremely superstitious among the backward and horrifically poor peasantry (considering the glittering court at Versailles) but also at the highest levels of society. The rot went all the way through the classes, the four estates and the ordinary public. Voltaire later demanded that superstition be destroyed root and branch, but that could not be.

The superstition of the customers added immense psychological power to even the non-deadly concoctions that were made up. Even during The Enlightenment witchcraft poisoned the mind, as well as many unfortunate bodies.

Later, when science was coming to the fore, there was Mesmer and his animal magnetism (hypnosis), electrified beds to stimulate conception, and, during the post-Romantic latter part of the nineteenth century, the rise of the decadents, a huge underground of poets devoted to the black arts, following the lead of Paul Verlaine, among them Arthur Rimbaud and Francis Jammes.

RED SHOES

Did that heading make you think of a film about ballet with Moira Shearer? Or Dorothy's ruby slippers? Superstition says red shoes or a red hat means a woman is not wearing panties, an idea probably related to the term *red-light district* and to Mae West's famous remark, "Only two kinds of women wear red dresses and you ain't no Spanish dancer!"

RIGHT

Right side is right, left side is wrong, sinister. So we see misogyny in superstitions about boy babies being carried on the right side, conceived in the right ovary and in the right way on the right night, etc.

Here is "Jane Sharp" (who may have been a male writer using a pseudonym) in *The Compleat Midwife's Companion* (1724) with a superstition still alive:

If it be a Boy, she [a pregnant woman] is better Coloured, her Right Breast will swell more, for Males lie most on the on the right side and her Belly especially on that side lieth rounder and more tumefied [swollen] and the Child will be first felt to move on that side, the Woman is more cheerful and in better Heath, her pains are not so often or so great.

RINGS

The superstitions attached to rings could fill a book, but the commonest is that if a woman loses her wedding ring she will lose her husband's love.

It is superstition to believe that the wedding ring is worn on the third finger of the left hand because a *vena amoris* [vein of love] runs from there to the heart, the seat of love. Rings are worn on the third finger of the left hand because there they are the least likely to fall off.

An unmarried girl could fill a glass with water that was flowing south only and over it suspend a borrowed wedding ring by a hair of her head. If the ring swung slowly around she would be married and if it hit the side of the glass she would not.

RUSALKA

The Bulgarians believe in *vilas*, souls of dead babies or girl children. The Slavs have the same kind of thing and call it *rusalka*. There is an extremely boring opera by Dvorák in which a woman gets into a tree and sings interminably in Czech. The *rusalka* generally died by drowning but when it seduces a man it tickles him to death. The folklore of Bohemia has the usual kind of forest creature or water sprite bringing seduction and destruction to men. The Swedes have country maidens or *hulder* who do the same, as have many other cultures all over.

SEVEN

Everybody's favorite lucky number (except among the Arabs) leads to the idea that the seventh son or seventh daughter has healing powers (the boy used to be called Doctor). The seventh son of a seventh son is very rare in these days of DINKs (Double Incomes, No Kids) and 2.3 children (ever met any of the .3s?) but he is said to be able to prophesy. A woman's seventh child, they say in Eastern Europe, may be a vampire.

Seven is an odd number; odd numbers are luckier than even ones. Men, add up the number of letters in your name and your wife's name. If the result is odd, you will outlive your wife.

If you need the number of God (YAHWEH) it is 26.

But when people start on superstitions involving numbers what comes to my mind is the takeoff on Ripley by Eric Metaxis in a *New York Times Magazine* "Endpaper" for 4 June 1995 that caught my eye because I once wrote a book for the Ripley people. On numbers Metaxis said: "Luke Fibonacci, famed mathematician, argued until his dying day that the numbers 22 and 23 were reversed. He also believed that the number 6 was a hoax."

SIZE MATTERS

Superstition says that by the size of a nose or feet or hand span one can tell the size of a man's more private part. A big mouth on a woman is said to mean a loose vagina. Research continues.

SNEEZE ON SATURDAY

One sneeze is a good omen, unless it is in bed. One sneeze and your wish will be granted, but you have to make the wish before you sneeze. Three sneezes in a row are said to be unlucky, but Truman Capote used to say that seven sneezes in a row was more satisfying than orgasm.

However many sneezes you indulge in, always have someone say "Bless you" or "*Gesundheit*" [Health] because for a moment your soul flies out of the body and without those protections The Devil could get in then. Try to keep your sneezes for Saturday:

Sneeze on a Monday, sneeze for danger,
Sneeze on a Tuesday, kiss a stranger.
Sneeze on a Wednesday, get a letter,
Sneeze on a Thursday, something better.
Sneeze on a Friday, sneeze for sorrow,
Sneeze on a Saturday, see your true love tomorrow.
Sneeze on a Sunday, safety seek,
Or The Devil will have you the rest of the week.

TABLE THE MOTION

A woman will never get a husband if she sits at the corner of the table.

TOMBS

These things go by contraries. Just as it is good news to dream of a funeral, so dreaming of a tomb, as long as it is in good condition, means good news of weddings and births.

TUESDAY

This is a good day to get married, unless you are Greek. Greeks don't even like to say their name for Tuesday; they call it "Day Three."

UNCOMMON SMOKE

Incense rises to the gods, or God, like prayers. The Amerindians often used ground cedar for incense and it was their custom to "smoke against someone." Their tobacco pipes were ceremonial, beautifully made and treasured, smoked to bind a peace or to perform magic (draw a person's picture on the ground, place your pipe on top of the picture, etc.), but not for the pleasure of smoking. You could smoke to put a spell on a person or just to get a person to accept you sexually. Now you may have to quit smoking to get sex.

UNFAITHFUL

Crusaders tried chastity belts and spells to keep their wives faithful back home. Witches did a brisk business in keeping husbands from straying or punishing them if and when they did. Elephant hunters in Africa (says P. Richard in *Deutsch-Östafrika* [German East Africa], 1892) feared that the pachyderms would kill them if the wives back in the *kraal* cheated on them. Camphor collectors in Sarawak believed that if their wives were cheating while the men were off in the forest, the camphor would evaporate. Sir James G. Frazer (*Psyche's Task*, second edition 1913) wrote that fear of adultery in Bengal caused epidemics.

Now the U.S. has an epidemic—of adultery.

UNICORN

The belief was that only virgins captured this fabulous beast. As you will hear later, unicorn horn was a medicine. In China there was a one-horned fabulous creature called the Lin, the embodiment of perfection. It had the body of a deer, the tail of an ox, and that single horn, and it lived 1000 years. Legend says there is a unicorn-like creature in the *lochs* (lakes) of the Isle of Skye, Scotland. It is from Celtic myth and is called the *Biasd na Scrogaig*.

VIRGINITY

The absence of sex certainly belongs in a discussion of the subject. Someone once wisely described virginity as "an overemphasis on sex." A virgin has many uses: she can make a candle that has nearly gone out flare up again. She may be able to create a flame in an old roué who thought he would never shine again.

How do you know if a girl is no longer a virgin? Easy: she forgets to put the saltcellar on the table.

WATER

Magicians had some gruesome uses for the water that breaks before an infant is born, but you don't want to know about their practices, as sensational as they were superstitious. You might like to know that if for any sex magic recipe you are called upon to use water, it should come from a stream flowing from the North, which was where evil was supposed to be strongest. If you are making a poppet to stick full of pins and be placed in a stream, a south-flowing stream is best. The head of the poppet ought to be submerged with its head to the current. Float candles downstream with intentions.

WATER OF JEALOUSY

According to *Five Philosophical Questions Answered* (1623), the Water of Jealousy was a beverage you could use to test whether a woman had committed adultery. Upon drinking it an adulteress would "burst." I do not have the recipe.

WEDDINGS

Don't go to church to hear the banns read before the wedding. Your child might be born deaf.

Pick a day when the sun shines. "Happy the bride the sun shines in today." An open grave in the churchyard suggests you choose another church. This goes also for meeting a funeral on the way to church. If your twin is being married on the same day, make sure the two of you are married in different churches. Never marry anyone whose surname begins with the same letter as your own. This may be convenient if you have monogrammed things but it is considered very bad luck, a superstition that probably rises from some old fear of incest.

> If you change the name and not the letter
> You marry for worse and not for better.

The first piece of a wedding cake brings luck. Put a piece of someone else's wedding cake under your pillow so you can dream of whom you will marry. Or place a piece of cheese given to you by the new father at the party celebrating the birth of his child—it is called groaning cheese because of the mother's pains at delivery—and you will get the same dreams. However eating cheese before sleeping causes nightmares.

Sir John Harsick and his wife from a monumental brass at Southacre in Norfolk, 1384.

The very best time to get married is on a Wednesday afternoon in June but be sure it is after the half hour so that the minute hand on the clock is rising, not falling.

WELLS

So-called holy wells, left over from pagan times or dedicated to local or even non-existent saints (as in the west of Britain), are not only considered good for making wishes but can actually be used to practice sex magic.

At the Silver Well in Llanblethian (Glamorganshire) lovers threw blackthorn twigs into the well. If the twig sank you knew your lover was faithful; if it didn't, they weren't. Use a heavy twig.

Every year Britain has well dressing festivals when ancient wells are decked with garlands. Drop a coin in a wishing well, make a wish, and see if you can see your future lover's face in the water.

WHITSUNTIDE

Pentecost was called White Sunday or Whitsun and superstition said that people, especially lovers, ought to appear on that church festival in new clothes. Those who did not, people said, were sure to have a breakup or other bad luck. Now we don new outfits for the Easter Parade but attach no superstition to that.

The Fool Marries a She-Devil from *Von der grossen Lutherischen Narren* c. 1518.

It's just a fashion show and pressure to be in tune with the new season. Snakes shed last year's skin.

SOME LOVELY THOUGHTS

From the American folk, here are some trenchant thoughts on what all the sex magic is about: love and lovers.

Telling lies is a fault in a boy, an art in a lover, an accomplishment in a bachelor, and second nature in a married woman.

Love is the only fire against which there is no insurance.
Love is a malady without a cure.
What you can't stand in your partner now is precisely what attracted you in the first place.
Love between two people is a beautiful thing and between three is a gas.
A small love forgives much, a great love forgives little, and a perfect love forgives all.
All is fair in love and war.
You cannot produce a baby in one month by getting nine women pregnant.

Love takes away the sight. Matrimony restores it.

Love knows hidden paths.

There is more pleasure in loving than in being in love.

Father's Day comes nine months before Mother's Day.

Love does much, money does more.

Sex, even when bad, is good.

Who can quote law to lovers?

No marriage ever fails; it's the people who fail.

Bigamy is having one spouse too many; so is marriage.

As in bridge, most mistakes are the fault of your partner.

A man can make a mistake and not know it, unless he is married.

The best chaperone a girl can have is to be in love with another fellow.

The lover is often lost in the husband.

It is unusual in Hollywood ever to get married for the first time.

If you marry for money you'll earn it.

Where it is impossible to walk love will creep.

It works better if you put the plug in.

Man cannot live by broad alone.

Puppy love leads to a dog's life.

Marry in lent, live to repent.

Big fat dimwit women make better wives and mothers than
neurotic college graduates.

Remarriage is the triumph of hope over experience.

Love 'em and leave 'em.

Catfights are rough but there are always plenty of kittens.

Marriage is a great institution if you have to be
committed to an institution.

If you marry for love instead of money you may have bad days
but you'll have good nights.

It's not the men in your life; it's the life in your men.

Alimony is the high cost of leaving.

When poverty comes in the door love flies out the window.

If you want to be loved, then love and be loveable.

Old chemists never get impotent; they just fail to react.

You wind up spending all night doing what you used to be able to do all
night.

Never sleep with anyone poorer or crazier than yourself.

Men and beasts are all alike.

Freedom is when all the children leave home and the dog dies.

She is as hot as a June bride in a feather bed.

Men are only good for one thing and who cares about parallel parking?

Marriages are made in heaven but you have few friends there.

If youth but knew and age but could.

It just takes two to make a marriage: a girl and her mother.
One major cause of divorce is successful communication in marriage.
A nice wife, a back door, often makes a rich man poor.
Sex is a misdemeanor: the more you miss it de meaner you get.
Middle age comes between the time when you don't know how and the
time when you can't.
Girls with fat cheeks have hearts like flint.
Women let you chase them until you are caught.
Where there is marriage without love there will be love without marriage.
The noblest sight on earth is a man talking reason and his wife listening.
When he says "frog," she jumps.
She wears the pants in the family.
Sex is like bridge; if you don't have a good partner you must
have a good hand.
Love can be a blessing or a curse.
A woman needs a man like a fish needs a bicycle.
If the fire isn't poked regularly, it goes out.
Men and dogs for the barn. Women and cats for the kitchen.
When independence is bliss, 'tis folly to be wives.
A woman is a calamity (say the Persians) but no house must
be without this evil.
When women are honored, the gods are pleased.
An echo is the only thing that ever cheated a wife out of the last word.

THE ORIGINS OF SUPERSTITIONS

I have not had space to attempt explanations. Some you can figure out for yourself, or you can consult books such as the Opies & Moira Tatum's *A Dictionary of Superstitions* (1989) and T. Sharper Knowlson's *The Origins of Popular Superstitions* (2000) or old books such as the following:

Adams, W. H. D. *Curiosities of Superstition and Sketches of Some Unrevealed Religions* (1882)
Basset, Fletcher. *Legends and Superstitions of the Sea and Sailors* (1885)
Balsalobre, Gonçalo de. *Relación auténtica de las supersticiones de los índios* [Authentic Report of the Superstitions of the Indians] (1892)
Baudet, P. *Superstition populaire* [Popular Superstition] (1907)
In 1969 Biren Bonnerjea's *Dictionary of Superstitions and Mythology* (originally published in 1927) was printed and I have read it all with great profit

A TREASURY OF

American Superstitions

BY

Claudia de Lys

THE PHILOSOPHICAL LIBRARY

New York

and recommend it. But there are a great many rudimentary books of a similar nature.

"CATCH A FALLING STAR"

A shooting star means that someone is going to ejaculate (preferably on a wedding night).

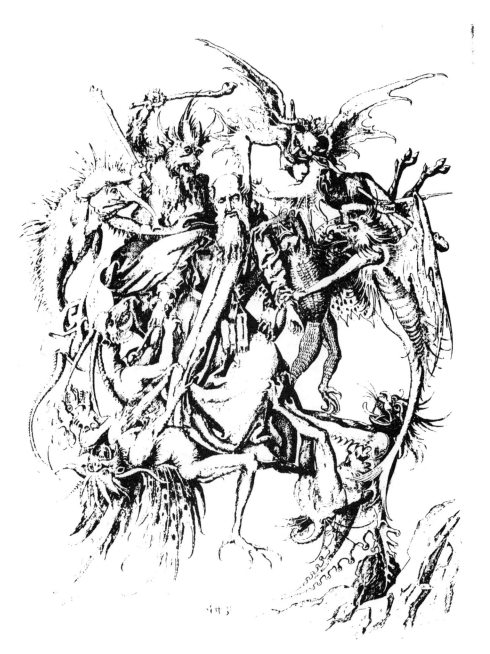

A saint assailed by grotesque demons.

LES CLAVICULES
DE SALOMON

Traduit de l'Hébreux en Langue Latine,
Par le Rabin Abognazar,
ET
Mis en langue Vulgaire Par M. BARAULT Archevêque d'Arles.

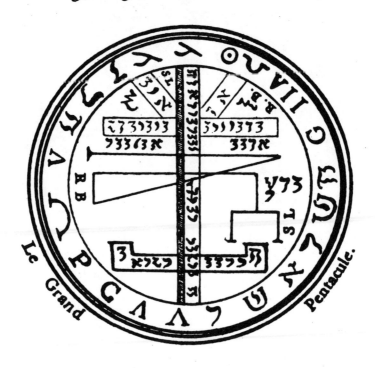

Le Grand Pentacule.

M. DC. XXXIV.

3

Spells and Charms

LOVE SPELLS

Magic seeks to make desired things happen. You must expect a great deal of it to involve love spells and love charms, amulets and talismans, chants and incantations, words and inscriptions, even gestures and acts such as crossing your fingers, spitting, or turning in circles. Witches were busy at their cauldrons (an activity not unrelated to the Holy Grail—but that's another story).

All are sex magic aspects that bring together, keep together, or sometimes part, lovers.

In this chapter I may repeat some of the material found in another book in this series, *The Complete Book of Spells, Curses, and Magical Recipes* (1997), published in both the U.S. and the UK. In *Sex Magic*, readers will find all I

D	O	D	I	M
O				
D				
I				
M				

"Love's Pleasures"
Love of a Spouse

S	I	C	O	F	B	T
I						
C	E	N	A	L	I	F
O	R	A	M	A	R	O
F						
B						
T						

To Gain the Love of
a Particular Female

C	A	L	L	A	H
A					
L	O	R	A	I	L
L					
A	G	O	U	P	A
H	A	L	L	A	C

"Married Woman"
Particular One

C	A	T	A	N
A				
T				
A				
N				

Adulteries in
General

From *The Sacred Magic of Abramelin the Mage* as translated (and adapted) by S. L. MacGregor Mathers.

know about the art, its practice and even other varieties forbidden by pagan and Jewish, Christian, and Islamic religion.

Of course neither my publishers nor myself recommend any reader to practice magical rites. Serious followers of magic say that the grammars of the craft must be handwritten, never printed, as well as given, never sold. What you have here is history of people's odd beliefs. You are not invited to dabble in the occult, simply to see how varied, strange, and related to psychology it can be.

WHY SPELLS AND CHARMS WORK

"David Conway"—pseudonyms are frequent in magic: "Papus," "Paul Christian," "Éliphas Lévy" were all famous Frenchmen in the craft—has an excellent book on *Ritual Magic* (1972, 1987). I am of the opinion that most if not all ritual magic, which aspires to difficult tasks like raising the dead, invisibility, *envoûtement* (killing at a distance by magical means), and so on, fails.

Proponents argue that its frequent failures are due to the fact that it is so demanding, and that practitioners are too often of an independent mind and will not follow a rigorous series of instructions. But they claim it can and sometimes does work. "David Conway" is on firmer ground when he asserts that love spells, amulets and talismans, charms, etc., do work. He writes:

> There are probably more love charms in existence than stars in the sky. Some are quaint, some crude and a few quite beautiful, but all are potentially effective. Their merit lies not so much in the procedures they recommend as in the effect they have on the mind of whoever performs them. Firstly, they concentrate his attention on the person of his choice, in whose mind a reciprocal interest is telepathically aroused. Secondly, they link the adept's intention with the "love-aspect" of the universal mind. The charm he is engaged on then draws down the force needed to accomplish the intention behind it. From this it will be clear that a talisman, suitably consecrated, is an indispensable weapon in the lover's armoury. In addition, however, he has a vast stock of other charms, spells and incantations to assist him.

It was once thought that when the mandrake was pulled from the earth it would emit a scream of such horror that a man hearing it would go insane, and that is why mandrakes were collected by tying them firmly to a dog's tail and then running out of earshot until the dog pulled up the plant. The supposed power of the mandrake as a love charm must derive from the resemblance of the root to the figure of a man.

"Conway" (pp. 205–208, 1978 paperback edition) gives a love charm that "belongs to Celtic magic" and has incantations in Welsh with English translations. It should be noted that magic usually says that no changes, such as translations, must be made at all in magical incantations. Therefore, for instance, this love charm might not work except with Welsh. In fact, if one were thoroughly to apply this dictum, the transubstantiation of the Mass would not work except in Latin, which would be disturbing to Roman Catholics, who regard the consecration as a magical act. For them it is not a mere Protestant memorialization of the Last Supper but an actual transformation of the bread and wine into the body and blood of Christ Himself.

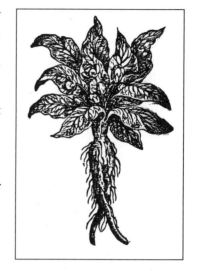

A Mandrake.

WIZARD

This word, meaning "wonderful" or "first-rate," I learned from English boys' papers. Later I found it means a male witch. It comes from the same source for *wise* that we see in "wise woman" meaning a witch, though often a white rather than a black witch, a healer rather than a hurter. The most famous wizard of our culture was born through magic and we call him Merlin.

The Venusian inscription to be placed on the paper in which the mandrake for the love charm is to be dried.

HIGH JOHN THE CONQUEROR

There is an herb called St. John's Wort (*wort* a plant), taken over by that saint when pagan use was replaced by Christian use, both in medicine and in magic. St. John's Wort is now used a great deal by the people who gobble vitamins and capsules of ground-up herbs, but it is a charm and not a medication when it is sewn into a little bag and worn around the neck to bring love or to effect some other desired end. The bag ought to be chamois or red cloth and water-proof, since we take more baths these days than people did in the Middle Ages, when they might take a bath before getting married. The little bag should never be taken off.

DON'T ASK, DON'T TELL

When it comes to sex magic it is wise never to tell the person involved and probably to never tell anyone else that you are thinking of using it or (worse) have already decided to. The targets of sex magic, along with auditors for the IRS and several other sorts, can never be told too little. Whether you get good results or not just keep mum.

INVISIBILITY

Voyeurs would find this power very useful. There are a great many magical rites that claim to guarantee it and some are gruesome (involving, for instance, a dead man's hand). A consecrated ring is said to grant invisibility. Here is one story about such a magical ring. It comes from Plato:

> Gyges was king of Lydia [in part of what is now Turkey] in the sev-
> enth century BC. He went down into an opening of the earth and there
> he found a brazen horse, inside of which was the corpse of a man. On
> the man's finger was a magic ring, which Gyges took and used to make
> himself invisible whenever he wished.

Another way to gain invisibility is to use fern seed. Near the start of Beaumont & Fletcher's play *The Fair Maid of the Inn* a character asks, "Why, did you think that you had Gyges' ring. Or the herb that gives invisibility?"

CHARM

The word comes from the Latin *carmen*, "song," and so we see that charms worked by the incantation. Now they may be consecrated by a little song but then they can also be mute tokens of good luck. Blessed medals are really charms. Charms on charm bracelets are not.

LOOKING FOR A GOOD TIME?

If so, you really need to do your sex magic at a good time, the hour of Venus. Here are the best times to operate with spells, prayers, candles, incense, etc.:

	AM	*PM*	*Your best day*
Sunday	2:00, 9:00	4:00, 11:00	everyone
Monday	6:00	1:00, 8:00	Leo, Capricorn
Tuesday	3:00, 10:00	5:00, midnight	Cancer, Taurus
Wednesday	7:00	2:00, 9:00	Pisces, Virgo
Thursday	4:00, 11:00	6:00	Aries, Libra
Friday	1:00, 8:00	3:00, 11:00	Sagittarius, Aquarius
Saturday	5:00, noon	7:00	Scorpio, Gemini

CHRIST SYMBOLS

Even in black magic, symbols of Christ might be used. He is represented on certain amulets, charms, etc., in many ways: the figure of a fish, in reference to the Greek name; the figure of a lamb, innocent sacrificial Lamb of God, *Agnus Dei*; the pelican, superstition said the pelican pierced its breast to provide its own blood to its chicks, a symbol of self-sacrifice; the unicorn, a symbol of virginity, for Christ was pure; or the Greek letters *Chi Rho* (P with an X superimposed) or IHS (Latin *Iesu Hominem Savior*, Jesus the Savior of Men).

The fish charm was called by the Greek word *ichthys* (Greek, *ichthus*) and that is from *Iesous Christos Theou Uios Soter* (Jesus Christ Son of God Savior). Examples have been found dating as early as the first or second century after Christ.

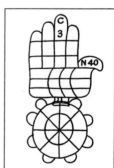

GYPSIES

Their name suggests they came from Egypt, though they have also been thought to come from Flanders (the Spanish *flamencos*) or Bohemia (the English *bohemians*).

Actually, they were the dark people who originally came from India. Nonetheless, they continued to be associated with almost anywhere but there. In Henry Wadsworth Longfellow's poem *The Spanish Student* we find these lines:

> . . . the Egyptian and Chaldean strangers,
> Known by the name of Gypsies, shall henceforth
> Be banished from the realm, as vagabonds.

The gypsies wandered widely in Europe and lived as itinerant tinkers, horse traders, and fortune tellers. To them was attributed great skill in creating charms, creating spells and curses, reading The Tarot or other cards, and reading palms (if you crossed their palms with silver). For this they were feared and distrusted but often consulted. They might scry for you (look into crystal balls or simply basins of water to see the future).

The gypsies were accused of everything from selling their souls to The Devil in order to play the violin magnificently, to pilfering property (linen left to dry on the hedges) and kidnapping children, sometimes leaving behind one of their own. Charms and spells abounded to protect non-gypsy children, to avoid changelings, and to get your own child back if stolen by the gypsies. The commonest way to force a gypsy who had stolen your child and left one of her own was to put the changeling into a hot oven. It was said that the mother would appear and bring you your child to save the life of her own. If she didn't, of course, the unfortunate child died.

A gypsy's curse was often said to be the worst curse possible.

HIMALAH AND *TILSAM*

Himalah is the Arabic word for the cord by which you attached your copy of The Koran to your person. The sacred book was regarded as a protection against evil. The Latin was *amuletum*, a charm or amulet. *Tilsam* is the Arabic word from Greek *telesma* "mystery" and the origin of our word *talisman*.

IN CŒNA DOMINI

This translates as "At The Lord's Supper." It is a bull of the Roman Catholic Church. Papal directives are called "bulls" (from the *bulla*, seal) and identified by their opening words, always in Latin. This one was first issued in the thirteenth century and remained and in effect for about 500 years, until 1773. It was directed against heresies, sacrilege, infringement of traditional papal privileges. On occasion it was taken as warrant for putting down amulets, talismans and charms. After such rules were more or less inactive for about a century, a new version came from Pope Pius IX (1869). It was called *Apostolicæ Sedis* [From the Seat of the Apostles].

CARRY WITH YOU FOR CARRYINGS ON

Lavender, Lovage, Queen's root, Vervain, the root of the Yaw. These are a mere tasting of the plethora of powerful herbs of attraction, amulets and seals of attraction and power, lucky gems or scarabs, your favorite ordinary good-luck piece, the name of a lover you seek on a piece of paper you have prayed over, one of the love oils from your local *botánica* worn, inconspicuously, and with an obvious air of confidence, good humor, and optimism. Visualize success achieved through these means. Keep that idea of success in your mind at all times. Remember, with all this baggage, that the will is what makes magic work best.

Seal of Mephistopheles.

If your faith flags, burn some John the Conqueror incense and work harder at visualizing success and improving your good-luck package. If you think you are hexed, bathe with unhexing oils in your bath, use controlling oils and uncrossing powders, put up some mistletoe or other cleansing herbs in your home, and (if things are really bad) add a Seal of Mephistopheles to your pocket. Occult shops peddle more materials and if you can bring yourself to trust in them they may free you from your fears.

That done, all that attraction paraphernalia ought to have some effect, and you can help it along with Incense of Attraction burned with strong visualization of success at the PM hours of the Sun, as follows:

Sunday	8:00
Monday	5:00, midnight
Tuesday	9:00
Wednesday	6:00
Thursday	3:00, 10:00
Friday	8:00
Saturday	4:00, 11:00

CAN YOU SWALLOW THIS?

A love spell written on rice paper can be dissolved in water and the result added to a drink. Some people believe that in this way you can create a potent love potion. Some spells were written on cheese and eaten. The worst magical cure I can think of offhand was baked vermin on toast.

COPPER

Many amulets and talismans have to be made in gold or silver but alchemists say copper is associated with Venus, so copper is good for love charms. Cheaper, too.

PINK

Some associated this color, most damnably the Nazis, with homosexuality: think of the pink triangles homosexuals were forced to wear in the extermination camps. But magic associates pink with love, so if you want to cast a love spell you burn a pink candle. Lots of people to this day believe medicine that is pink works better. If you say so.

The pink candle thing is preferably one not bought but made by you and charged with power by incantations and visualizations. The more personal a magical object the more powerful it becomes.

DON'T BOTHER TO CALL ME IN THE MORNING

Some practitioners of magic, even sex magic, claim to be able to work over the cell phone and in days gone by used the radio. Before that they simply received messengers, heard the problem, and sent the messenger back—usually to discover that the desired effect had been achieved.

I heard of one person who sent someone to a New York City magician to say that the client wanted "a blond." The messenger did not happen to inform the magus that the client was gay. The client discovered that a lovely blonde woman had fallen for him. He was much disturbed, because he had been hoping for a muscular surfer-type. The way the disappointed lover put it was rather crude: "I was prepared for highlights but not headlights."

TO BRING A LOVER TO YOU

Take a shoulder bone from a sheep, pierce it with a sharp knife, and intone:

It's not this bone I wish to stick.
But the heart of N[ame] I wish to prick.
Be he asleep or wide awake,
I'd have him come to me and speak.

Notice that I said, "intone." Magical enchantments (as that word suggests) have to be chanted.

Q	E	B	H	I	R
E	R	A	I	S	A
B	A	Q	O	L	I
H	I	O	L	I	A
I	S	L	I	A	C
R	A	I	A	C	A

Magic square used by a woman to make her employer love her.

TO HOLD ONTO A LOVER

Cut an Adam and Eve root in two and each of you carry half on the person. Get some Love Powder and use it generously. Women can wear Scullcap to keep hubby home. Heart's Ease may help.

TO BUILD LOVE OF YOURSELF

Buy a pot of Narcissus and talk to it. I would give you an incantation to increase self-love but you are so egotistical already you want to make up your own. Unflaggingly pursued, a love affair with yourself can be lonely but sustaining.

TO BRING BACK A LOVER WHO HAS GONE

Mix dragon's blood, sulphur, mercury, and saltpeter and throw the mixture into the fire in small quantities, intoning the lover's name with each gesture, chanting:

> May [NAME] never pleasure see
> Until s/he comes back to me.
> May [NAME] never be at rest
> 'Til s/he sees that I'm the best.

This is bad poetry and these are dangerous ingredients to play with, so do this only if you are desperate. I put it in this chapter for information rather than in the Witchcraft chapter where you might look if you wanted to go to this extreme.

An easier option involves soaking damiana in red wine and sprinkling a little of the liquid at your front and back doors every night at dusk faithfully, for three weeks running. If that doesn't work, do it for another three weeks or go get another lover.

PUZZLING CHANTS

Readers have written to ask, "What language is it and how do you translate it?" about this quotation. I don't know. But this is it:

Anck thazi n epibatha cheouch cha amok.

A passage of The Koran carried as an amulet.

Your guess is as good as mine, but remember that magic is supposed to depend a great deal on the force and sincerity with which the enchanter pronounces the magical formula, whatever it may mean, and the exact meaning is considered less significant than belief in the efficacy of the formula.

Here is another truly occult, supposedly wonderworking sentence:

Kafé, kasira non kafela et publia fili omnibus suis.

Some kind of Latin, but the thing to remember is that it will make a female "obey you in all that you desire." That almost certainly means sex. You are supposed to hold her hand as you say, "*Besteraberto corrumpit ejius mulieris*" and you are not to repeat or explain the remark (as if you easily could!).

WISE WOMEN

Witches are often divided into good (white) and bad (black), but all witchcraft is condemned in Christianity. A bishop of Exeter once condemned all women "who profess to be able to change men's minds by sorcery and enchantments, as from hate to love or from love to hate." Notice that the good bishop did not go so far as to state that this could actually be done by witches or (presumably) wizards; he simply said that attempting it was flying in the face of God. In Christianity it is not necessary to actually accomplish evil; the desire to do so is sin enough.

If you intend to commit a sin but do not get around to it (perhaps it was raining and you didn't want to go out), you have sinned anyway. Christianity has sins of commission, sins of omission, and sins of intention.

Some so-called wise women did not mean to sin. They were just old women who knew folk medicines, made from herbs and other things. Their simple cures seemed miraculous to simple people and the women were regarded with awe. When the locals turned against them, the old women and their pets were destroyed as witches and familiars. They would have been better off not helping the ignorant in the first place.

BOTANICALS

These are still sold in *botánicas* and other places, to attract love, among other desired effects. Chinese herbalists use the top, middle, or bottom of a plant depending upon where the medicinal effect is desired in the body. For love matters you would concentrate on the middle of the plants, if not on their reproductive organs. You might want to consider orchids, because their name is related to testicles.

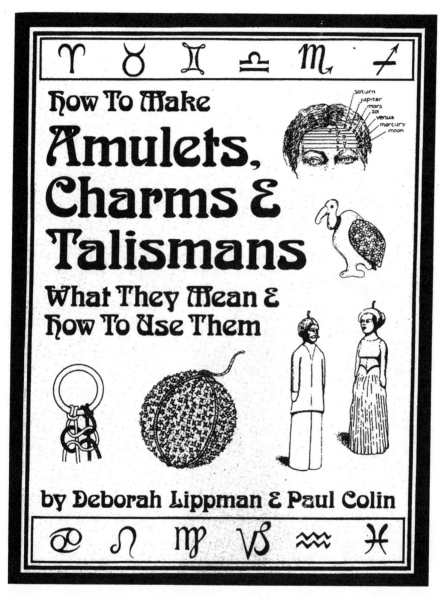

They are many guides to manufacturing amulets and talismans and charms of all sorts. This is a typical book, from 1974.

There is a host of plants with powers. The Christian clergy used to be very knowledgeable about the properties of them but that changed. That was because the Council of Clérmont (1130) declared that Roman Catholic clergy were not to dabble in pharmacy or make botanical medicines, ever. It smacked, to church authorities, of the "wise women" of witchcraft.

Folk medicine flourishes even today. The followers of Wicca are numerous. Wiccans and witches (not the same thing as Wiccans) create and use botanical magical mixtures. Put a little Aloe on your chosen lad's big toe or on the end of his phallus if things have progressed that far. Balm of Gilead mends broken hearts. Bamboo springs right up, and fast. Bay leaves have several magical properties and might prevent rape, for Daphne was saved from rape by being turned into a bay tree. Bernini has a dazzling sculpture of the event: her fingers are turning into twigs with tiny leaves on them.

If you share a broken twig from the green bay tree with a lover, it will not split you in two; indeed, it is claimed to keep you together. Put three leaves into your target's pocket without being observed and the target is yours. Bittersweet twigs under your pillow will help you recover if the lover suddenly stops being yours.

Samson snakeroot is supposed to soften a woman's heart and make a male's member hard, but Borage is more common and is said to work equally well. It also makes a tasty drink. Carnation petals (color of flesh, as the name suggests) may stimulate fleshly appetites. The reputation, though, may come from the fact that the smell resembles Cloves, often suggested as a turn-on, along with Bergamot (Earl Grey tea), mint (juleps), Juniper berry (gin), Sandalwood as in incense, and Teak, which is extremely hard. Simply chosen for its name are Bachelor's Buttons. Couch Grass is supposed to help get someone to go to bed with you.

Heart's Ease may ease the troubled heart, long imagined to be the seat of emotions. Dog Grass will dog lovers you do not like. Gladiolus takes its name from a sword but also looks phallic, so it has been used as an aphrodisiac. Slip some Lavender into your jockstrap and women will pursue you, despite the fact that the color of this plant is now projected onto homosexuality. Musk works on all sexes.

Lovage brings love, naturally. Here's one for you Southerners: put Magnolia leaves under the mattress to improve your sex life. Periwinkle also brings more excitement to the bedroom. Sprinkle dried, powdered Periwinkle under the bed (ignore the dust balls). Maybe Queen's Root will attract women and effeminate gays.

Sage not only brings wisdom (of course) but if you can hold a little under your tongue, women will find you irresistible—maybe just because you turn into the strong, silent type.

Witch Hazel and Witches' Grass will assist witches in all their spells, good and evil. Coriander is used in spells of hate (for example, breaking up sexual relationships) but I don't know the reason for that.

Sometimes there seems to no explanation for the choice of herbs and flowers in black and white magic. If there ever was an explanation it has been lost in the mists of time, for these spells go back ages and ages. Tormentilla looks explicable: this root's name has suggested to some witches that it can cause torment. They recommend it be sprinkled on a photograph of a wayward lover. The photograph, as you know, is the same as the person in these occult operations. If you have no tormentilla to hand, you can always drip some hot wax on the photo or stick a pin in the picture of the person you wish to harm. Poke out the eyes.

The characters should be graven on the inner side of the Ring

For love.

Since photographic plates, film and now digital photography have arrived, there is no need for you to make images of your victim out of wax, human tallow, clay (maybe with a little human blood mixed in), and so on. The poppets (magical dolls) of old-fashioned black magic and the little dolls of voodoo are *so* over. Now we can put Kodak moments right into our computers.

The botanicals most often employed are overtly or covertly administered aphrodisiacs, but they can be just plants assumed to have some kind of magical powers, especially powers of attraction.

You may not know the complete magical formula for what a bride must wear:

> Something old, something new,
> Something borrowed, something blue,
> And a sprig of furze.

The first things are still pretty much in evidence today, but the omission of the furze, some may argue, is the reason for the high incidence of failed marriages and divorce in our modern world.

CESTUS

You may know the Latin word *cestus* as the brass-knuckle kind of boxing glove used by very tough Roman pugilists but the word also refers to the Girdle of Venus. This was a kind of chastity belt that her husband Vulcan had fashioned for her and it fell off when Mars made his move. It was supposed to have landed on the so-called Acidalian Mount and to possess the power to incite passion.

SAPPHIRES AND OPALS

If using these in sex magic, remember that sapphires are supposed to be male. Opals are female, and extremely bad luck: Alfonso XII, a nineteenth-century king of Spain, knocked off several members of the royal family one after another as he passed around an opal ring, eventually wearing it himself and dropping dead. The ring was donated to a church to be hung on a ribbon around the neck of the Blessed Virgin, presumably immune from sex magic. In India sapphires are said to be extremely bad for you, particularly for your love life, whatever your birthstone.

The Secret Seal of Solomon.

STRINGING THEM ALONG

Tie five chestnuts together with a red string (red being the color of blood, of the heart). Put three (a magical number) knots in the string between each of the chestnuts. As you tie each knot, recite:

> I tie this knot to snare the heart of N[ame].
> Let her [or him] neither sleep nor rest
> Until she [or he] turns to me.

An old Celtic love charm uses six chestnuts, three knots between each on the string, and requires you to burn a red (for ardor, not a pink for affection) candle as you recite:

> O Diana, goddess of love and the hunt,
> I pray to thee!
> I pray these knots will tie up the heart of N[ame].
> May she neither rest nor sleep
> Until she sleeps with me!
> Until she submits to my will, my love,
> O Diana, bring about our love, and bless it!

I suppose you can submit the name of a male and substitute *he* for *she* but as a Christian or a Jew or a Muslim you cannot pray to any heathen goddess with impunity.

Having delivered the incantation, you must throw the chestnuts and string into the fire. People believed that you would get results before the embers grew cold. All magic seems to be extreme and always in a hurry, hence the *presto!* (Quick!") shouted by stage magicians.

Ordinarily, tying knots in a string is supposed to create impotence, not desire. Untying the knots they had made in cords, witches raised fearful winds to wreck ships at sea. Plants such as True-Love Knots were supposed to protect lovers.

MICAH ROOD'S APPLES

Micah Rood had an orchard on his farm a couple of centuries ago in Pennsylvania. It is said that when the peddler came to his house, the farmer murdered him for his stock. His body was found under an apple tree in the orchard. People say there must have been a curse put on Micah Rood. He died soon after, and to this day the Micah Rood variety of apple has a red spot (blood?) at its heart.

What is the relevance here? It is that apples are so connected with love and love magic that were Farmer Rood's case was not so sensational, some other folktale would have sprung up.

HOW DOES YOUR GARDEN GROW?

Here is a little *hortus siccus* of not-too-dry facts about plants. When planning next year's garden, why not plant a protective row of red flowers (red like the coats of British soldiers) to stand guard against witches at your house? As we say in Brooklyn, "it couldn't hurt." Unless, of course, you think that giving in to age-old superstition erodes your grasp on reality. Don't plant orange flowers; the dead are said to be attracted to them and may return, sometimes bringing trouble.

Vetiver is one of many plants used to reverse spells. Ginger root strengthens them.

VEGETABLES, FRUITS, AND NUTS

Cucumber is often considered cooling but its shape likewise recommends it to those interested in the phallus. Rhubarb is also said to have gratifying sexual powers.

Walnut juice was once thought to be especially efficacious in causing impotence. It presumably was what we call sympathetic magic, relating things that look alike—in this case walnuts and testicles. Tonka Beans are good. Love Seed (oddly) guarantees only Platonic friendship, as do Lemon, Sweet Pea, and, strangely, Passion Fruit.

Pistachios are said to be efficacious in breaking love spells. Apples may be associated with sex (look what happened to Eve) and are said to have an odor that will turn men on. Also good are Avocado (from *Nahuatl ahuacatl*, "testicle") and Strawberries.

Mullaska Beans, worn as amulets, will not work in any usual way: they do not protect against evil but will at least warn you of being attacked. If evil comes to you, the white bean turns black. There is no bean I can find that will tell you when someone will fall in or out of love with you, so use your own bean.

THIS TAKES THE CAKE

The expression, in case you didn't know, is from the old cakewalk competitions. Here is a way to get someone to love you, though you have to throw a party for children and hope that Taebo and Kainde, the twin sons of Macumba (god of thunder) will turn up. Worshipped in the Macumba cults of Brazil, he is expected to partake of the goodies served. A few crumbs of the cake or cookies, if secretly strewn near your intended, draw him or her to you. However, if you are observed doing it the magic will not work.

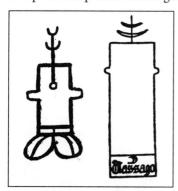

BODY FLUIDS

Magic makes great use of body fluids of both persons and animals. The most frequently used fluids are menstrual blood (considered the essence of life in the West Indies and elsewhere), and semen, once believed to come from the heart. These fluids, when surreptitiously added to drinks or food, have been widely credited with making the imbiber love you. Even spit is said to have magically curative powers. Jesus used his saliva in this way. It, like blood and semen, is a part of you, a piece of your being or soul.

The demon Vassago is said to declare "things past, present, and future" and is invoked by these signs in the *Lesser Key of Solomon*. That for black magic (left) looks more phallic than that white magic (right).

Semen is used in the "Love Ritual for Teenage Lust" on pp. 314–315 in my *Spells* book and was a big part of the sex magic that "The Beast," Aleister Crowley, used to drive a number of men and women with whom he copulated in magical rites completely round the bend, often to suicide. Suicide is of course strictly forbidden in all non-pagan religions, even the Muslim, something modern terrorists who claim to be following The Koran have ignored.

Blood is even more common in magical rites, which seldom involve human sacrifice, except in honest-to-goodness (or should we say honest-to-evil?) Satanic ceremonies. The fact that they require a baby to be sacrificed tells you that black magic is nothing to fool around with.

The Devil and his demons are said to crave the blood of humans at least as much as vampires do (in both cases the blood represents the soul of the victim). Evil magicians may have to sacrifice some of their blood or the blood of others to the powers of darkness to gain their nefarious purposes. We shall probably encounter blood and semen often in discussions of sex magic. They symbolize current and potential life.

ASHES

We often treat the ashes of the cremated dead with the respect due the living person. Sex magic makes use of ashes, human particularly. The vampire defeated by sunlight in a movie may leave nothing but ashes, sometimes in the form of a cross. Blood added to a vampire's ashes gave us Instant Dracula in a British horror flick, and in a Mexican one the ashes of Nostradamus destroyed his vampiric descendant.

BOOK

While we are mentioning movies (200 are coming up in Chapter 6) let me remark on Hollywood's claim that if you find a magical book, you shouldn't read it aloud. In *Equinox* (known to videotape renters as *The Beast*) a foolish professor translates aloud a passage from an old *grimoire* and, whammo! demons and The Devil himself are on the scene.

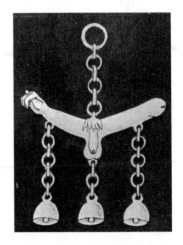

A Roman doorbell.

CANDLES

Scented or unscented, candles serve as useful phallic symbols and their flames suggest ardor so they are used in sex magic. The scented ones add the power of the botanical. Candles are ritually burned as in traditional religions. They can also be used for curses and breaking up lovers. Try curses on a Friday, the day Christ died, if you insist on transgressing and are Christian, because that Friday was "good," and you want to be "bad."

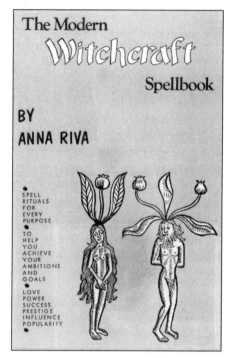

It is the sense of transgression that creates the heightened emotions believed to make magic possible. You know you are doing wrong. That is why I dislike the term "white magic," which tries to do good and clings to the idea that you can do as you please "so long as you harm none." I would define trying to help and never intentionally harming as the practice of medicine.

To do something bad and bust up lovers, take two candles, preferably black. Somehow associate each with the name of a lover in the pair you want to split asunder. Maybe you could write one name on each of the candles. One of the candles may represent a former lover, now shacked up with someone else. This one you want to injure especially, you unforgiving thing!

Now comes the essential act revered by witches as the hardest and best part. Visualize the breakup of the pair with special pain to the more "guilty" of the two. As you do so, day after day, move the candles a little farther apart. This works best at the waning moon so that the love of the pair will wane, "as above, so below" being one of magic's central beliefs.

I quote in another book "Sarah Lyddon Morrison's rather camp, chatty *Modern Witch's Spellbook*." I have to say, however, that she sometimes exhibits a mean side, as when she writes:

> If you have need of punishing a faithless lover, draw the curtains and at midnight light a candle. Take a needle and prick the candle many times, saying: "As I prick this candle, I prick thee. Break your heart, unhappy be!"

Sticking a pin in what is essentially a voodoo doll is standard in black magic. The candle seems phallic to me. The act of pricking the prick, as it were, is undoubtedly vengeful and desirous of hurting him "where he lives." It is probably wishing impotence on the wayward lover. It surely must give the angry lover some kind of nasty satisfaction, if not the desired results.

As in all magic, everything costs something, so you had better consider if you want to hurt your victim to the extent that you are willing to get hurt yourself. On top of that, if the target of black magic becomes aware of who is bringing evil upon him, he can get a witch to retaliate. *Honi soit qui mal y pense:* "Shame to him who evil thinks," and maybe a hell of a lot worse. He might bounce the spell right back at you, especially if you have been in a gay relationship and the spell caster has a phallus, too.

One way to bounce the spell back is to light two black candles at the exact moment of sunset on a Friday—your Jewish friends may be able to give you this information because they require it to start their Sabbath—and recite the following:

Beelzebub, and all ye evil spirits, in the name of Astaroth and the Light and the Dark and the gods of the Netherworld, remove thy curse and thy sting from my heart and mine, and against whomsoever casts a curse at me let it be reversed upon them. Let these candles be their candles, this burning their burning, this curse a curse upon them. Let the pain they direct upon me and mine fall upon them.

Let the candles burn down completely and, it is said, the person or persons attacking will be themselves diminished. A candle gutting is a sure sign, they say, of an end. In exorcism bell, book, and candle are used, you know, and the blowing out of the candle is supposed to cinch the driving out of evil.

At the top, Aurelius Augustinus, author of *De Trinitate, De Civitate Dei* (1489), and at the bottom (left) Zion is attacked by Babylon (right), angels and demons battle.

Repeat this candle business five times, ideally on five successive Fridays if you think you have the time for that procedure or need to keep at your enemies over a long period. As recommended in my *Spells* book, do not use giant pillar candles, because though they burn safely they burn too long. Never, of course, leave a burning candle unattended or your bad luck may arrive in the form of a fire.

An easy way to break a spell is to light a candle that is ideally of the same color as the one used against you. If it is a love matter you might well guess at red or black rather than white and then turn it upside down, blow out the lit end, and light the other. Magic often deals in reversals to undo magic, as when you turn your jacket inside out, retrace your steps, or simply turn around a few times when a black cat crosses your path or some other bad omen turns up.

Witchcraft, which will be dealt with in another chapter, basically reverses things: the white candles of the Mass are black at the Black Mass, the crucifix is upside down, and the Host is defiled rather than worshipped. In covens, witches dance "widdershins," an old word that means "in the opposite direction to the movement of the sun." That is because the sun, which used to be worshipped as God, is "good" and witchcraft is of The Prince of Darkness.

Someone writing as "Anna Riva" is a prolific author of booklets on the occult. His or her *Candle Burning Magic* is just one of many books about this popular subject. In some neighborhoods you can get "magic" candles in the supermarkets, each marked with the purpose for which it is said to be sovereign. Love ones sell especially well.

Here is the way the candle is "dressed" for Goddess rites in Wicca:

Take an unlit pure beeswax taper. It may be white or another suitable color. Use olive oil or almond oil to anoint it. Start at the middle and stroke upward with the oil; then rub downward. Add whatever markings you like, with a pin, and then roll the candle in a powdered herb. Once dressed and set into its holder, the candle is ready to be lit for spell work and charged with power.

Wiccans deal a lot in symbolism, some of which you may have noted in the instructions just given. The most obvious Wiccan gesture comes in The Great Rite in which a female holds a cup, a male holds a dagger, and the dagger is plunged into the cup. (This may or may not be followed by coition.)

CHARMS

The religious wear medals with images of saints/Blessed Virgin, crucifixes, and the Hebrew letter that begins the word for "life" (*ch'aim*). There are also Jewish phylacteries, worn during prayer, or the Hand of Fatima for Muslims. In other religions teeth, claws, feathers of certain birds, seashells, pink coral or precious and semi-precious gems act as charms. Carnelian helps with menstruation. One potent charm is the winged phallus.

I once listed among "The Ten Most Disgusting Amulets" (objects worn for protection) a dried phallus, which is replaced today by a miniature in silver; a smear of menstrual blood; or some part of a dead person, such as a piece from a corpse whose brothers one had to face in battle.

Simple protection comes from putting open scissors on the windowsill to prevent bad influences from getting into your house and under your pillow as you sleep to prevent demons from getting

The names of three angels appear on this cabalistic amulet.

at you while you are in repose. An acorn on a windowsill can ward off evil. That's why the pulls on blinds sometimes are adorned with wooden representations of acorns.

YOU SMELL SO GOOD

Sweet smells bring sweet results. Burn incense to get love: choices include amber, cardamom, copal, gardenia, jasmine, lavender, musk, patchouli (besides smelling attractive it is a prime ingredient in unhexing mixtures), rose, strawberry, vanilla, vetiver, violet, or ylang-ylang. Put some of these in your bathtub or directly on your person. Apply perfumes at pulse points. They say thyme is the best thing to smell of if you want to be desired. Love takes thyme.

A can't-fail come-on from my book on magic and witchcraft proposes a little green silk bag, into which you sew vervain (an ingredient to restore youth that is less messy than bathing in the blood of virgins), southernwood, and orrisroot. But you have to grind the ingredient with sandstone. Maybe there's a front stoop on your block you could knock a chip off of.

You have to make the bag on a Friday and pin it to your underwear. A scented charm next to the body, where heat exploits odor to the fullest, is considered a kind of pheromone that makes people inexplicably and irresistibly drawn to you. This one is a lot nicer than the old practice of carrying a piece of raw meat in your armpit.

A little Dill weed in your bathwater is said to help make you irresistible.

ONE WAY TO KEEP A LIVE–IN LOVER HAPPY

A happy home is a great aid to sexual content, so put a few or many violets in the corners but never bring less than a big bunch into the home. When they dry out, burn and replace them. It is good luck to burn violets and certain other dried flowers and herbs, but some things ought never to be burned in a home. Eggshells, for instance.

HARTSHORN

Grind up some hartshorn, mix it with cow gall, and carry it on the person. If I said take it orally, that would be folk medicine, not magic. But this is magic, and it is supposed to make an impotent or uninterested husband very horny. Then you may need another preparation to keep him from straying. Woman's work is never done.

ANIMAL MAGNETISM

Have you tried magnetized iron filings in your love potions to draw someone to you?

TIMING IS EVERYTHING

Here are the names of some demons that can be appealed to in working your sex magic spells, along with the best times to get to them:

- Astaroth, very nasty and often involved in sex magic (August)
- Baalberith (not really a name but a title), master of marriages (June)
- Belial, demon of pederasty (January)
- Hecate, queen of the witches for feminist revenges (November)
- Leviathan, said to have assumed different sexes to tempt Adam and Eve (February)

Each has detailed rituals such as colors of magical robes, incense, etc. Astrological conditions and certain times of day or night must all be taken into account. All this takes immense preparation, dedication, perhaps obsession.

TAR

Bishop Berkeley (whose name still holds weight in California) believed that tar water was an extremely efficacious medicine. Many people, from Sweden to Africa, believe that to keep evil creatures away you must paint a cross in tar on your home, to protect yourself and your loved ones, and on your barn, to protect your animals.

NUMBERS

To get your hands on that cute number, I say forget about numerology. If you have to play numbers, stick to the lottery. Experts recommend numbers over 31 so you don't compete too much with people who like to play birth dates, anniversary

Minor devils, demons, satyrs and hobgoblins.

dates, etc. Also, people have what I consider to be the crazy idea that 3 and 7 are lucky. Try 1, 2, 8, 9, and 0.

Lotteries, someone wise has said, are a tax on ignorance. To employ an overexposed and often misused word, it is *ironic* that proceeds from some lotteries are used for public education. Nonetheless, people both uneducated and educated play numerological games with the dates for hot dates, names of hot prospects, etc.

TO WARD OFF THE EVIL EYE

You can, like the Italians, make the hand gesture in which the thumb and little finger are thrust forward while the other fingers are bent to the palm: you are directing a pointer at each of the *malocchia*. Or you can try this incantation translated from Spanish:

> The shepherd went to the fountain
> And returned from the fountain.
> Take away the evil eye
> From the person on which you placed it.

This presumably bounces back the evil intended.

LORICA

This originally meant a kind of leather body armor. In magic a *lorica* is what Christians call "the armor of righteousness." It is a quite detailed written charm that people wore for protection in the same way Muslims carried a magical quotation from The Koran to make themselves invulnerable.

An old *lorica* of St. Patrick invoked the protection of God:

> Against incantations of false prophets,
> Against the black laws of paganism,
> Against spells of women, smiths and druids,
> Against all knowledge that is forbidden the human soul.

Notice, as in line three, that blacksmiths were often credited with magical powers, and women come first when one speaks of casting spells.

ROSEBUD

A key word in the movie *Citizen Kane*, you know, but did you know you can use rosebuds like daisies to play "loves me, loves me not"? Peel off the petals one by one.

THE ROWAN TREE

Put a branch of the Rowan over the main door to your house to keep evil spirits from coming in. Plant a Rowan on a grave. Rowan trees and Yews (symbols of immortality) are often seen in British churchyards.

NO CASH, NO CREDIT CARDS

Many people believe that no spell or charm will work if any money passes hands. The gift that the magician or witch has is to be used without charge. Tell that to the so-called psychics who advertise on TV or the storefront readers and advisors you find in any town. In Britain, many such people are prosecuted under laws forbidding fraud but in the U.S. it is *caveat emptor* and free enterprise unchecked.

Maybe a "Thank You, St. Jude" ad in the personals column is okay if your prayers have been answered. The best way to pay for a good deed is to do one for someone else.

Maybe it is not true that money can't buy love but it indubitably is true that money can't buy effective sex magic.

HARE TODAY, GONE TOMORROW

Remember the bit about witches turning into hares? (You *are* memorizing this material, aren't you?) Here are the charms:

> Changing: I shall go into a hare
> With sorrow and sighing and mickle care,
> And I shall go in The Devil's name
> 'Til I come home again.

Mickle means "much." To revert to human form:

> Hare, hare, God send thee care.
> I am in a hare's likeness now
> But I shall be in a woman's likeness even now.

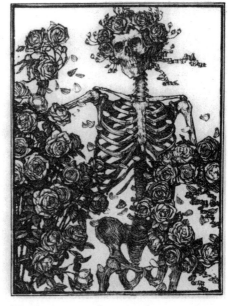

Notice how shape-shifting stresses the often-missed point that the spirit and the body are separate. In magic, the spirit can travel out of the body, sometimes leaving it in a state of suspended animation, as when the spirit accomplishes astral projection or enters into a wolf to become a werewolf. Sometimes the human body vanishes while a new corporeal form is assumed.

The concept of the human being's mind and spirit as part and parcel of the human body is a fairly recent one and still not accepted by many because it means that when the body dies the individual ceases to be. "Dead as a doornail" does not appeal to most people. We want to somehow be immortal, as angels or even vampires. "Thou wast not made for death. . . ."

CINQUEFOIL

Remove the contents of an egg and stuff the shell with Cinquefoil, taping it up with cellophane tape. Keep this hidden away in the house for good luck and protection and love.

CLOVES

Hold seven in one hand and concentrate on making someone love you. Then burn them. The cloves, I mean.

WICCAN CEREMONIES

I put these here rather than with Witchcraft (which comes later) because I want to emphasize that Wiccans are not practitioners of black magic. Thanks to "Myth Woodling" of Free Spirit Alliance (Baltimore, MD), I offer the following:

Wiccan Rede
Eight words the Wiccan rede fulfill:
"An it harm none, do what you will."

Drawing Down the Moon

I invoke thee and call upon thee, Mighty Mother of Us All, bringer of all fruitfulness, by seed and root, by bud and stem, by leaf and flower and fruit, by life and love do I invoke thee to descend upon the body of thy servant and priestess. Hear with her ears, see with her eyes, speak with her lips, breathe with her nostrils, touch with her hands, that thy servants be fulfilled.

The Great Rite

At the sabbat of Beltane it is recorded that a lit brand was lowered into a cauldron of water to bless the land. Today in Wicca we use the athame [sacred knife, a phallic symbol] and the cup [a female symbol] in The Great Rite. A woman shall hold a cup and a man the athame. She kneels before the man and extends the cup and he turns his blade over the cup and lowers it in. They say: "As the cup is to the female, the athame is to the male, the cauldron to the spear, the grail to the lance. The beloved to the lover, earth and sun, they are one." They kiss and the wine is shared with all present and the cakes are blessed and eaten by all.

10 SUGGESTIONS FOR FURTHER READING

Budge, E. A. Wallis. *Amulets and Superstitions* (reprint 1978)
Farrar, Stewart & Janet. *Spells and How They Work* (1990)
Heartman, Charles F. *Aphrodisiac Culinary Manual* (nd)

Lockhart, J. G. *Curses, Luck, and Talismans* (reprint 1971)
MacKenzie, William. *Gaelic Incantation . . . Hebrides* (1895)
Marlborough, Ray L. *Charms, Spells, and Formulas* (1987)
Mickaharic, Draja. *A Century of Spells* (1988)
Rechung, Lama. *Tibetan Medicine* (1972)
Teal, John. *Wiccan Sex Magick* (1999)
Wall, O.A. *Sex and Sex Worship* (1919)

TAKE-OUT

If you do not wish to bother making your own amulets and talismans, blessing your own candles, or creating your own magical charms, you will find suppliers in many cities or on the internet.

Suppliers are particularly plentiful in the area of the voodoo beloved of Haitians, expatriates from the Dominican Republic (who practice a kind of Haitian voodoo), and so on. Followers of *Santería* and similar religions in the U.S. can buy ready-made everything, from candles of various colors to elaborate banners of the *orishas* (deities) and *seite potencias* (Seven Powers) or the *vodun* (voodoo) Bondye (*le bon Dieu*, Good God). There are also some South American imports, such as *obeah*. These are not as old as the Native American religions but are far more active and just as fundamentally American.

Using certain pamphlets sold by occult suppliers you can get by without a leader in quite a few religions. You can be your own *curandero* (witch doctor); *santero* (priest of *Santería*); *bruja* (witch); or lead Yoruba groups, Christianity cults of various kinds, or the Congolese Christianity *palo mayombé*. You can be one of *babalaos* yourself and devote yourself to sex magic with the goddess of love (sometimes disguised as—*Nuestra Señora de la Caridád*). Another possibility is becoming priestess of the Nigerian Efik Christian religion of *Abakuá*, which incorporates a surprising touch of Freemasonry found in a lot of made-in-America religions, even Mormonism.

The *reglas* (rites) are supposed to be secret but you can read all about it if you are persistent. Do not be frightened by the idea of orgies. Celebrants engage in personal ecstasies, not group sex. There are sacrifices of animals and birds but even Satanists usually do not kill people. For example, Obadala disguised as Our Lady of Mercy demands white doves.

The wild dances look more like disco than demon worship. I find the *cultos afro-americanos* fascinating. They're much more interesting than our typically puritan and neo-pagan American religions, one of which is amusing for its forbidding young girls to wear patent-leather shoes lest they reflect what was under their dresses. They are also not nearly as barbaric as those involving the sexual mutilation of males, a ritual observed despite the fact that the U.S. recoils in horror at African customs of circumcising females.

Read the following and shock your reference librarian with requests about more:

> Cabrera, Lydia. *El monte: notas sobre las religiones, la mágia, las supersticiones y el folklore de los negros criolles y del pueblo de Cuba* [The Country: Notes about Religions, Magic, Superstitions and Folklore of the Black Creoles and the Cuban People] (1954)
> ———. *La Sociedad secreta Abakuá* [The Abakuá, A Secret Society] (1958)
> Miller, Timothy. *America's Alternate Religions* (1995)
> Rigaud, Milo. *Secrets of Voodoo* (reprinted 1985)

SPIRITUAL WARFARE

Recently Christians have been less apologetic about beliefs in devils and demons and the Pope has personally performed exorcism. Frank Marzullo's *Incubus and Succubus* (1995) is from the Protestant side, the Christian Covenant Fellowship, in fact, but his work also emphasizes that Christians of all types consider themselves to be in a war with evil spirits, quite as real as those that were so feared and fought in the Age of Faith.

APHRODISIAC COOKING

There is an amazing amount of publication about herbal potions—Will H. Lee's *Herbal Love Potions* (1990) is typical—and cooking that is supposed to turn on sex partners. In the eighties there was the like of Eric Hill's *The Aphrodisiac Gourmet* (1982) and in the nineties books like B. Carlson's *Aphrodisiac Cooking* (1994), while the pace seems to have picked up since the turn of the millennium. In fact, although various spices and herbs have traditionally been believed to increase sexual desire, the only really reliable aphrodisiac is raw oysters. Nothing you can cook up competes. "Spanish fly" merely irritates the sexual organs, and causes pain. It should be avoided. Because in sex there is nothing either on or off but thinking makes it so, if you happen to have faith in some herb dedicated to the goddess of love, or believe that nutmeg or cinnamon or some other spice can spice up your love life, go ahead and use it. It may work if you think it will. But taking someone out to a romantic dinner in an expensive restaurant probably is a better bet than attempting to whip up a sexy meal at home. For one thing, such an adventure shows you are willing to spend money, and money is one of the strongest of all aphrodisiacs.

THERE'S MORE

Don't imagine that I waited until volume 10 in this Barricade Books' series to bring up the subject of sex magic. Naturally there is a lot of sex and magic in earlier books, particularly *The Complete Book of Vampires* and *The Complete Book of Werewolves*, dealing as they do respectively with evil seduction and rape and involving supernatural characters. I hope you will look there, if you are interested. The history of witchcraft is the history of misogyny. The practitioners of magic have often been sexual outsiders, whether vestal virgins or cross-dressing shamans. Sex and magic are both creative and transformative, and hedged about with taboos. Sex and magic are inextricably tied together. And as always there are magical recipes. Read on.

4
Magical Recipes

LISTENING TO EXPERTS

In magic there are more fools than real gurus. Be careful whose word you take.
An old and sage counsel runs like this:

> He who knows not, and knows not he knows not, is a fool. Shun him.
> He who knows not, and knows that he knows not, may be willing.
> Teach him.
> He who knows, and knows not that he knows, sleeps. Awaken him.
> He who knows, and knows he knows, is wise. Follow him.

As I have frequently remarked in print, those in the occult who know, and
know they know, may not wish you to know, or, as it has been said, "He who
knows does not tell, and he who tells does not know."

APHRODISIACS

Maybe you turned to this chapter first, looking for these, so we had best get
them out of the way. The history of sex magic is littered with recipes for stim-
ulants to passion, particularly for men but for women too. This book could
be filled with them. It will not be. Permit me to give you just one—how many
do you need?—requiring no astrological timing or elaborate cooking and containing none of the common but dangerous ingredients like cantharides.

Ready? Here is my one single favorite recipe. I do not urge you to take it but if you absolutely must take something I suppose this is best. Chinese emperors swore by it and, though many of their close advisors were eunuchs, they probably knew what they were doing. Those with the Mandate of Heaven were accustomed to the best of everything.

Here goes: Take 100 peacocks' tongues and season well with hot chili powder. That's it. The magic element is the *frisson* produced by knowing that 100 peacocks were so barbarously treated. The active ingredient of the chemical variety is the hot chili pepper. That also works on a basic magical principle: if it is hot how could it not make you hot to trot?

If you do not happen to have peacocks ready to hand, I suggest you forget the *frisson* and just put plenty of red-hot chili pepper on your popcorn as you watch the late movie. That will work as well as yohimbe, whose effects are not fully understood anyway, or any other popular ingredient. Want to be hot? Eat something hot. It is the same idea that has driven those who want to be horny to kill black rhinos so that their horns can be powdered and put into drinks.

Even the pragmatic William James used to stress that in psychology, if you want something, sheer willpower may very well succeed. So the following may be the ingredient you need. From Salman Rushdie's failed novel *Fury:*

Mercury mates with Sulfur in this symbolic picture of alchemical union from *Le Rosier des philosophes*.

Fury—sexual, Oedipal, political, magical, brutal—drives us to our finest heights and coarsest depths. Out of *furia* comes creation, inspiration, originality, passion, but also violence, pain, pure unafraid destruction.

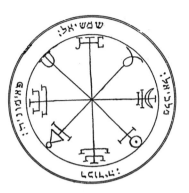

The Crown of Resplendence.

Magical recipes have to be energized. They are not just pharmaceutical; they are often accompanied by spells and curses and incantations and always informed by the spirit of the witch or wizard. You have to put something of other creatures into the mix but also something of yourself if you expect the recipe to work.

So complete confidence and red-hot chili pepper in equal amounts. Very, very hot. Good health, an attractive and cooperative partner, and lack of stress are useful too.

For more reading with an emphasis on the folklore, see Ernst Lehner's *The Folklore and Symbolism of Plants and Trees*, and Sangiradi Júnior's *Plantas eróticas*. People have come up with some fine medicines in the search for sexier lives. There is a world of wonder in plant life, from the Jesuit bark that missionaries found in the jungles of South America to the banana peel that improves your leather furniture by oiling it.

Magic always believed in a Doctrine of Signs. They were right. Some of the aphrodisiacs you would be crazy to take, like Spanish fly, but any of them works if you *believe*. Faith can move mountains *and* produce erections.

THE JOY OF TEXT

This is not the *elisir d'amore* (elixir of love) that all the operatic brouhaha is about but the very elixir of life that the alchemists were searching for, along with the philosopher's stone that was able to effect transformations like base metal into gold. Alchemy had one barrier that chemistry does not: to be a successful alchemist you had first to transform yourself from sinful to pure as gold itself. Not many, if any, occult scientists were able to do that.

The following recipe does not seem to me to breach the secrecy that alchemists worked so hard to foster. It was written down in the seventeenth

The Magician gives The Devil a copy of The Bible and
receives in exchange the Black Book of Sorcery.

century by one Jean d'Esponet of Bordeaux. I cannot make it out but it does
appear to refer to the Four Elements of Galen, whose theory adopted for more
than a millennium held that everything is made of fire, water, earth, and air.
It does not really identify the ingredients; that is a basic flaw, surely, in any
recipe. It starts like this:

"Take three parts of red earth, water and air, six parts all together, mix
them thoroughly and prepare a metallic paste like butter." The ingredients
are disguised, as is often the case, in alchemy, but mercury comes into it somewhere. To add insult to injury at the end we are told to use the elixir for the
glory of God and "keep the secret." The secret? I don't know what the secret
is! If I gave you the whole long rigmarole you wouldn't know it either.

TAN

This was the elixir of gold said to have been created by the Chinese and to
confer immortality on anyone who drank half of it. (Half of how much?) If
you drank the whole thing you would not live forever on earth but immediately ascend to dwell among the gods. For immortality you could also go to
the island of Yang Chow and drink the water, which tastes like wine.

PORK

Instead of creating all kinds of contraceptive drinks, all you really have to do is touch a woman *when she is not looking* with a piece of pork. That makes her barren. If in the past your contraception did not work you might go to a wise woman or witch to get something to cause an abortion. The Witchcraft Act (1541) in England soon caught people like Elizabeth Francis for making and selling a magical abortion portion. Her familiar, a cat, was called Satan.

Mother Earth nurses mankind, a goat nurses Hercules, and a wolf nurses Romulus and Remus.

COCKLEBREAD

A woman makes cockle bread by kneading it against her genitals and with her thighs. If a man eats the baked bread, he is hers. A man could make bagels.

KITTY LIVER

The poet William Butler Yeats dabbled in the occult, as a member of The Golden Dawn in fact, and provided one of the most annoying recipes I have ever included in my books on the occult. You will see why the ASPCA and

Druids about to perform human sacrifice.

moggie-lovers everywhere object to it, why I received hate mail, and why I hasten to say I do not recommend, simply report, the recipe. Yeats said that lovers could make love potions by drying and grinding into powder the liver of a black cat. Mixed with tea, and poured from a black teapot, it is infallible.

I want to add that I do happen to own a black basalt Wedgwood teapot, which some eighteenth-century widow must have used while mourning, but I do not grind up cats' livers. I do not even feed liver to my cat. I have been told that cats cannot digest it (or milk, by the way).

HERE IS ONE I DON'T LIKE

H. Ploss in *Das Weib in der Natur und Volkskunde* [The Wife in Nature and Folklore, 1895) says that if a woman pees in a man's shoe, he's hers.

DEADLY POTIONS

From the earliest times witches were notorious for making poisons. Tired of a rival or a spouse? Consult the wise woman. Tired of waiting for a promotion or an inheritance? Got a grudge? Better life through chemistry. Of course if a love potion was purchased but something went wrong and the imbiber died, the witch would be accused of poisoning.

Francesco Maria Guazzo's witches' encyclopedia, the *Compendium maleficarum*, based upon 322 principal "authorities" on the subject, had this to say about witches and poisoning:

> The poisons used by witches are compounded and mixed from many sorts of poisons, such as the leaves and stalks and roots of plants; from animals, fishes, and venomous reptiles, stones and metals; sometimes these are reduced to powder and sometimes to an ointment. It must also be known that witches administer such poisons either by causing them to be swallowed, or by external application. In the first instance  they usually mix some poisonous powder with the food or drink: in the second they bewitch their victim, whether man or woman, while he is sleeping by anointing him with their lotions, wafers, oils and unguents which contain many and various poisons. They anoint the thighs, or belly, or head, throat, breast, ribs, or some

other part of the body of the person to be bewitched, who being asleep feels nothing; but such is the potency of that unguent that, as it is slowly absorbed by the heat of the sleeper's body, it enters his flesh and penetrates his vitals, causing him the greatest bodily pain. . . . They have also a third method of administering poison, namely, by inhalation: and this is the worst of all kinds of poison, for by reason of its tenuity it is readily drawn in through the mouth and so quickly reaches the heart.

In Italy, the Fratricelli were accused of crushing babies with their bare hands and later grinding them to powder to be used in poisons. In the Denmark of *Hamlet*, poison is liquid placed in a drink, on the tops of fencing foils, and poured in the ear of the old King Hamlet while he is asleep because the corpse of a monarch had to be exhibited so that his liege lords could be certain he was dead before shifting their allegiance. Any corrosion from the poison would not be noticed in the ear, covered by long hair.

The same demand for traceless murder methods led to Edward II of England's murder by virtue of a red-hot poker thrust up his rectum. The idea may have seemed appropriate to his angry wife, Isabella, the She-Wolf of France, so titled because Edward had left her for his boyfriend, Piers Gaveston.

Poisonous gasses did not only inspire the oracles of old, they are used today in magical rites by burning poisonous plants. A small amount of this incense can easily alter the minds of the participants.

A common method not noted by Guazzo was the poisoning of clothes, especially gloves and shirts given as presents to inconvenient husbands or lovers. Witches had a lot of preparations you could buy for this. First they sold you a love potion to get someone; later you would buy a poison to get rid of them. Then someone would figure out what you had done and purchase a means of getting you out of the way.

Label for a bottle of poison, late fifteenth century.

Drugs that are not poisonous but are dangerous have been used as hallucinogens in magical ceremonies from time immemorial. Gay witches worshipped Bapthomet in New York City late in the twentieth century using LSD and what was dubbed "anal nightride." Neither drug was uncommon in the general population at the time. At least two early twenty-first century lesbian covens use Ecstasy.

Naturally many drunks and druggies were attracted to sexual and other transgressive indulgences of witchcraft. People speak of the "magic" of "getting out of yourself"—one of the reasons people turned to witchcraft in the first place.

It must be added that witches and Wiccans are hardly ever pagan poisoners of themselves or others, and that many poison peddlers may have tried to give the impression their products were magical but themselves were not really witches. They were simply criminals with some primitive (or even sophisticated) knowledge of chemistry and physiology.

Out of both non-poisonous and poisonous concoctions of the alchemists, witches, herbalists and sorcerers, the world gained recipes for Benedictine, Chartreuse, and addictive and dangerous potables such as absinthe.

WHITE MAGIC CONDEMNED

"Cunning women" had many recipes for herbal and other medicines but some people did not like the public going to them, even though they were white witches; helpers and healers, neither poisoners nor in league with the Evil One.

W. Perkins in his *Discourse of the Damned Art of Witchcraft* (1608) thought white witches were as bad or worse than black and he writes that

> it were a thousand times better for the land if all witches, but especially the *blessing witch*, might suffer death. Men doe commonly hate and spit at the *damnifying sorcerer*, as unworthy to live among them, whereas they flie unto the other in necessitie, they depend upon him as their God, and by this meanes thousands are carried away to their finall confusion. Death, therefore, is the just and deserved portion of the good witch.

These "good" witches were perhaps the only source of medicines and treatments that certain poor people had. Witches' potions may have been tainted with superstition and magic, but they helped many, and belief in their efficacy was one of the reasons they worked.

Wormwood, sometimes called Old Woman, was used not only to call up spirits and for protection from spirits and sea serpents but also in a dangerous love potion that eventually became absinthe.

Those who said the wise women were guilty of using devilish things to accomplish good were not considering the sick bodies, just the immortal souls. The most frequent dangers to witches came not from the churches but from the villagers who suddenly turned on a witch, even for as blatant a reason as wanting what little property she had, or disagreeing with some effect they believe she'd achieved. The most vicious persecutors of the witches were those whose love potions did not work or who were refused poisons. They used the witch's services and then turned on her, suffering the guilt from older, pre-Christian ways.

DRUID CEREMONY AND DRINK

We know very little about the druids. Tacitus barely mentions them. Archeologists have found little in the ruins of their buildings, though a druidic circle on Iona revealed that they used the barbaric old custom of strengthening buildings by placing human sacrifices in the foundations. We stand in awe of Stonehenge but are not all agreed on what its purpose was—or how the huge stones were brought from so far away.

We tend to think of the druids as Welsh bards at their annual festivals, peaceful and poetry-loving people. They were believed to own a large store of herbal medicines, and here is a mention of just one. It is from Pliny's *Natural History* XVI:

The Druids—for so they call their magicians—hold nothing more sacred than mistletoe and a tree upon which it is growing, provided that it is a Volonia oak. . . . Mistletoe is rare and when it is found it is gathered with great ceremony, especially on the sixth day of the moon. . . . They prepare a ritual sacrifice together with a banquet underneath a tree and bring two white bulls whose horns are bound for the first time. A priest, dressed in white vestments, climbs up the tree and with a golden sickle cuts down the mistletoe, which is caught in a white cloak. Then finally they kill the victims [bulls], praying to their gods to send gifts propitious to those upon whom

Sex (four playful amoretti) goads the witch to ride her broomstick to the sabbat.

they have bestowed them. They [the druids] believe that mistletoe, administered in a drink, will impart fertility to any animal that is barren and that it is an antidote to all poisons.

In another old religion the white berries of the mistletoe are said to be the tears of a goddess. Today, when kissing under the mistletoe, we are not asking for fertility.

TO PRESERVE VIRILITY AND LENGTHEN THE LIFE OF MALES

Here is one prescription that may appeal more to older males than to older women: old men should sleep with young girls. It's not just fun, it's healthy. An ancient memorial tablet erected in Rome is translated as follows:

TO ÆSCULAPIUS AND HEALTH

[Æsculapius was a human physician raised to divinity for his apparently miraculous cures]

this is erected by
L [UCIUS]. CLODIUS HERMIPPUS
who by the breath of young girls lived
115 years and 5 days
at which physicians were no little surprised.
Succeeding generations lead such a life.

EAT YOUR CAKE AND HAVE IT, TOO

The modern world has "masturbakers" who will make you pornographic cakes, but the idea is old. The Greeks at their Thesmophoria celebrations ate cakes of phallic shape. You do not need a recipe, just use a cake mix, but mould the cake or cookies, etc., in sexual shapes. You might add figs because they have many seeds.

Herodotus and other early historians comments on phallic and other sexual idols, as well as food, reflected the sexual desires of early people. The Jews, the Christians, and the followers of Islam all destroyed as many phallic idols as they could. Hot-cross buns at Easter are not phallic in shape but marked with a Christian symbol. They remain symbolic of resurrection if not erection.

TO AVOID FERTILITY

Superstition and sex magic offer many ways of causing abortion, but the simplest recipes are those that promise to avoid pregnancy. You can take some or all of the following herbs: parsley, pennyroyal, nettles, or saffron. The British used to swear by hot gin. Earlier still, they said that you should drink vinegar in which twelve pennies obtained from the "church money" (I suppose they meant the poor box or Peter's Pence). Is this medicine or magic? In early days it was hard to distinguish between them, but I repeat that if you were told to take the potion at a certain astrological time or with a certain incantation, you were using magic.

STOMACH CRAMPS

Pregnant women were advised to soothe stomach pains by eating a powder made of dried chicken gizzards. That was medicine. But it was sex magic to believe that if the pregnant woman crawled over her husband to get into bed it would cause him to have sympathetic pains when the time for delivery arose. In a number of cultures men do have such pains.

SEX MAGIC HERBS

To get the most power in your herbs for any kind of magic, gather them on Ascension Day, 40 days after Easter. Easter varies: the first Sunday after the first full moon after the vernal equinox. No wonder you always have to look at the calendar. It took the church quite a while to agree on a date for Easter. After that, setting Ash Wednesday (the beginning of 40 days of Lent) and Ascension Day was easy.

The Magic Of Herbs

By Donna Rose

RAT POISON

This can be dangerous to have around, not only for rats. Pray to St. Gertrude instead. She might also help with sex problems.

BIRTHMARK REMOVAL

Birthmarks were thought to come from magic, as when a woman was not given blueberries she craved and there were purple marks on the baby, and so could be removed by magic. Rubbing the birthmark with a duck's foot might be understood as medical treatment but certainly the idea that you had to wipe the birthmark with a towel and put the towel into a coffin about to be buried in consecrated ground was magic.

You were supposed to say as you put in the towel, "Oh, Lord, take with Thee what harmeth Thee not but harmeth me."

NEVERMORE

To get rid of evil permanently, nail up a raven in your barn. But some ravens were good: they fed Elijah and will foster lost children.

Cupid Among the Flowers, from the *Loves of the Flowers*, by Erasmus Darwin.

SANTERÍA LOVE MAGIC

Santería is a mixture of African religion and Roman Catholicism. It is the principal religion of Cuba's mixed population. It is also very active among Hispanics in the U.S. Its ceremonies have been thoroughly studied by Joseph M. Murphy for a doctoral dissertation (Rutgers University) and have been the subject of many studies by writers from Cuba and elsewhere.

In the chapter on Witchcraft you will find some of this religion's sex magic, but here we can note a few recipes that do not involve the gods and goddesses of Santería (usually disguised as Roman Catholic saints like St. Barbara, St. Cosmos and St. Damian). Here is one of the "Ebos for Love": "Chew a small stick of Jamaica rosewood and . . . leave it inside your mouth while you speak to a person you are trying to seduce." Here is another easy one: to "resolve romantic problems," mix parsley, honey, cinnamon sticks, and dry corn kernels. Then: Place the mixture in a high place in your house. Every time you speak with the one you love, you must have a sprig of parsley with you.

Many Santería concoctions are less tasty, typically involving human secretions, as you will see later. In this religion as in all magic there is a doctrine of "like affects like," as when worms are boiled and the water given to children who are suffering from worms.

ELIXIR OF POTENCY

Lady Wilde, Oscar's mum, gives us another Irish recipe:

> rind of 10 Oranges
> 2 oz. Cochineal
> 1 oz. Gentian root
> 2 drachms Saffron
> 2 drachms Snakeroot
> 2 drachms Salt of Wormwood

I must confess I am not sure what "Salt of Wormwood" is, but you put the mixture into a quart of brandy and it is "kept for use." Maybe you could simply use Wormwood, but that ingredient is precisely why I wouldn't advise anyone to drink this stuff. Wormwood

From Lys de Bray's *Fantastic Garlands* (1982), Shakespeare's "love-in-idleness" (Heart's ease) and "Dian's bud" (Wormwood), mentioned as magical in *A Midsummer Night's Dream*. Also seen is Fern, because fern seed was supposed to make one magically invisible. The fact is that since it does not flower Fern has no seeds.

(*Artemesia*) was the reason absinthe was banned: the slimy green oil eats the brain. In the eighteenth century, there seems to have been a distinction between Roman and Pontick Wormwood. Magical recipes seem to call for the Roman. Use whatever kind you have around the house.

BOOSTING PERFORMANCE

Viagra is just one of the recent attempts to improve sexual performance, but it follows on a great many natural substances, such as yohimbe. This is medicine. It is only when such substances are taken with incantations, or in conjunction with astrological "best times" that sex magic is involved.

Women can take angelica, its powers supposedly revealed to a seventeenth-century Benedictine monk as the Herb of the Angels. The Chinese were using it long before that for the kidneys and other organs said to affect female sexuality, but never when pregnant and (unfortunately) not with great regularity.

Angelica.

MAKING A GYPSY MAGIC
HANDKERCHIEF

'Tis true; there's magic in the web of it;
A sibyl, which had number'd in the world
The sun to course two hundred compasses,
In her prophetic fury sew'd the work;
The worms were hallow'd that did breed the silk,
And it was dy'd in mummy which the skilful
Conserv'd of maiden's hearts.

This is the magic handkerchief that helps to bring disaster upon the love of Othello and Desdemona in Shakespeare's most melodramatic play, the moral of which (cuttingly remarked Thomas Rhymer) is that one should pay careful attention to one's "Linen."

There may have been a curse put on Othello's family by the Egyptian who gave his mother the handkerchief embroidered with a design of strawberries, or it may be that superstition undermines one's ability to see truth from falsehood in our lives and loves.

DANGER

I am always leery about something that offers more than one deserves. Magic promises unearned rewards and tremendous profits. If a thing seems too good to be true, it is true that it may not be good. There are, in my view, injustice and evil in magical formulae, and magic seems to very much resemble the members of the Russian embassy who were described by Lord Macaulay in his *History of England* as "so gorgeous that all London crowded to stare at them, and so filthy that nobody dared to touch them. They came to the court balls dropping pearls and vermin."

As you are presented with the fascinating promises in magical recipes, think how the vermin may be there among the pearls, and do not permit yourself to be dazzled. If you make investments, remember that you only gain in the market by taking risks, so don't take more risks than you can afford. Remember also that almost everyone who gambles long enough dies broke.

RED

In most cultures red means danger. To the Chinese it means happiness (but their royal purple is yellow, so expect them always to be different). If you want a demon to seduce you, dress in red. If that is what he's after, the demon will be dressed in red also.

AN EXORCISM BY ROBERT HERRICK (1591–1674)

> Holy Water come and bring;
> Cast in Salt, for seasoning;
> Set the Brush for sprinkling;
> Meale and it now mix together;

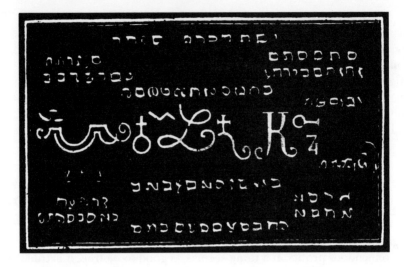

Seal of Knowledge.

> Add a little Oyl to either;
> Give the Tapers here their light;
> Ring the Saints-Bell to affright
> Far from here the evil Sprite.

BINDING A LOVER

Burn a sock of the lover with some Heart's Ease at the full moon. Heart's Ease sneaked into his shoe will also whip a man into line if he walks on it.

HEAD START PROGRAM

Before education became a way of prolonging adolescence way past its end, it was said that age seven was the time to start a child on its professional career. Some believed that the playthings given to the smallest infants would influence their choice of professions.

CLOSE SHAVE

If you are a man and someone close to you dies, you should shave. That way the Angel of Death may not recognize you as a relative.

LET EVIL ESCAPE

In Africa, some women cut into a sick baby's skin to let the evil out, and add pepper to the wounds to make it uncomfortable for the evil spirits to stay. When mixed with clarified butter, pepper even cures the wounds created by venomous snakes. Trouble might have been avoided had the baby received a name such as Worthless so that demons would pass it by.

SANTERÍA SEXINESS

Grind up five corals and five hairs from a stray bitch (canine) and mix with Talisman body talc. Add five pinches of a powder made of eggshell from an unfertilized dove egg, ground antler (used like rhino horn as an aphrodisiac for men), two lodestones reduced to powder, iron filings (to create the desired magnetism), five cowrie shells powdered (a common ingredient in African decoration and in magic), a little incense, a little borax, a little cinnamon, some dried and powdered valerian. Apply this powder to your body. You will be tired from the effort but irresistible.

Another recipe calls for cinnamon, valerian, holy water, and (unfortunately) mercury, so it would be unwise to use it. Valerian, by the way, can always be used as an easily obtained substitute in the Santería or, more commonly, voodoo (*vodun*) recipes that call for "graveyard dirt."

SHEN

Put this Chinese character over the door to keep love in and evil out. You might wish to make the path to your front door zigzag: Chinese demons can only move in straight lines.

PROTECTION BEFORE BAPTISM

The Devil will get a baby if you don't promise it to Christ quickly. Or trolls might steal it, occasionally leaving a changeling in its place. At least as far back as Roman times (as Petronius says) the baby might be stolen by witches and a poppet, usually made of straw, left in its place.

People were very afraid of the innocent newborn being spirited away. In Scandinavia, it was the custom to save any water in which the infant was washed so that witchcraft could not be worked with it. They were also careful never to let the fire go out in the room where the baby was kept, and to put a pin or something iron (anathema to witches) in the baby's wrappings. Naturally, country people might have to wait some time before a priest could come along to baptize the baby, but the Roman Catholic rule is that in an emergency any Catholic can baptize a baby into the faith. Surely evil forces could qualify as an emergency, so these precautions could be put aside if one simply poured water over the baby's head and recited the very simple formula, "I baptize thee in the name of The Father, The Son, and The Holy Ghost." (Today, "Holy Spirit" is substituted for the term "Holy Ghost.")

There are extant quite a number of magic recipes to protect the infant and the new mother with things they can eat and drink to make them repulsive to evil spirits but they are wholly unnecessary. I think people liked to play with the horrific idea of an innocent babe being snatched by evil, the way one tends to keep poking a painful tooth.

Even after baptism, it was common for amulets to be hung around the baby's neck. The peasantry, particularly, lived in a world of fearful possibilities.

JUST SAY NO

If sex is taking too much time from your work, or golf, you can take a tincture of *Vitex agnus-castas* berries (Monk's pepper) the way women (to serve the goddess of chastity) or celibate clergy used to do. If you are in a hurry to become comfortably chaste, you will have to find another medication or distraction: this "chaste berry" must be taken for quite a long while before it produces any effect.

When it was involved in sacrificing to Ceres, this was something like superstition. Today it is herbal medicine. Problem: the "chaste berry" may actually counteract the effect of birth control pills. It does seem to help with hot flashes and post-menstrual syndrome, as do black cohosh, evening primrose, milk thistle, motherwort, and (strangely?) passionflower, among other botanicals.

SUCCESS IN LOVE AND EVERYTHING

Take an egg laid by a black hen. Take care and remove as much of the white as is the size of a small bean. Replace that amount with fresh semen. Stick a bit of never-used parchment on to seal the egg. Put it in a pile of dung on the first day of the March moon. After incubating for 30 days, the egg will break open to release a homunculus (a little creature that resembles a human being).

You must keep the creature carefully hidden from prying eyes and harm. Feed it on lavender seeds and earthworms. As long as it lives you will enjoy success in everything, including your love life. This is more demanding than keeping a cat or a dog in your apartment, because you cannot go away and ask a neighbor to feed your pet. If you take it with you, customs could be most inconvenient and of course the little fellow has no passport.

NO COOKING REQUIRED

To attract a husband you could cook something for him using this spice, but if that is too much trouble invite him over, order in and sprinkle marjoram behind the couch. It will be fine, unless you are a real witch, in which case you cannot bear the smell of marjoram.

Put a powder made from eggshells on your hands before shaking hands with a new would-be conquest.

Take seven earthworms and put them in the sun to dry. Also dry some of your menstrual blood in the sun, with a few pubic hairs, a few hairs from your head, and a bit of your excrement. When all ingredients are well dried, powder the lot. Put some of the powder into a man's food.

Eat a kernel of corn without chewing it. Retrieve it from your stool and put it into the unsuspecting person's food.

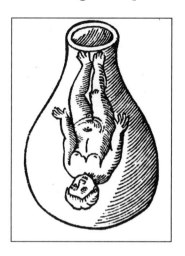

An early test-tube baby? Our knowledge of attempts to make a homunculus stem from folktales and alchemy.

Here is a recipe with even stranger ingredients. Take some of your menstrual blood (or semen), trimmings from each of your fingernails, hairs from your head, your armpits and your pubic region. Dry and grind to a fine powder. Put this next to your Santería idol for three days. Then put it in a person's food or drink.

If you are suspicious that someone is trying to slip you a Magic Mickey, hold keys in your left hand or, less conspicuously, put some in the stocking on your left foot and witchcraft will not work on you. There are at least as many ways to counter sex magic as there are to perpetrate it. Among the natives of Africa half of the witch doctors are taking off hexes and countering sex magic spells as fast as the other half creates them.

The magic ingredient slipped into what we eat or drink is hard to deal with until after the damage has been done. It is not as simple a trick as writing your name on a piece of paper or a photograph, giving it the *mojo* boost, and then tearing a piece of it off each day.

BLASPHEMY

This is, sad to say, a powerful ingredient in sex magic recipes and indeed in all black magic. The most disgusting habit was probably piercing or otherwise defiling the Eucharist. As early as the Middle Ages one Konrad of Marburg went on a hunt for witches who did that. The same blasphemy was being repeated by insane Frenchmen fighting their little magical wars in nineteenth-century Paris. Blasphemy, whether in the Black Mass, the ingredients of sex potions, or the gestures that surround their manufacture, is one of the most unnerving of all sex magic ingredients.

THE COOKING OF JOY

Another Santería recipe requires a bit of odd cooking and a sacrifice, but Santería sacrifices animals only.

In a clay pot place seven drops of your urine, seven teaspoons of red wine, seven teaspoons of lemon juice, seven pieces of rock candy, and seven drops of mercury (a poison, you must be warned). Kill a black dove over the pot and let its blood drip in. Fill the pot with cooking oil. Write the name of the desired person backwards on a piece of paper. Wrap the heart of the dove in the paper and pierce it with seven needles. Place the wrapped heart in the pot. Insert a wick and burn the lot a little every day for seven days. Meanwhile dry seven earthworms, some menstrual blood, and some of your hair in the sun. On the seventh day, remove the dove's heart and bake it. Dry it and add to it dried worms, dried blood, and dried hair. Powder the lot. Put it in the food or drink of the desired person. If a man is making this concoction, he uses semen instead of menstrual blood. The idea is to literally infuse it with a bit of you.

THESE BOOTS WERE MADE FOR WALKING

Boil water and throw in some snakeroot. Turn off the heat and let the snakeroot steep in the water until it is cool. Strain out the snakeroot and bottle the water for seven days. After that voodoo says you can rub it on your shoes and your feet will take you to whatever or whomever you desire.

VETIVER

Used in many sex magic recipes, vetiver can also take a sex hex off you. Here's what you do. Take a small box that will pass as a kind of coffin and line it with black cloth. If you are feeling ambitious, make the outside resemble a coffin, with handles painted on and all. Into the "coffin" place a doll representing the person whom you suspect of the sex hex or, better, a photo or lock of hair, unwashed used handkerchiefs, etc. Close up the box. Tie it with black cord, making nine knots. Take the box unobserved to some place it will not be soon found—if anyone unties the knots it will undo the spell. Dispose of it and do not look back.

VERBENA

You can probably get a version of this, though not the vervain of olden times used to cleanse altars and in the rites of Isis, Thor, Jupiter, Mars, Venus, and Aradia and her witches. Use it in recipes to promote chastity and love, sleep and healing, peace and prosperity. It is also called a *herba sacra* (holy herb), Herb of Enchantment, Herb of Grace, and Herb of the Cross. It is lately being taken up as a supposed druidic crown—they would be better off with oak leaves—by certain New Age pagan cults who want to establish a connection with druidic rites.

A DRINK TO CREATE LOVE

Forget about cocktails named Maiden's Prayer or even Sex on the Beach. Try powdered cinnamon, coral, and anise. Mix with crème de menthe.

Another recipe for passion is dried and powdered sea turtle eggs added to tea made with cinnamon, sweetened with honey. Administer several times a day.

CHERRIES

If you happen not to have enough human or menstrual blood around the house, you can (some so-called authorities say) substitute cherry juice. I do not agree.

Strawberry juice is likewise a bad idea. Using blood creates a certain emotional as well as physical investment that cherry juice, or even kirsch, does not equal. This leaves the recipe wanting.

CATNIP

Almost anything that will disguise the taste can have catnip added to it. After all, it turns on cats. So if you want someone to start tomcatting around, give it a try, but don't tell them.

If you have any catnip leaves left over that are big enough, they are traditionally used as bookmarks in magical books.

CAMPHOR AND ASAFETIDA

Both of these smelly substances were thought to keep away the demons of disease and were included in recipes with that in mind. Later still, camphor or asafetida was enclosed in tiny bags and placed around the necks of children to ward off infection. If they really did work it must have been by keeping others from coming close.

CANDLES

Some recipes require that a candle (often of a particular color or scent) burn while the ingredients of some magic recipe are blended. Ritual magic goes much farther and demands consecrated tools, blessed vestments, heavy clouds of incense and more, for these things are as necessary as the miters and copes of the Catholics or the jeweled crowns of the Greek Orthodox. Indeed all religions have or had ceremonies with lots of trappings.

When I was young I had a friend who was Christian like myself but sang at the services of an Orthodox Jewish synagogue. He invited me to hear him and I naïvely looked forward to seeing the Jewish priest in horned headdress, bejeweled breastplate, and full outfit.

Three Old Wives in Battle with the Devil, by Daniel Hopfer.

I was disappointed to see the rabbi in a business suit, resembling Abba Eban on television and not the bishop in my mother's family. I learned that the synagogue is often called a temple but it is basically a school (*shul*); the priests, the Levis and the Cohens, will not appear until The Temple is rebuilt. In the meantime the ancient rites are not celebrated with pageantry. Some ancient customs remain: the groom smashes the glass from which he and his new bride have drunk after being united under a canopy that protects them from evil at that crucial moment. Some traditions and symbols do survive in the religion, whether orthodox, conservative, or reformed.

Similarly, they survive in witchcraft. Often modern practitioners have no idea what they once meant, or when and why they were adopted. I tend to omit such things here. This chapter is about recipes, not rituals.

In black magic candles draw evil spirits, yet they are always called for in daily prayers of thanks to God. Candles are called for to bring goodness and protection to the rooms of newborns and at the biers at wakes, perhaps derived from the idea of the god of light to battle the powers of darkness in some Manichean fashion.

Candles are required in all rooms where a corpse lies, the idea being evil spirits will be kept at bay. If you thought that the candles at the altar during Mass or other divine services were there solely to give light, you're wrong.

Candles can be holy and seem to carry prayers on high, which is what we intend by votive lights. It is not the candle but your state of mind as you light one that is important. The candle is just a symbol.

Magic goes farther and insists that there can be power in the object itself, a belief that goes back to mankind's earliest days when it was thought that mysterious powers resided everywhere in Nature—Pantheism; gods everywhere.

Some magicians I know do like to cook up their magical brews by candlelight. They say it creates an appropriate atmosphere for the work. For sex magic, candles are romantic.

An *ex voto* of 1675 testifies to a man and his wife having been vouchsafed an appearance of the Blessed Mother with the Christ Child.

VAMPIROS EN LA HABANA

Juan Antonio García Borrero kindly gave me a copy of his excellent *Guía crítica del cine cubano de ficción* (Critical Guide to Cuban Fictional Cinema, which means it tells you everything about everything except the documentaries, 2001). It brought to my attention Juan Padrón's cult film *Vampiros en la Habana* [Vampires in Havana] of 1985. A clutch of the undead go to Havana in search of the formula that will enable vampires to live by day, like most people.

Many horror films have some magical formula at the center of the plot. Who can forget the early British vampire film where an exotic flower from Tibet is sought as a cure? Or the tanna leaves brew and Boris Karloff in *The Mummy*? The most famous magic potion—well, it's supposed to be science but the metamorphosis is basically magical—is the one Dr. Jekyll cooks up. If you are a movie fan, make a list of magical recipes in films. Notice how few of them are sex magic.

Horrors of the Spanish Inquisition from K. T. Greisinqer's book of 1869.

SYMPATHETIC MAGIC

In some societies wild sexual abandon has been engaged in to stimulate crops. In societies where sex is looked on as evil or debilitating, people may refrain from intercourse to "purify" themselves and to earn spiritual Brownie Points. The problem is that too much sexual repression (for holiness, in war, in mourning, etc.) can bring about disastrous results.

THREE FROM TRINIDAD

Here are three sex recipes from Trinidad. Any country could give you similar folk remedies. I am told these are used both medicinally and magically—but that accompanying incantations are superfluous. The first is for an aphrodisiac described to me as "like the magic purse that is always full of money no matter how much you spend":

> Boil water containing anise seeds, mace (the outside of a nutmeg), and bark from a marbay (a tree in Trinidad). Add sugar to make the taste a little more acceptable. Mind you, superstition says if things don't taste bad they seldom work well. Drink a wineglass of it, my informant urges, "every day!"

The second is for an abortion:

> Cut up a green pineapple, peel and leaves, and boil with flowers from the silk fig, a type of banana tree. Drink a wineglass of this "tea" for several days.

The third is for venereal disease:

> Boil the following roots together: yon rasso, sarsaparilla, minnie, gully, zeb à femme, and wild coffee. Continue to boil adding St. John leaves and senna leaves, the inside of a young calabah, sosofa bark, and "graveyard bush leaves." That is a Trinidadian name for a certain kind of bush, but also means any bush that grows in a graveyard. This is sex magic, not folk pharmacy. You strain this concoction after boiling for a while and add some Epsom salts. The instruction is to take a wineglass full "every three days" but fails to mention how long you should keep it up.

CUNA INDIANS OF DARIEN

Not Connecticut—Central America, as described by Donald S. Marshall in an unpublished MS. (Harvard University, 1950). There in Panama, husbands who have had fights with their wives take a magic potion to restore domestic harmony.

IF YOUR MAGICAL RECIPE DOES NOT WORK

This may be attributable to the lack of the right atmosphere or, more likely, the absence of the correct state of mind in the operator. Magic is supposed to work, because magic is compulsion, while prayer and religion deal in begging and propitiation. Most recipes fail these days, confirmed magicians tell me. The difficulties spring from the same urges that make cooks deviate from their cookbooks.

From a prehistoric cave in France, a sorcerer dressed in the skin of an animal, presumably trying to bring food to his people by magical means.

Except for certain professional chefs, people should do no more and no less than the reliable cookbook says. This is a kind of cooking that hardly appeals to would-be creative types.

Witchcraft attracts the outsider and rule-breaker. That is why, when I had created a Wiccan ritual in a book I was doing and was asked to compile a whole book, I had to decline. Wiccans are too independent to submit to set rituals, even if these would help the religion.

Gerald Gardner's Wiccans came out of the post-World War I desire to break, not create, conventions. Wiccans flourished in the U.S. during the do-your-own-thing era of the sixties. I did not want to create rules for them. Ever try to herd rabbits?

If people want their recipes to work they must bow to authority, do what they are told and put their faith in the result, not in experimenting. As the old saying goes, if all else fails, read the directions.

DO NOT WORRY

Lack of confidence and presence of anxiety are death to magic. Good stuff comes to the bold and upbeat. In Japan, Shinto and Buddhism combined to produce Seven Deities of Luck, the *Shichi Fukujin*. They are: Benten (arts, beauty, bounty); Bishamonten (wealth); Daikoku (inexhaustible wealth); Ebishu (fishing, food, honest dealing); Fukurokuju (longevity, fortune); Jorojin (longevity, health); and Hotei (wealth). Of these you probably know just one: Hotei, with his big fat belly and sack of goodies, which he distributes to those who are carefree.

SOME RECENT BOOKS OF MAGICAL RECIPES

Of a great many, I can only list a few. Here are some that followed upon my own book of 1997 on the subject. See also the book lists throughout this book.

Ashley, Leonard R. N. *The Complete Book of Spells, Curses, and Magical Recipes* (Barricade Books, 1997)
Bower, Susan. *Notions and Potions* (Sterling Publishing Company, 1997)
Morrison, Sarah L. *The Modern Witch's Book of Herbs and Healing* (Carol Publishing Group, 1998)
Telesco, Patricia. *A Witch's Beverages and Brews* (Career Press, 2000)
Woodward, Jamie C. *Wicca Cookbook* (Carol Publishing Group, 1999)

Jugudhatri, the Hindu goddess of love. The finger and ring are symbols of sexual union.

DON'T TRY THIS AT HOME

Need I repeat? Do not try magical recipes for sex, nor combine aphrodisiacs with hard drugs, as some people do. The foods and descriptions of the sex magic activities given here are for your information, not your use. Some are dangerous to your physical health and all can be dangerous to your mental health. Please heed warnings. Unless there is something physically wrong with you, if you don't turn on sexually you don't need aphrodisiacs you need sexier partners.

DIET

The Romans prepared for orgies by consuming cuttlefish, octopus, oysters, red mullet, even electric eels, all seasoned with plenty of hot pepper and myrrh.

England's King John died of "a surfeit of lampreys," Pius V preferred a pie of bulls' testicles. The French liked bean and truffle soup.

Anything resembling a phallus is thought to be good, such as snake, lizards, and worms, or (for the squeamish) carrots, leeks and parsnips.

Blood is always useful. Initiates of Mithraism (a pre-Christian mystery religion with disturbing parallels to Christianity) were treated as "dead" and "brought back to life" by baptism with blood; you might say born again. A similar ceremony "raises" the initiate to Freemasonry after he is ritually "slain" as was the great architect of the Temple of Solomon, Hiram Abiff.

Such "resurrections" recall the cult of Isis and Osiris (divinities of female and male) and earlier. The power to erect the phallus by magic or by substances eaten, imbibed, or applied reminds one of the mysteries of creation of the universe, of fertility, of seed and harvest, of life and death. The female is also much symbolized as the creator and sometimes the "gateway of evil," the perilous temptress and the essential propagator of the human race.

Eros by Thorwaldsen.

MILK

Obviously milk has many sexual connotations and is a powerful ingredient in some magical potions. The milk of women's breasts is especially so. One male saint has been depicted receiving a squirt from the breast of the Blessed Virgin but the "milk of males" (semen) is more common. Among the Zulus, dead ancestors are offered milk and beer to gain fertility for their descendants.

ROWAN BERRIES

Elsewhere I mention rowan, or mountain ash, also called witch wood and witchbane. It's attributed the power to protect and heal. Its leaves, branches, or twigs are used, especially when tied into the shape

Mistletoe.

of a cross by red thread and carried as an amulet. Berries can be eaten to strengthen one's sexual and psychic powers.

THE DIFFERENCE BETWEEN MAGIC AND MEDICINE

To take a part of mistletoe and apply it to a wound would be medicinal, but to cure a wound by simply carrying it in your pocket is magical. To ingest a substance is medicinal but to do so only at the appropriate astrological hour with an incantation is magical. Now that I have repeated that enough times I hope that is clear.

To drink a potion is medicinal but to have a witch doctor apply it to a fetish you keep on your house is magical. Sex Magic is not about substances that actually increase sexual desire or potency but about those that put a little imagination behind it.

A "Black Book."

In Scandinavia magical recipes were found in "black books," such as this old example from Sweden, that brought sorcery from Germany to the North.

5

Witchcraft and Ritual Magic

GENDER, CLASS, RACE, POLITICS AND CULTURE

The first thing to say about witchcraft and its carnal lusts is that it is absolutely not some trivial topic. It pinpoints the current major concerns of intellectuals and the general public. Its issues are many: gender, through its attitudes toward women's "frailties" and an assumed predisposition to use sex against men; class, the poor reacting to the privileged classes and institutions designed to subjugate them; race, magic as the refuge of the despised outsider; and many more.

When asked by other scholars why I'm "fooling around" with topics like magic and witchcraft, which naturally extend into issues of theology and demonology, I cite Freud's statement late in his career that if he had it to do over he would specialize in parapsychology.

Although some scholars have denounced Freud as a coked-up fraud, I must in all fairness grant him the honor of bringing certain questions to light. His work was of vast importance to people and the mental worlds in which they live. Freud opened doors through which his successors entered and advanced our knowledge.

So the study of witchcraft is far more than a popular topic among those interested in the history of repression and rebellion. The study of witchcraft is a crucial introduction to the most important questions asked by modern thinkers.

With that in mind, let us look at some of the oddities of sex magic.

Exalted on a throne of royal state, Satan receives new witches who have submitted to his power. From Gérard d'Euphrate's, *Livre de L'histoire et ancienne cronique* (1549).

MAGICAL CHEMICAL

The general purpose, industrial strength magic oil or salve in sex magic can be prepared with olive oil or an Abolene or other cold cream base from the combination of the following ingredients, some of which are poisonous or hallucinogenic: cornbind, deadly nightshade, Devil's claw, elder, hemlock, traveler's joy, wolf's milk, and wormwood. Ramping fumitory or red spur valerian may be substituted for most of the ingredients, excluding deadly nightshade and hemlock.

If you cannot find deadly nightshade (belladonna) or hemlock, substitute the equally poisonous henbane. Always remember that western witchcraft climaxed with the rise of major advances in chemistry and medicine.

Really nasty sex magic such as offing your rejecter or their subsequent significant other requires the witches' brew of frogs or poisonous toads, black millet, flesh of unbaptized baby (substitute flesh of hanged criminal if you do not wish to kill babies), and what is called witches' powder (the ingredients of which I never print because I fear someone would try this stuff). Witches were often proponents of alternative medicine. They were primitive alchemists, and in their own way scientists. They could also be murderers.

RAISING HELL

If you are so reckless as to sell your soul to please your body, you can try sex magic with Lucifer himself. At midnight on a Thursday, at the appropriate hour for your astrological sign, draw a circle nine feet in diameter with a consecrated knife and inscribe it with the names of power while datura and henbane burn in nearby braziers.

Satan presides as a black goat at the witches' sabbat at Blocksberg in this illustration from Johannes Praetorius LIGATUREAE, *Blockes Berges Verrichtung*, printed at Leipzig in 1669.

Once you have entered the circle with the appropriate magical robes and your well-inscribed magic wand, do not dare to leave it until the apparition you summon has finished its appearance. The apparition will appear in a triangle large enough for a man to stand in, which you have drawn *outside* the circle of protection. There should be lit black candles marking the two base angles of the triangle.

Hold your magic wand in one hand and a handful of vervain in the other. Use magical inscriptions on parchment (not paper) and whatever silver amulets or talismans you rely upon. Summon your courage and recite the following incantation three times.

Just to be safe, read it once, and once only.

> O Lucifer! Appear before me!
> I give you my heart!
> I give you my soul!
> I give you my body!
> My desires and my service are yours!
> Look favorably upon me!

The Seven Deadly Sins by Hans Baldung Grien, from the *Buch Granatapfel* (1511).

Thereupon Lucifer (or a subordinate sent by him) will appear to you. You can ask for anything evil. Obviously, The Devil does not have goodness to offer. Remember also that The Devil is the lord of lies, so you will probably be cheated. If this is all for sex, ask yourself: is she or he "to die for," really?

ANOTHER WAY TO SELL YOUR SOUL

For those insanely in love but too lazy or incompetent to try the elaborate ceremony just described, here is something simpler. I do not recommend you try this one either:

Satan at the witches' sabbat.

Take two handfuls of wormwood. With the left (or sinister) hand, throw the first handful up. This is acceptance of evil, a gesture to The Devil. With the right hand, throw the second handful down. This is rejection of good, a gesture toward God.

Then recite the Lord's Prayer, backwards. (You may have to write it down for this purpose.) This constitutes a pact with The Devil and an insult to God Almighty. The word *Almighty* ought to make you think twice about using black magic just to get someone into your sexual grip. Are you sure a more venial sin, such as the occasional escort service, might not be enough?

HECATE

Other people's gods and goddesses can become our evil forces personified. Thus Mazda, the god of light of their enemies, became evil to the Jews. We contradict ourselves by calling The Devil, Lucifer (from the Latin "light-bearer"). In a similar fashion we took a pre-Greek goddess of the underworld, afterwards associated with Artemis, and made her into the potent witch Hecate. Few if any religions spring, like Minerva, full-grown out of someone's head. They usually consist of selected elements of earlier religions, sometimes reversing things, as does black magic.

Hecate is essentially the evil spirit invoked in sorcery by Medea in the Greek tragedy that bears her name. Hecate appears in a revision of Shakespeare's *Macbeth* by another hand. In that revised version Hecate is imposed upon Shakespeare's three unnamed witches. She is sometimes referred to as the queen of the witches. Worship of her can be confused with that of Artemis. According to Homer she is the daughter of the chief god Zeus and the goddess Leto.

Hecate is also confused with the worship of Diana, goddess of the hunt; Selene, goddess of the moon; Orthia, a Spartan goddess; and several others. In Christian religion, where God is tripartite and all three Persons are male, we tend to lose sight of the fact that other religions had goddesses and even The Goddess. To me, it seems natural to think of a Creator or a creative force as female.

Those who worship The Goddess in rejection of patriarchy say they are returning to a time before our God the Father. They think of God the Mother, of a time lost in the fogs of antiquity when matriarchy ruled and witches drew creative or destructive powers from female divinity.

Standing within the protective magic circle, an eighteenth-century magician has summoned Beelzebub. From *Le Diable amoreux* of J. Cazotte.

JEWISH SEX MAGIC

The most famous book of magic is called *The Key of Solomon*, but Solomon, if he really was an historical character, had nothing to do with it. The book was medieval in its first form, as are several other magic books fathered on important names. The legend that Solomon used magic to built his Temple is false. In my opinion the *sigil*, called Seal of Solomon, will perform no more magic for you than the flower of the same name.

Supposedly there was a man called Saul. I doubt his existence because the meaning of his name, "Desire," is too apt, like Adam's "Clay." He was allegedly the one who hired the Witch of Endor to perform black magic for the purpose of necromancy (raising a spirit from the dead).

The Jews believed rising from the dead could be done, though they abhorred the idea. For them dead is dead. At death a person ceases to be; the person lives on only in descendants. Even Abraham died, but the family of Abraham survives, as the Jewish God promised it would.

From time immemorial Jews have used magic. They received amulets, talismans and magical incantations from the Chaldeans and other neighbors but maintained the idea of prayer (begging) rather than force ("God cannot be coerced"). At the same time, the Jewish religion, by forbidding "other gods," seems to suggest that their "jealous God" recognizes that people might turn

elsewhere for help. In fact, Jewish ortho-
doxy recognizes the *possibility* of magic but
warns its punishment will be dire.

One could write several volumes on
the sexual aspect, essential to the idea of
descendants and the Chosen People, but
I'll hit and run with one single quotation:
"*Zikh aleyn vi men vil, a vayb a kind muz
men makhn,*" which I translate as "Do
whatever you please but keep your wife
pregnant."

Sex, for Orthodox Jews, operates fundamentally "to increase the tribe of
Israel" so that it can protect itself and be
a viable political entity. It is not for magical manipulations.

The High Priest of the Jews
conducting a ceremony at The
Ark of the Covenant.

CHRISTIAN OPPOSITION TO MAGIC

Emerson remarked that "the religions we call false were once true." Some old
religions are true to believers even today. We find the same paradoxical con-
demnation and integration of magic in modern times as that which pervades
religious history.

First off, any religion has to assert its superiority, and is very likely to assert
its power, over any competing dogma. From the start, Christianity, accused
of magic itself, came down on pagans as hard as it could. In the first century
AD it battled magicians, in the second century it was accused of magic by a
series of competitors, and in the third century, beginning with the Synod of
Elvira (around 306 AD), it was flinging anathemas at Christians who maintained certain magical practices. Such Christians were persecuted because the
practices mostly dealt with sex.

St. John Chrysostom, whom you have met, fulminated against Christians
in Antioch using Jewish "charms, incantations, and amulets." One can assert
that Christianity was a Jewish religion for the first few centuries, and with that
came certain Jewish magical practices.

Other early church dignitaries had trouble with magic. There were St.
Augustine, Gregory of Nazianus, Gregory of Nyasa, and St. Jerome, whose
Vulgate brought The Bible to the civilized world in Latin. These holy men
vehemently condemned the use of magic.

Still, they were unable to abolish it. Some popes even tried magic. Those
who did not dabble in it still risked being charged with the use of magic. How
else, their opponents asked, could they have seized the Chair of Peter?

Along came Islam and more foreign religion rife with magic, to threaten the Christianity of Europe. In Spain, Isidore of Seville fought against all non-Christian magic, just as that other St. Augustine partially converted the heathen in Britain. However, he seems at the same time to have believed in the magic of numbers.

In time Christianity was overthrown in its strongest location: Rome, the very place that was seen as its *locus classicus*. Flavius Claudius Julianus, emperor of Rome (AD 360–366) dumped the Christianity that Constantine had adopted as the empire's religion. Julianus' return to paganism thereafter labeled him Julian the Apostate.

In the early centuries Christians worried that at any time Christianity might be abandoned in favor of paganism and magic. The price of its survival was constant vigilance, which culminated in the Holy Inquisition and the all-out war on heresy.

Magicians were always heretics. If Christians were not careful, it was thought, the uneducated public might well find the

St. Augustine, Bishop of Hippo, harmonized classical and Christian thought.

church without authority and the masses would revert to devils and demons to get what they wanted. They would worship idols, as the Jews did even while Moses was up the mountain getting the Ten Commandments.

Dangerous possibilities lay in the evil magic of Babylon and Egypt as well as that of the Magi, the magicians who arose among the Medes and the Persians, by whom Christ was honored but whom He put out of business.

In a poem about the journey of the Magi, whose astrology told them of the birth of Christ, T. S. Eliot describes one of them wishing for "another death," years after the Nativity. It is not known if this one of the three kings is referring to his death or that of Jesus, who has threatened all he knew.

The Magi were once immensely powerful in the east. At first the Persians of the *Avesta* condemned the wizards of Babylon but in the long run gave rise to their own Magi. Their world of demons was especially horrible. And the demons did not stay in Persia. Certain Roman emperors brought in insidious magical doctrines from the east.

Emperors such as Alexander Severus were willing to grant magic a sort of official status, aligning magicians with those who wore the imperial purple. That understandably made the church very anxious.

In addition, the cherished beliefs from pre-Christian Europe were always present, underground but powerful. They included worship of a horned god very much like The Devil himself. Many of the superstitions recounted in this book survived pre-Christian European magical beliefs. So did innocuous and non-sexual superstitions such as wassailing apple trees and putting up Christmas trees. Sober puritans in early New England banned such pagan traditions, even mince pies.

We do not mind telling the bees—you have to inform them when a member of the household dies—but we do object to grandmothers telling susceptible children about age-old, non-Christian magic. It is one thing to carry a bent penny for good luck (preferably one with the date of your birth on it) but

Demons bother a heretic (after Holbein).

quite another to incline the children toward non-godly activities.

A few children who learned voodoo from a black servant caused the greatest of American witch-hunt crises, the blot on our history that is Salem. Historically, people were accused of burning witches in Salem. They did not; they hanged them, and pressed to death anyone who obstructed what they considered to be simple justice. We have to remember that the Puritans were zealous but not weird: they merely acted on what a great many other people believed was right. They were afraid of magic, but were by no means the only ones who feared it or saw it as a threat to their way of life. What we tend to condemn in Puritans is their acting on their principles and going to extremes where most of us stop short in putting our ideals into action. It is disturbing to face the fact that in our lax modern ways we dismiss as Fundamentalists those who used to be called True Believers, preferring tolerance to terrorism.

Every religion, even the Buddhist, has some magical components, but the Christian religion has feared magic more than most and certainly has done more than the Jews or the Muslims to crush it. In the name of putting down magic, Christian religion has killed millions upon millions of people, heretics or other persons suspected of the sin of witchcraft.

This is an even greater outrage in church history than the so-called Black History of the *conquistadors* in America. In both cases, the victims (witches in Europe, the *índios* in the Americas) were regarded as hardly human and treated with great inhumanity.

And now we come to an individual who was all too human but is usually called "The Beast."

THE BEAST

That is what his own mother called the magus and mountebank Aleister Crowley (1875–1947), who was proud of that title and wanted to be known as the most dangerous man alive. He enjoyed being called "The Wickedest Man in the World" by the tabloids.

His sex magic most certainly made him dangerous to those who got into affairs with him, whether they were his Scarlet Woman friend or his homosexual lovers. They ended up badly, some insane or dead from too many drugs and too much debauchery.

Satan enthroned—his crown looks rather like the pope's—with a witch (left) and a wizard. *Histoires prodigieuses* (1597).

Magic's concept that you can do what you like provided you harm nobody did not cut much ice with this egomaniac. He started out young by seducing the servant girls of his own wealthy family. He then moved on to taking advantage of everyone he met. His strict upbringing in the Plymouth Brethren only sharpened his outrageousness. There is nothing so wild as a prude gone rude.

He argued in his unrepentant *Confessions* that men and women "are not free to love decently until they have analyzed themselves completely and swept away any mystery from sex . . . [achieving] a profound philosophical theory based on wide reading of anthropology and enlightened practice." In actuality, his sexual escapades were far from any aspect of "loving decently," and he used sexual perversity and narcissistic self-indulgence to fuel his magical ambitions.

If it can be said that a man can be the most cold, selfish and calculating about fierce, unbridled and unprincipled passions, such a man was "The Beast" out of *Revelations*. He called himself by the Greek equivalent, Therion, the personification of wickedness. He turned to sex and drugs (mostly heroin) and the obscene worship of Baphomet.

Crowley wrote in the same book that Magick (which he always spelled with a *k* to distinguish it from the illusions created by stage magicians) is one of

Aleister Crowley looking a trifle less frightening than usual.

the subtlest and most difficult of the sciences and arts. There is more opportunity for errors of comprehension, judgment and practice than in any other branch of physics.

Crowley was probably the wildest practitioner of sex magic(k) of the twentieth century. No intellectual slouch, he also authored what was probably the best book on this topic of the century, *Magick in Theory and Practice*. Although he did not sacrifice hundreds of people to his crazy ambitions, as did Gilles de Rais and the Countess Báthory in earlier centuries, he indubitably brought destruction upon a great many followers with his reckless and obscene "do what thou wilt" notions and practices.

Both of his wives went insane (if indeed they were not insane to be near him in the first place) and five of his mistresses were driven to suicide. At the same time I suppose it has to be said that all pioneers and enthusiasts have something in them that, if only at first, seems ridiculous and unjustified to the majority of people. To be honest about it, Crowley was only after what a great many other people sought: sex and power, money and fame. The difference was that he went after what he wanted with total disregard for others. His dedication, whatever you think of his goals, was amazing. His mind was focused, but deranged.

Crowley wrote about 100 books. I think he shared something of Nawal el-Saadawi ("Like prophets and gods I reach for life after death by writing") with the book and something of the sadistic schoolmaster with the birch. He went so far as to break the solemn vow of members of the hermetic society The Golden Dawn made to keep the secrets of the order ("the KEY"). But considering those involved it seems inevitable that someone would do so. Crowley was not as gifted with words as Yeats, but Yeats' *A Vision* is a great deal more unreadable than any book by Crowley. Crowley had more gumption than A. E. Waite and even more drive than S. L. MacGregor Mathers.

Mathers was another oddball and a very devious one. He was once photographed in the getup of a priest of the Egyptian goddess Isis. He was one of the founders of the mishmash of old religions, Freemasonry and folklore called The Order of the Golden Dawn, actually went to court to get an injunction against Crowley publishing the secrets in his occult magazine *The Equinox*. But Crowley used magic(k), he claimed, and had the court order reversed.

There are many magical spells for getting judges to decide in one's favor. I guess Crowley's were better than Mathers'. I would like to float the suggestion that the reason Crowley's magic always worked better was simply that Crowley believed less in that sort of thing than his opponents did. However, I confess I am never quite sure when he is pretending and when he is sincere—the same sort of problem I run into with one Mme. Blavatsky, whom I once called "a genuine fake" in contradistinction to a pretender who never believes her or his own fabrications thereby never gaining authentic results. Cocksure as Crowley always seems, he must have privately been surprised at his public success as often as not.

Whatever he did, Crowley never apologized. After revealing "the KEY" (and not very much of it), many associates, including William Butler Yeats, A. E. Waite, Algernon Blackwood, Arthur Machen, and other literary types of The Golden Dawn, ostracized him. But Crowley, always desirous of running any organization of which he was a member, did not much care. He founded a new order, *Argentinum Astrum*. He collected disciples from Britain and the U.S. Eventually one of them [Francis] Israel Regardie, who had moved to California for its extensive occult activities, spilled the beans on The Golden Dawn and Crowley's "Silver Constellation" as well. Regardie was thereafter heartily despised by some, despite his undoubted talents and useful books on magic.

Regardie did not seek out enemies, whereas Crowley was the kind of man who loved opposition and could act against opponents with glee. When Mathers set a vampire on him, Crowley replied with Beelzebub and a large host of demons. Not since ritual magicians battled with each other in nineteenth-century France (using curses, Black Masses and blasphemies of the consecrated host) had the occult world seen anything like the Mathers/Crowley battle. The schisms between modern Satanists do not compare to the French rivalries, perhaps because the educated masses of today are less vulnerable to the power of suggestion.

In magic, as in voodoo, you open yourself to the power of magical suggestion when you are a believer. You can do great damage to your own psyche if and when you learn that some magical curse has been perpetrated against you. It is a sort of mental jujitsu; your own strength (in this case strength of belief) is used against you. W. C. Fields used to say, "you can't cheat an honest man." I say it is difficult if not impossible to hex a nonbeliever.

Crowley attracted many believers. He deliberately degraded disciples and mistreated friends and mistresses. Colleagues were sure he had killed Mathers in 1918 by witchcraft.

Crowley's weakness lay in his gluttony. He was sometimes strung out on too much sex and too many drugs. He drove himself temporarily insane at times and ruined the minds of those he drew into Satanic and sexual orgies at his Abbey of Thelema (meaning "Will" or maybe "Choice" in Greek) at Cefalù on the coast of Sicily. Eventually animal sacrifices (which Crowley started at the age of 12, aroused sexually by them) roused the Italian government's ire. "The Beast" was deported from Italy. He was later to be in the U.S. where he christened a toad Jesus Christ and killed it, and Britain.

Crowley had undeniable charisma. He strengthened his fatal attraction with Ruthvah, otherwise known as the Perfume of Immortality or The Perfume of Satyr. Because it has three ingredients, it is also called the Perfume of The Triad. Supposedly, when Crowley wore it men and women were irresistibly drawn to him and horses neighed as he passed them in the street. I unwisely printed it in my book on magic and witchcraft, and a friend of mine made some. He was murdered in the street a short time later. I cannot say the perfume was the cause but I do feel obliged to warn you not to try it. Put pheromones into your regular aftershave, if you must. Or just use musk.

But in trying to get head, or ahead, don't lose your mind or your immortal soul. If "immortal soul" means nothing to you, consider that the life of any outsider is difficult. Are you masochistic? Are you evil? Do you want to be like Crowley a "Black Magician"? For God's sake, why?

Whichever way you look at Crowley, consider the advice of what is probably the oldest book that has survived: *The Book of Resurrection*, better known today as *The Book of the Dead*. It says: "Consult the ignorant and the wise." Which do you think Crowley was?

ALLEN BENNETT

One of Crowley's strange disciples, who thought him wise indeed despite many justifications for altering his opinion, was Allen Bennett. He got a bad start when it came to sex and it took a long time to recover.

When just a teenager, Bennett had turned against God because Bennett's school friends disabused him of the misconception that human beings were born of angels. When he discovered how humans were conceived, and how the plumbing worked, Bennett thought God had created a "loathsome" method of reproduction. "Therefore," he reasoned, "this God must be a devil!"

Bennett had already attempted to call up The Devil by reciting the Lord's Prayer backwards. "Something happened which frightened him," Crowley said of the incident. "Having now rejected Catholicism, he took up Magick and at once attained extraordinary success."

So a sexual shock had launched Bennett on a career of sex magic. It was not to turn out well. Bennett was a very intelligent man and did much to introduce certain Buddhist ideas to the west, but he wasted himself on Crowley.

The Order of the Golden Dawn.

VICTOR NEUBERG

The stories of Crowley's heterosexual rampages are better known than his awful if temporary ruination of Victor Neuberg during "The Paris Working" of sex magic—24 orgies in which Crowley played the feminine role in January and February of 1914. Here is how Nat Freedland in *The Occult Explosion* (1972) describes the first of Crowley and Neuberg's homosexual encounters, years before:

> Neuberg was a starry-eyed young Cambridge student who accompanied Crowley on a trek across the Algerian desert in 1909 when they conjured up the "mighty devil Choronzon" with the aid of quantities of hashish and performance of a homosexual rite on an improvised sand altar "in the sight of the sun." With Neuberg protected inside a magic circle, Crowley crouched in a Triangle of Solomon and allowed the demon to take possession of him; appearing in turn as a hairy, horned beast, a beautiful whore, a wriggling snake, and a naked pseudo-Crowley who broke into the protected circle and tried to bite Neuberg's throat.

Neuberg broke with Crowley after "The Paris Working." Crowley put a curse on him, effecting

> a two-year nervous breakdown. Neuberg recovered and fought for his country in World War I [Crowley fled to the U.S. and didn't participate beyond writing pro-German propaganda]. He [Neuberg] married, and became a father. He was an important poetry editor during the 1930s and responsible for publishing the first printed verse of Dylan Thomas.

Not all of Crowley's contacts did as well as Neuberg. Some were supposed to have been active in a coven Crowley founded in California which long outlasted 1947, the year of Crowley's death.

My favorite Crowley contact was Lam, an "entity" he says he contacted. The sketch Crowley drew of Lam (1910) looks very much like the standard egghead space aliens of decades later. Crowley, for all his medieval "magick," was ahead of his time.

JACK PARSONS

Inevitably, a certain amount of material on sex magic will come from my earlier publications. In the case of that incredible Jack Parsons, an American disciple of "The Beast" Crowley, I hope I may be excused for quoting from an earlier work. If you've read it before, it is colorful enough to look at again. In any case, here goes:

> The *Ordo Templi Orientis* that Aleister Crowley established in Europe [I take this opportunity to correct my error: *OTO* was a German group founded by others and Crowley was the appointed head of the British branch] had certain appeals to Americans, especially those interested in sex magic. These disciples formed a group in California called Agape Lodge, but the Greek word *agape* (selfless and outgoing love) had little reference to their real activities, especially those of Jack Parsons, a brilliant physical chemist. Parson's sex life with real women convinced him that he would be far better off with an "elemental" woman conjured up by sex magic. For a while Parsons had to be content with Crowleyan ceremonies that involved a lot of boring ritual magic and no sex but masturbation, but in the long run—lo and behold!—the "elemental" was produced. Some people said she was a would-be poetess from New York, but Parsons was ready to believe she was his promised magical bride. With this attractive woman . . . vivacious, red-haired and green-eyed, Parsons undertook to produce in her womb Babalon, the Crowleyan "female principle" itself. Parsons and his girlfriend advanced the cause of heterosexual sex magic to the fullest extent of their energies, but no Babalon was conceived. Ultimately (1952) Parsons blew himself up in an experiment with fulminate of mercury. He is remembered chiefly not for his sexual or magical prowess but for his legal name change—from "Jack Parsons" to "Balarion Armiluss al Daijal Antichrist."

To those few paragraphs from *The Complete Book of Magic and Witchcraft* (1986) I perhaps should add a definition of "elemental." This is a creature entirely summoned by the visualizations of the magician, not personification of the elemental spirit or god but projection of the will of the magician. Many persons claiming magical powers swear they have created such creatures. "Dion Fortune," an English woman, even claimed to have frightened herself by producing a large and dangerous "elemental" animal that got on her bed.

I have to say that Jack Parson's (or Mr. Antichrist's) "elemental" was as far as almost anyone besides himself could see an ordinary female from the East Coast who went out to get caught up on the occult doings of a state in which there were innumerable loonies. California had seen several Messiahs, Neo-Rosicrucians (H. S. Lewis and his Ancient and Mystical Order of the Rosy Cross or AMORC, founded 1915), the

Minute Men of St. Germain (Guy Warren Ballard and his friends), Satanists (and the pseudo-Satanists of the Church of Satan) and some more bizarro cults. California was snidely referred to as "the land of fruits and nuts."

Cults were more or less welcomed in that sunny and relaxed country. They succeeded in becoming tax-free because they are counted as religions. As they say in California, "whatever!" It was in California that the first (and as far as I know, only) B.A. with a "major in Magic" was awarded (to Isaac Bonewits). I have seen Bonewits on television. He seems like a perfectly sane individual. Many in the occult world do not give that impression at all. Many of them live in California.

For more on Jack Parsons, see the book written under what I think must be a pseudonym ("John Carter"), *Sex and Rockets: The Occult World of Jack Parsons.*

This book of mine will introduce interesting individuals about whom you can get the whole story in any bookstore or library, if you're interested. Crowley and his friends are some of those colorful characters. I trust I do no one a great injustice by giving my personal opinions without qualifying evidence but I feel entitled to them, and I urge you to inform yourself and then make up your own mind too.

"NOT FOR LOVE NOR MONEY"

Love and money are not always so unconnected. In magic some people use love or sex to get money, just as women used to prostitute themselves for religious purposes, offering themselves to anyone who came to the temple.

There are numerous examples of people using sex magic for personal wealth. A famous one is that of Lucius Apuleius, author of *The Golden Ass* (sometimes entitled *Metamorphoses*). Apuleius was born about AD 123 in North Africa, and educated in Carthage and Greece. He went to Rome and wrote *The Golden Ass*, the earliest of Latin novels to survive. But writing novels was not bringing him a lot of money and he, like his hero in the novel, may have been a sorcerer's apprentice.

In any case he was accused of using witchcraft to get into marriage with a rich old widow. Did he use his extensive knowledge of the rites of the Egyptian goddess Isis to get himself a wealthy wife? He claimed that he had simply applied a few little tricks picked up from the Magi, and, after all, wasn't marrying for money a Roman custom? Whether he used seduction or sorcery, they forgave him.

THOSE HARES

I was listening to an old musical, *Golden Apple*, and in it there is a witch-like old woman called Mother Hare. This brought to my mind the British tradition wherein witches are said to turn themselves into hares. I wonder if there could be any connection between the sexual proclivities of rabbits and these metamorphoses? TV's Two Fat Ladies suggested eating rabbits might be a good idea to perk up life outside the kitchen.

In Scotland, where second sight and other superstitions were rife, it was believed that only a silver bullet could kill witches who had transformed themselves into hares. Or you could fire a silver coin at them (ideally a bent one).

ASHES AND ALOES

Today aloes are mostly associated with skin care. They used to be used in sexual attraction of a magical sort.

Write the name of a person you desire in ink, or in dove's blood if you are an adept, on a piece of virgin parchment (paper will do). Take three hairs of your head and place them one by one on the parchment, saying the following with each such placement, because this is not a mere recipe but an act of sex magic. It heretically calls on pre-Christian divinities:

By the power of the goddess Diana, by the power of the mighty Horned God [Cerunos], let all of mine and all of thine be now and forever more as one. This boon I seek in the name of the goddess Diana.

Fold the hairs into the parchment and burn it. Add the ashes to some aloes and scatter this mixture in equal parts to the four cardinal points of the compass in this order: north, east, south, and west.

The Burning Time.

THE SEX OF THE DEVIL

Jeffrey Burton Russell, author of several scholarly books on the Devil is perhaps the leading expert on the history of the subject. In *Satan* (1981), the one dealing with The Devil in Early Christian history, Russell writes:

> Religious tradition has spoken of the Devil, as it has of the Lord, in masculine terms. In English and most other languages, the Devil is "he." Tradition suggests numerous subsidiary female spirits of evil but symbolizes the chief of these spirits as masculine. Yet theology does not require a masculine Devil, and in fact theologians have traditionally argued that the Devil, being an [arch]angel, has no specific sex.

This means that in sex magic The Devil is considered to be capable of taking either the male or female role, and so, presumably, can his diabolical minions.

ASTROLOGERS AND MAGICIANS

Astrology is perhaps the largest magic component of any so-called occult science, which did not prevent popes from keeping or being astrologers even at the height of witchcraft persecution. Astrology is in every daily newspaper. If you want to see where it came from, and convince yourself that it is intimately connected with black magic read R. C. Thompson's *Reports of the Magicians and*

Astrologers of Nineveh and Babylon (two volumes, 1900). If you can read French and want a more authoritative commentary on astrology than you might get from most modern books, consult Alfred Maury's *Magie et astrologie* [Magic and Astrology]. Expert "Paul Christian" [Jean-Baptiste-Christian Pitois] has a book that has been translated and revised under the general editorship of Ross Nicholls as *The History and Practice of Magic* (1963). It has two very relevant chapters: "General Theory of the Horoscope" and "General Keys of Astrology," brilliantly researched by a dedicated librarian of the occult. This information is way beyond most modern "professional" astrologers who cannot do the math required for casting horoscopes, not even with computer programs. If you will consider the detail of the natal horoscope of Louis XVI (and he has not even included the "keys" of Juctine de Florence) you will appreciate the immense work of casting a horoscope, if not the fact that it is easier to predict after the event.

The Art Deco Devil of Aleister Crowley's Tarot.

TWIGGY

We hear of ash twigs in chapter two. If you have an extra one, perhaps left over from babies and cauls, put it under your pillow and dream of whom you will marry, according to the incantation you must recite before going to sleep:

> Not in his vest, not in his best,
> But in the clothes of everyday.

Unfortunately, for seeing the person nude in your dream, I have no method.

THE VAMPIRE AND SEX

As the werewolf springs from the idea of bestiality, so vampires stress the archetype of the immortal soul. Both supernatural creatures are closely connected to sex. Werewolves remind us of rape; the werewolf ravages the innocent. Vampires evoke thoughts of seduction; you have to invite the vampire in. Both are connected to witchcraft. In this series, I've devoted a book each to werewolves and vampires, and the sex angle must have been one of, if not *the* most important reason, the reason that those books were successful here and abroad.

VAMPIRI PRESENTA
IL FILM DI MEZZANOTTE

3 e 4 aprile IL CONTE DRACULA
(El Conde Dracula) - Spagna /Italia, 1971 - In italiano
Di Jess Franco. Con Christopher Lee, Klaus Kinski, Maria Rohan, Herbert Lom.
Lee impersona come sempre Dracula. Un Dracula che ringiovanisce sempre più dopo
ogni bevuta di sangue. Lom è Van Helsing e Kinski il pazzo Renfield.

10 e 11 aprile LA VENDETTA DEL VAMPIRO
(El Mundo de los Vampiros) Messico, 1962 - In italiano
Di Henry G.Richards. Con Edward B. Tucker, Lydia Larson.
L'ultimo di una casata di vampiri tenta di distruggere i suoi persecutori. Ma, come
sempre, sarà lui ad essere distrutto.

17 e 18 aprile VAMPIRI AMANTI
(The Vampire Lovers) Gran Bretagna, 1970 - In italiano
Di Roy Ward Baker. Con Ingrid Pitt, George Cole, Peter Cushing.
E' il primo dei tre film che la Hammer ha realizzato basandosi sulla figura di Carmilla
creata da Sheridan Le Fanu. Questo film ha beneficiato del budget più alto mai attribuito
a un film di vampiri della casa di produzione inglese. E si vede.

24 e 25 aprile INTERVISTA COL VAMPIRO
(Interview with the Vampire) USA 1994 - In italiano
Di Neil Jordan. Con Tom Cruise, Brad Pitt, Antonio Banderas.
Un nuovo vampiro si affaccia sullo schermo. Il vampiro tormentato creato da Anne Rice e
protagonista di una delle saghe più amate dai lettori di mezzo mondo.

1 e 2 maggio DRACULA IL VAMPIRO
(Horror of Dracula) Gran Bretagna, 1958 - In italiano
Di Terence Fisher. Con Peter Cushing, Cristopher Lee, Melissa Stribling.
Il primo film della Hammer dedicato al Vampiro. Il trampolino di lancio per Lee (Il Conte
Dracula) e una consacrazione per Cushing nel ruolo di Van Helsing. Da non perdere.

L'appuntamento è al cinema Mexico (Via Savona, 57 – 48951802)
ovviamente alle 24.00. Il prezzo del biglietto, per ogni proiezione, è di 9.000
lire ma per i possessori della VAMPIRI card sarà di 7.000 lire.

Everyone knows the curse of the werewolf and the sexy appeal of the vampire. They may not realize the extent to which the werewolf and vampire of peasant folk tradition were promoted to a sexier and higher class in popular fiction and film. Mr. L. Talbot (played by Lon Chaney, Jr.) and The Count (played by a long string of actors, including Christopher Lee and George Hamilton) are not peasants. They are suave, sophisticated landowners.

My books list a great number of stories and films that present the raging human turned into a wolf and the undead human who seeks the blood and the souls of the living. Everyone knows of Count Dracula, and aficionados of vampire lore know *Varney, The Vampire*, the character responsible for one of the most terrific opening scenes in literature: the savage attack of a beautiful woman as she lies in bed, her hair (a Victorian symbol of sex) sprawled about the coverlet while the monster takes his "repast." That opening chapter is a highlight in the field of what the British used to call the *penny dreadful*. The novel of 1847 was later published in penny parts, so the first chapter had to sell the book with a stunning opening tableau. The first few pages are brief and bloody. Blood, as Freud's biographer Ernest Jones put it, is the equivalent of semen in our psychology.

Another of these creatures' connection with sex is that werewolves and vampires can be born of illicit sexual congress. In Smyth Upton's obscure novel *The Last of the Vampires* (1845), the vampire baron has to kill a young woman every ten years and drink her blood to maintain his youth. As you well know, that bad baron was by no means the last of the sex-mad, undead monsters. The vampire still stalks, undead indeed. Bram Stoker's *Dracula* has celebrated its 100th birthday and has never been out if print. The literature of vampirism as well as the vampire in cinema and on television is more popular than ever. My vampire book in this series was chosen as a feature by a British book club.

Witchcraft has been used throughout the centuries to create the man-wolf and undead and then to try to cope with these horrors. Like witchcraft itself, werewolfery and vampirism are about power and sex.

WEREWOLVES

In this series' book on werewolves, I tell the story of the Gandillion family in the Jura district of France in 1584. They confessed to being werewolves. They said they not only attended sabbats but also had sex with The Devil in the form of a goat.

Sex orgies at sabbats were featured in many witchcraft confessions—confessions sometimes made at the business end of red-hot pincers. Most witches said they had sex with The Devil (apart from the traditional kissing of his rear end in homage) in a semi-human form, not that of a goat, despite the fact that black goats were often seen at sabbats.

The myth of female werewolves existed, but was more rare. The werewolf committed a sort of ravage or rape on his or her victims and was usually killed by one of his or her loved ones.

"THE WAY TO A MAN'S HEART IS THROUGH HIS STOMACH"

If it happens to be Midsummer's Eve, a woman can follow the old magical custom of setting out bread, cheese and ale on a clean white cloth and leave the front door open. A lover (or just a hungry male) will appear.

TANTRIC YOGA

When I tell people I am writing a book on sex magic, they often ask if I am going to address Tantric yoga. Not really. That belongs somewhere else, although it does have to do with sex and the supernatural, because in Indian religion Shiva and Shakti are male and female deities from whose interaction come the cosmos. In that story, it is through the sexual union of divinities and the sexuality of human beings that everything works and "the dance of life" continues.

Tantrism in Hindu and Buddhist elements are connected to a number of religious and magical beliefs and rituals. The lower tantras concern themselves with mundane and occult issues, including magic powers, especially in the Tibetan beliefs. The higher tantras deal with meditation and psychosexual powers, and with delaying the completion of the sex act producing a state of ecstasy. The *chakras* (wheels) and the female force of *kundalina* in the human body are far too complex a subject for a brief entry here. You need another book, such as Sir John Woodroffe's *Principles of Tantra* (second edition, 1952) before you can undertake the yogic practices of meditation, breath control, and management of the sexual energies.

There is really no simple shortcut to enlightenment. Those who are seeking good sex rather than transcendental awareness of the unity, of non-duality, of completeness, are on the wrong track fiddling with these esoteric ideas. If they insist on good sex they might be better off (though I doubt it) dealing with Aleister Crowley's mangled tantrism and the sexual trance he portentously called "eroto-comatose lucidity." It was not really the product of religious ecstasy but of sexual exhaustion and drug-induced hallucinations. Where others sought enlightenment and self-realization in abstemious practices he, characteristically, sought it in debauchery and overindulgence. You can, to put it crudely, "screw yourself out of your mind," but if you think that thereby you are getting yourself in a position to command all the forces of Nature and commune with Higher Powers, I think you are dangerously mistaken.

[Henry] Havelock Ellis wrote a big (and for its time extremely shocking) book called *Psychopathia Sexualis* and seven volumes of *The Psychology of Sex* (1898–1928). I think that basically Crowley was a sexual psychopath and weirder than any of Ellis' cases. Through him we see what Tantric practices put to evil, sadistic purposes can result in: not serene and beautiful harmony but destructive insanity. There are still followers around, though probably none so extreme.

I know my opinion will not be universally accepted, but there it is. I say study Tantric yoga or any other system of belief if you like, but don't pervert it. Sex badly handled, as Hesiod said, "overcomes the mind." Don't go crazy.

MORE SANTERÍA SEX MAGIC

To attract a lover you can burn some strange concoctions. One goes as follows. Write the lover's name at the bottom of a pot and nearly fill it with cooking oil. Add a little indigo (a blue dye) dissolved in brine, syrup of sugar cane or some rock candy, corojo butter and cocoa butter, pork lard, a dash of vegetable oil, and a candlewick. Take it to the seashore with seven pins tied together with blue thread and walk into the water holding the pins at eye level in front of you while you say the desired person's name seven times.

Light the wick and take the burning lamp back home. Let it burn off and on for seven days. At the end of that time take it back to the seashore and consign it to the deep. Pray to Yemaya. (Some say you need to put mercury in the pot. I say mercury is dangerous and that you must keep away from it.)

Another one goes as follows and requires less water. Take a glass of water and put into it a piece of paper with the desired person's name written on it, along with camphor, poppies, and honey. (Once again mercury is called for. Try omitting it.) Light a candle and place it beside the glass. Pray to a Santería divinity of choice.

There are many Santería formulae for holding onto a lover once you have one.

Take ribbons of different colors representing seven African divinities (white, black, red, blue, yellow, green, and brown). Braid them together. Smear the cord with corojo butter and coconut oil. Make seven knots in the cord. Place it with a photograph or drawing of the desired person. Burn candles beside it for seven days.

Take a pot and drop in a piece of paper with your lover's name and five needles and five pins. On top of this put honey, brown sugar, and rock candy for your sweetheart. Fill up the pot with oil and insert five candlewicks. It had better be a lot of oil because this has to burn for five days, presumably nonstop. Or maybe recipes like this intend you to burn the pots for only a short time each day for five days. I don't know. If one way doesn't work, try another.

Take anise, cumin, saffron and salt and make a very thick paste with a little wine. Form a poppet of the desired person out of this. Gather seven small stones and three small twigs from the four corners of the street nearest where the desired person lives. At the seashore catch a hermit crab. Wherever you can, sweep up a little dust from the desired person's footprints. Write the person's name on a piece of paper and put it in a bag with all the other items. Put that bag inside another bag and sew it up. Sprinkle it with wine. One recipe I read specified "dry wine" and added "leave it at a street corner." I presume what is meant is his or her street corner.

Here's one to hold onto a husband. Fill a gourd nearly full of oil of almonds. Add small amounts of honey and holy water and add the yoke of one egg. Insert a candlewick. As you light the lamp, pray to the god Oshun. Take a length of yellow cloth, wrap it around your waist, and tie it with a red ribbon. Wear this for five days.

If he got away, here is one to "have a lover return." Write his name on a piece of paper (resist the temptation to add nasty remarks). Place a large gourd on top of the paper and into the gourd put five nails from a chicken, one egg, paprika, marjoram, a dash of Florida water, and a lot of linseed oil, plus something belonging to the vanished rogue. Add a candlewick, light it while you pray to the powerful god Oshun, and "burn for five days." Then throw the thing into the river.

Let me reiterate before we leave this religion from Africa, which has continued into the New World along the same lines as obeah and voodoo, that the African gods of Santería are disguised by the Americas in the "religion of saints." So you will see statues of St. Barbara or St. Francis of Assisi (an alias for Ifa, the god of divination, who is never wrong) and others you recognize but may not realize whose help the devotees are invoking.

Let me give you one example. In Africa there are the Ibehji; twin deities. Santería also worships them with red and blue banners and indeed voodoo recognizes them as the Marassa. But these gods, often called upon to protect infants, are concealed under the names of St. Cosmos and St. Damian. I use the word *legend* because these two are the thieves crucified with Jesus, who promised that they would be with Him in paradise the same day, so He, not the church, made them saints. The Gospels do not give them names any more than The Three

SANTERIA

A Practical Guide to Afro-Caribbean Magic

With a FOREWORD by MICHAEL VENTURA

Luis Manuel Núñez

Kings or the Roman soldier whose lance pierced the side of the crucified Redeemer. People simply invented names for these important if minor characters in the drama. By the magic of a name they made them more real.

READING SANTERÍA

General
González-Wippler, Migene. *The Santería Experience* (*c.* 1982)
Gregory, Steven. *Santería in New York City: A Study in Cultural Resistance* (1999)
Olmos, Fernández & Lizabeth Paravisini-Gebert, eds. *Sacred Possessions: Vodu, Santería, Obeah, and the Caribbean* (*c.* 1997)
Oyal'éti, Iyal'ocha Oloya. *The Three Doors of Ocha* (*c.* 2000)
Rose, Donna. *Santería, the Cuban-African Magical System* (*c.* 1980)

Cuban Santería
Bolivár Aróstegui, Natalia. *Cuba: imágenes y relatos de un mundo mágico* [Cuba: Images and Stories of a Magic World] (*c.* 1997)
Canet, Carlos. *Lucumi: religión de los Yorubas en Cuba* [Lucumi: Religion of the Yorubas in Cuba] (1973)
Canizares, Raúl. *Walking with the Night: The Afro-Cuban World of Santería* (1993)
Castellanos, Isabel [Mercedes]. *The Use of Language in Afro-Cuban Religion* (1976)
Dissertation, Georgetown University: Language Use in the Lucumi Cult of Cuba
Dornbach, María. *Orishas en soperas: los cultos de origen yoruba en Cuba* [Spirits in Soup Dishes: The Cults of Yoruba Origin in Cuba] (1993)
Guanche, Jesús. *Artesanía y religiosidad popular en el Santería cubana: el sol; el arcoy la flecha, la alfarería de uso ritual* [Workmanship and Popular Religiosity in Cuban Santería: The Sun, the Rainbow and the Arrow, the Ceramics for Ritual Use] (*c.* 2000)
Lachataíeré, Rómolo. *Manual de santería* [Manual of Santería] (1995)
Mason, Michael Atwood. *Practicing Santería, Performing the Self: The Social Construction of Subjectivity in Humans and Gods in Afro-Cuban Religion* (1997) [Dissertation, University of Indiana, 1997]
Pérez, Tómas. *La santería cubana: el camion de Osha; ceremonias, ritos y secretos* [Cuban Santería: The Road of Osha; Ceremonies, Rites and Secrets] (*c.* 1998)

WOMEN AND MAGIC

From Thomas Nashe's *The Terrors of the Night*, a bit of Elizabethan male chauvinism:

A number of men there be yet living, who have been haunted by their wives after their death, about forswearing themselves, and undoing their children, of whom they promised to be careful fathers: whereof I can gather no reason but this, that Women are born to torment a man both living and dead.

MORE READING

Anand, Margot. *The Art of Sexual Magic* (1995)
Faraone, Christopher A. *Ancient Greek Love Magic* (2002)
Holland, Eileen. *The Wicca Handbook* (2000)
Moloch, Brother. *Sexual Sorcery* (1997)
Russ, Joanna. *Magic Mommas, Trembling Sisters, Puritans & Perverts: Feminist Essays* (1985)
Williams, Brandy. *Ecstatic Ritual: Practical Sex Magic* (1990)

"PRICKED BY THE THORNS OF VENUS"

Partly out of prurience and scandal mongering, and partly out of recognition that sexual repression can produce some ugly behavior, history is full of stories about priests, monks and nuns going down the primrose path.

Usually it is nuns committing adultery as Brides of Christ. I trace the reports to at least as many reasons as there are deadly sins.

Venus by Alessandro Allori.

* First, people are people and the urge to have sex is strong, sometimes irresistible.
* Second, the life of chastity being difficult, celibates were admired but not always trusted, and it always gives some people satisfaction to see others who act superior fail.
* Third, even cloistered nuns were not entirely without opportunity, and close connections with their father confessors (directors of consciences), or the occasional man, could lead to unwonted (if not unwanted) intimacies. Moreover, though the convents may have given their occupants rather hard lives, women outside who were poor and hard-pressed must have been jealous of the better lives and security of the nuns. A major motive of scandal, as with magic, is envy.
* Fourth, other men might consider nuns a bigger notch in their belts than most women; as with magic, a sense of doing the outrageous adds zest. After all, if you want to deflower virgins as an ego trip, you go to a convent. As Willy Sutton might have said, "If you want virgins, rob the convent. That is where the virgins are."
* Fifth, the whole society believed the doctrines of the church, from ordination on down, that said women were weak passionate creatures, and therefore easy targets.
* Sixth, it is always more sensational when a female goes astray than when a man does. No matter what a wayward man is considered, a wayward woman is considered a slut.
* Seventh, some of those virgins are neurotic or psychotic and it may act out in wild sexuality. Maybe you are just what they have been praying would come along.
* And a Bonus: when a sexually naïve female is seduced, she may get pregnant, so keeping her activity a secret is harder.

There is more to say, and getting those factors in order of importance could fuel a lot of debate, but that is enough for now. I probably should add that there might have been less heterosexuality than homosexuality in same-sex institutions like convents and monasteries. However, the subject was not nearly as "out" as it is today.

The histories record suspiciously few executions of men and boys for sodomy or men and beasts involved in bestiality. The church dictated that the animal as well as the person be put to death. Of course *incubi* and *succubi* activity was also defined as bestiality because demons are not humans.

Many were the lustful nuns, and many more the victims of rape or cruel seductions. Often nuns brought clergymen to the stake for sexual sins, real or imagined. I deal with the hysterical nuns of Loudon and some other French convent scandals in my other books.

Here, from the great historian of France, Jules Michelet, is the passage that the title of this section promises, the details for which you have patiently been reading. I choose France, always anticlerical and often with the best of reasons, rather than Britain and the U.S. where such things are either rare or, more likely, hushed up when they occur.

In this passage, Michelet is writing about how "Satan Turns Ecclesiastic," quoting Massée's extraordinary *Chronique du monde* [World Chronicle] of 1540:

Mme. de Montespan.

> Not a few nuns fall victim to this new ruse [of The Devil] of borrowing the face and figure of a beloved confessor. We may instance the case of Jeanne Pothiere, a nun of Le Quesnoy, a woman of middle age, forty-five years old, but, alas! only too susceptible. She declares her passion for her father confessor, who takes good care not to listen to her, and runs away to Falempin, a place at some leagues' distance. The Devil, who never sleeps, at once recognizes his advantage, and seeing her (in the chronicle's words) "pricked by the thorns of Venus, he cunningly adopts the form of said father, and returning night after night to the convent, enjoys her favours, deceiving her so thoroughly that she declares herself to have been had by him—she had kept count—four hundred and thirty-four times. . . ." Her subsequent repentance met with no little compassion, and she was speedily relieved from the agonies of shame, a good walled dungeon being at once provided for her in the neighbourhood, at the Castle of Selles, where she expired in a few days, dying a peaceful, edifying death as a good Catholic should. What could be more touching?

We do not learn what happened to the confessor after the nun's last confession. In many other cases, the religious suffered greatly even to the extent of execution by the civil authorities as a warning to all potential sinners.

As we see in this case, some operations attributed to The Devil contain *no* suggestion of sex magic. We see also that, whatever the sixteenth- or the nineteenth-century historians believed, a twenty-first-century person might well see no participation at all of The Evil One in this sad and sordid affair. What could be more reasonable?

FOOD FOR THOUGHT

Speaking of nuns and clergymen brings to mind a point that you may find rather odd: I want to talk about magic and food . . . no, not the "magical" diets that have left so many Americans obese. I believe that scholars have not addressed an aspect of the history of magic that is hidden in plain sight: you are what you eat.

Historians do not dispute that ergot in diseased grain caused some populations in the Middle Ages to see visions, engage in orgies, etc. Medical men may agree that porfiria, although genetic, can be exacerbated by incorrect diet, creating symptoms that the superstitious consider signs of the vampire. Certain foods certainly trigger schizophrenic flare-ups and of course hard liquor or even too much beer can cause you to "see things." Ingest hallucinogenic substances and you may think you are flying.

I want to have you consider for a moment the food of those who were the strongest believers in and sometimes the greatest pursuers of the magicians.

In the early days of Christianity, men fled from society for the good of their souls and lived in the desert as hermits and anchorites. I suggest that dieting and self-flagellation can make you crazy—if you are not crazy in the first place so to "mortify the flesh"—and that what he had or did not have for dinner may explain quite a lot of the famous sexual temptations of St. Anthony.

Further, I draw to your attention the diet of the ordinary Greeks of ancient times, a regimen which consisted, as one wry British scholar put it, of two meals a day, "the first a kind of porridge, and the second a kind of porridge." I happen to think that "bread" or better "biscuit" ought to be substituted there for "porridge" but he is dead right that the diet was boring. Can it be that if your food is bland you seek spicier physical satisfactions in sex and may turn to magic to get them? Just asking.

In the Middle Ages the peasantry barely got by. Famines must have shaken their faith in God and driven them to seek desperate measures, even diabolical assistance. In the Middle Ages and in a more modern way than the anchorites, some men and women retired from the world into monasteries and nunneries. In most of those institutions they were "mortifying the flesh" to the extent that the flesh might well have rebelled. Think *incubi, succubi,* the visions of hungry (and sex hungry?) nuns, etc.

St. Benedict founded an order that was much higher-class and better living than most but except for the 200 fast days a year, when they were lucky to get one scant bite, they ate better than the peasantry. Benedictines at the start received two meals a day, not just bread and a thin soup or gruel like most clergy. Benedictines were offered two cooked dishes and one raw dish and a good amount of wine. Sundays and other holy days were celebrated with eggs, cheese and maybe even fish. Could this be the reason Benedictines were less superstitious, healthier in body and in mind, than most people of the time?

And how do you explain the nastiness of the Dominican order when it came to the persecution of witches? Was it to be attributed chiefly to the fact that Spain had a lot of Dominicans "tainted" by the mystical and magical writings of the Jews in their recent backgrounds or was it something in the Spanish kitchens?

I simply want to advance the theory that people who are healthy, well-balanced and well fed, who are having a happy sex life, whether as Jews whose folk saying celebrates wives who "talk less and clean more"; Muslims with lots more sex, even harems; or Christians with one cooperative partner, are less likely to turn to magic, especially sex magic. Do you agree? Could you accept as a corollary that the ill informed and ill-fed, not to mention ill-favored and ill-treated, might be disposed to seek gratifications through sex magic?

Lack of meat in the diet also coincided with the rise of sex magic. Mrs. Patrick Campbell once said of a famous vegetarian friend, George Bernard Shaw, that some day he might eat a pork chop, and then "God help women!" Those who turned in defiance or desperation to sex magic were certainly lacking *something*.

THE BOOK OF THOTH

At this point I feel it incumbent upon me to give you some information about the alleged source of so many magical spells. I am sure that the average reader will have little or no patience with the infighting of sex magicians and indeed all Magi who "peep and mutter," as one critic says, so it is not the modern and wholly unreliable *Necronomicon* of some pseudo-witches but the fabulous *Book of Thoth*. It was said the book of that Egyptian god was won at a board game by the scholar Setne Khamwas. It supposedly contains the secrets of Egyptian magic. Or so Clement of Alexandria reported. One source claimed:

> The book is lying on the bed of the Nile near Copros, in an iron box. Inside the iron box is one of copper, and in the copper is another, of juniper wood. Within that there is a box of ebony and inside that another of ivory, which contains a box of gold within a box of silver. The book is in the box of gold. Six miles of writhing snakes and innumerable scorpions guard it.

In my opinion, this is not to be taken literally: I think the successive boxes are merely poetic representations of the various degrees through which adepts must pass to get to the meaning of the text. The snakes are shifting interpretations, and the scorpions are fatal traps for the unwise or unwary.

In any case, we are told that a prince called Neferkaptah went after the box, despite all the dangers, in the Ptolemaic period of Egypt. After all, the book was supposed to contain the power to communicate with all living creatures in "their own languages" and held the keys to understanding everything about Nature.

The gods, defending the book, caused Neferkaptah's son's death by drowning but not before he resurfaced to proclaim that Ra, the sun god, was opposed to the expedition to get the book. The prince's wife likewise was drowned by the curse and in death spoke a warning. The prince nonetheless went on. He got the book and copied it on new papyrus before he tied the book to himself and, in despair, drowned in the Nile. His body was recovered, but the pharaoh ordered the book to be buried with him.

That was not the end of *The Book of Thoth*. It was supposedly found in later ages and revised as *Hermetica*. And there the story gets even more complicated. There have been many alleged discoveries and alleged misguided attempts to restore or revise *The Book of Thoth*. If the *Hermetica* is anything to go by, the *Thoth* holds much valuable information. After all, it was from the *Hermetica* that the Polish scientist we call by the Latin name Copernicus got his big idea!

Magical organizations and individuals have warred with each other over the possession of texts. Does any presently functioning magical group have their hands on the real *Book of Thoth*? Personally, I don't think so.

In fact, does any group have a corner on the one true religion? You answer that one. There is so much fighting. As Freud stated in his *Group Psychology and the Analysis of the Ego* (1921): "A religion, even if calls itself the religion of love, must be hard and unloving to those who do not belong to it."

"Must be"? I don't think so. Is? Yes. Have a look at the next two entries.

HOMOSEXUAL CHURCHES

Despite such organizations as Dignity (Roman Catholic), the Presbyterian Gay Caucus, and Integrity (Episcopalians, probably the most liberal on the subject), most traditional Christian denominations denounce homosex on the basis of church traditions. Both *Leviticus* 18: 22 and *Romans* 1: 27 have been interpreted as condemning homosexuality. So, many lesbians and gays who want to practice both homosexuality and religion have created their own sex-friendlier congregations, such as homosexual synagogues. For example, Beth Simchat Torah was founded in New York City in 1973.

The first gay evangelical Christian church to draw headlines recently certainly was that of Pentecostal minister Rev. Troy Perry. His Metropolitan Community Church, founded in Los Angeles in the sixties, and other homosexual churches are maligned if they are accused of sex magic. They all seek to provide the homosexual community with a spiritual center and no more attract the sexually promiscuous or the sex magicians than any other religious organization. Although they are not as uptight about sex as many of the Bible-thumping evangelicals.

If you want religious sex practices you do not go to any of these churches. You take up Tantric Yoga. But that is a subject for a different book. Another subject I wish to sidestep is one I really cannot, but on Satanism I shall be brief and as objective as possible.

SATANIC CHURCHES

There are more of these than most people might wish. The Church of Satan is probably the most famous, with grottoes (branches) licensed for sexual license by the San Francisco original, founded, it is said, by the late author of *The Satanic Bible*, Anton Szandor LaVay, on Walpurgisnacht (night of the witches) in 1966.

The church is not really a collection of Satanists holding black masses and sacrificing innocent babies even if LaVay did have a bit part in the film *Rosemary's Baby*. This Satanic church or Church of Satan is basically neo-Crowleyist, but not nearly as dangerous. If I say more I will probably get a rap from the magazine *The Cloven Hoof*.

A breakaway from the Church of Satan is the Church of Satan Brotherhood, with various branches more or less affiliated but always in danger of faction. This church's magazine is (or was, I have not heard much of them lately) *The True Grimoire*. That title underlines the fact that these schismatics disapprove of some aspects of LaVay's *The Satanic Rituals*. Arguments over that and other LaVay scriptures have raged continually since their inception.

Some former members of the Church of Satan Brotherhood split off to form the *Ordo Templi Satanas*. Joseph Daniels was one of the founders.

There are many others and it can get confusing. For example, The Brotherhood of the Ram, which was run last time I heard out of an occult bookshop in California, is ignorantly mistaken for the Neo-Nazi Order of the Black Ram. The Satanic Church gets confused with a Satanic Church and the Satanic Orthodox Church, etc. Occult bookshops tend to spawn occult groups in many places.

All of these organizations are dedicated to self-expression through sex and to one extent or another attempt to or actually do practice sex magic. San Francisco and Los Angeles in the west, various cities in New York and New Jersey in the east, New Orleans in the south, and in Detroit and Indianapolis among other Cities of the Plains—are the main locations of sex magic among those who have signed pacts (sometimes in their own blood) with The Devil.

They are absolutely not to be mistaken for Wiccan practitioners or Goddess witches' covens or for traditional magicians.

WORKING IN REVERSE

Probably because magicians help their spells by "feeling strongly" (in the Mary Wollstonecraft sense), many witchcraft operations are deliberately shocking, even blasphemous, and many ingredients are, magicians say, "negatives" (such as rat feces or other filth) that work "positively." Even some of the incantations that accompany what otherwise would be medicines and not magic potions are to be recited backwards.

A WICCAN CEREMONY

Wiccan groups, as I have said, generally make up their own ceremonies. Here is one from the New Reformed Orthodox Order of the Golden Dawn. It has nothing to do with the original Order of the Golden Dawn and by this complex name underlining the competing and schismatic Wiccan organizations.

In this ceremony for an infant coming into the group, 13 "fairy godparents" (the number of a coven, as well as the number at the Last Supper) gather. Each one carries a candle and as the participant makes a wish for the baby he (or usually she) blows out his (or her) candle. This seems to derive from no Golden Dawn ceremony but from birthday cakes and possibly the fairy tale *Sleeping Beauty*.

MORE CEREMONIES

Ankarloo, Bengt & Stuart Clark. *Witchcraft and Magic in Europe* (1999)
Dendle, Peter. *Satan Unbound: The Devil in Old English Narrative Literature* (2001)
Kelly, Aidan. *Crafting the Art of Magic . . . 1939–1964* (1991)
Kiekhefer, Richard. *Forbidden Rites* (1997)
Valiente, Doreen. *The Rebirth of Witchcraft* (1989)

THE WAY OF THE SECRET LOVER

This is the title of a mishmash of Tarot, Tantra, and "Enochian Magick" by Christopher S. Hyatt & Lon Milo DuQuette (1991). It purports to get you in touch with your Secret Lover, *i.e.* your Holy Guardian Angel. It allows that the individual can be of either sex, but traditionally the guardian angels (who accompany all Christians in a state of grace) are sexless. Usually angels are portrayed as men with wings and seldom as women, except when played by over-the-hill actresses on television.

This book will be useful to you if you want to attempt "The Ceremony of the Sun [priest] and Moon [priestess]," which is "a Ritual of Marriage designed for Conjuring of two souls in Nuit and Hadit," supplied by "David Cherubim." I suppose that as two heterosexuals, "embrace their bodies in pure passionate ecstasy and joy, ending all with a sacramental kiss of delicious delight as a final token of their Mystick" they are not doing much harm to others. I do worry a trifle about the author of the ceremony when he ends it with the participants proclaiming, "ABRAHADABRA!" which I think is meant to be "ABRACADABRA," a conjuror's word derived vaguely from an old pagan god called Abraxis.

For another operation called "The Royal Mass of the Secret Lover" we are told that, "the male shall be stimulated by the female a minimum of eleven times until his organ becomes his wand of inspiration." This fluffing suggests to me that either his partner is not sufficiently attractive or not quite ready for this activity, but "do as thou will an thou harm none."

VIRGIL AND FRIENDS

The great epic poet Virgil was reputed in the Middle Ages to have been a magician and his works used for bibliomancy (telling the future by dipping at random into a book). In Nicola de Pulford's recent *Spells & Charms*, we are told how to awaken creativity with St. John's wort and a copy of Virgil.

Many recipes like this, hardly magical, occur in modern works alleging to be about the subject of witchcraft. In Phyllis Currott's "spiritual guide," *Witchcrafting*, you are advised to go outside, breathe deeply, and say, "Spirits of air, bring me a clear and open mind." The "kitchen witch" Patricia Telesco's latest in an endless number of books tells the history of Candle Magick but involves wishful thinking more than witchcraft.

In *Love Magic* Sally Morningstar advises one to use crystals to divine their sexual future (or love life, as people like to say) but this is superstition, not working magic. These titles all come from Quality Paperback's latest flyer and so indicate to me a widespread interest in pseudo-witchcraft, part-time non-wicked Wicca (Phyllis Curott is both a New York lawyer *and* a Wiccan priestess), and pop paperbacks. They are all books about warm and fuzzy "occult empowerment." They are just an extension of the self-improvement movement.

Meanwhile, children of all ages are going wild over Harry Potter and many a kitchen has a Witches' Calendar on the wall. Nobody cooking up alleged love spells is onto the real stuff with such ingredients as, say, Cocillana bark (used in spells of sexual attraction, probably because of its smell of musk).

All this suggests to me a disturbing if minor irrationality in modern America but certainly not a desperately heretical frame of mind, whether the lady of the house is at the computer on www.witchvox.com or just adding some "witchy" ingredient to the ready-made cake mix.

I think the current mainstream popularity of witchcraft is one of those simple (albeit revealing) gestures, like tying yellow ribbons on trees or wearing lapel ribbons to indicate support for one cause or another.

THE CURE FOR THE COMMON SCOLD

They used to test witches by throwing them into water. If they sank, they were innocent (and maybe drowned). If they floated they were guilty (and maybe put to death).

A number of sex magicians repented of their folly when impotence gave them more time to think. A number responded to the invitation to renounce "the pomps" of The Devil when receiving the last rites of the church, though on that score the seventeenth-century wit John Selden wrote in *Table Talk:* "For a priest to turn a man when he lies a-dying, is just like one that for a long time solicits a woman, and cannot obtain his end; at length he makes her drunk, and so lies with her."

"Anna Riva," introduced at the end of chapter three, often suggests that one read certain psalms when working magic spells. I suggest that if you want to give up the Left Hand path you not wait until the last moment. Instead read *Romans* 3: 19 and 10: 9, *Acts* 3: 19 and 16: 30–31, and *John* 1: 12.

BOOKS ON SEX MAGIC

Campigny, Henri M. de. *Théorie et practique de la magie sexuelle: L'amour et occultisme* [Theory and Practice of Sex Magic: Love and Occultism] (1938)

Farren, David. *Sex and Magic* (1975)

Koszegi, Michael A. *Sexuality, Religion, and Magic: A Comprehensive Guide to Sources* (1994)

Muir, Charles & Caroline. *Tantra: The Art of Conscious Loving* (1989)

Randolph, Paschal Beverly. *Sexual Magic* [*Magia sexualis* translated and edited by Robert North] (1988)

Walker, Benjamin. *Sex and the Supernatural: Sexuality in Religion and Magic* (1970)

BOOKS ON VOODOO

There is a lot of garbage published on this topic and the best books were not
written in English, but some are conveniently and well translated, such as:

Aubourg, Michel & Leince Viaud. *Folklore Ceremony of Petro Rite* . . . (194?)
[This ceremony was celebrated 24 December 1944 in Port-au-Prince, Haiti.
Translated by E. Arthur. An authentic rather than tourist voodoo rite.]
Bryk, Felix. *Voodoo Eros: Ethnological Studies in the Sex-Life of the African Abo-
rigines (1933)* [Limited, private edition, translated from *Neger-eros*, Ger-
man, by Mayne T. Sexton, a copy in the New York Public Library.]
Kerboull, Jean. *Voodoo and Magic Practices* (1978) [Translated by John Shaw from
Vaudoo et practiques magiques.]
Rigaud, Milo. *Secrets of Voodoo* (1969) [Translated by Robert B. Cross from *Tra-
dition voudoo et le voudoo haïtien.*]

Of varying degrees of reliability, there are books originally in English from
Henry Gilfond to "Gay Witch" Leo Martello and some other books in which
voodoo plays a part. Examples:

Cajun, André. *Louisiana Voodoo* (1946)
Christensen, Barbara. *The Magic and Meaning of Voodoo* (1977)
Gilfond, Henry. *Voodoo: Its Origins and Practices* (1976)
Martello, Leo. *Black Magic, Satanism, Voodoo* (1973)
Martinez, Raymond J. *Mysterious Marie Laveau* (1956)
Pelton, Robert W. *The Complete Book of Voodoo* (1972)
Summers, Montague, ed. *The Supernatural Omnibus* (1982)

I single out Louisiana, because New Orleans is generally considered to
be the voodoo capital of the U.S. although there are more practitioners in New
York. Marie Laveau was a famous New Orleans character, especially since her
daughter succeeded her and many people thought the original had lived an
especially long time. The first Marie Laveau specialized in love charms and
in getting other people of color out of jail. There are many books about her.

By the nineteenth century the Three Graces of Greek mythology were selling corsets.

6
Sex and the Supernatural Onscreen

BAD, BAD, BAD ON THE BIG AND SMALL SCREEN

Here are featured 200 films about sex, magic and witchcraft with a number of others mentioned in passing. You can rent almost all to watch on videotape. If the prologue to one, *Dracula and Son* (1979), applies to you then this is your kind of stuff: "According to a recent survey, one in three people is a vampire. . . . Think of three of your closest friends; if they seem all right to you then *you're* the one." Ignore the mathematics. Get the gist of it.

THE TOP 200 WONDERFULLY BAD MOTION PICTURES AVAILABLE ON THE BIG AND SMALL SCREENS

Here are some films about magic and witchcraft that you can see on videotape. Presumably many will survive in DVD and future formats as they move from cinema and television to video and beyond. Not-bad stuff like *Black Sunday* (1960) and *Black Sabbath* (1964) were once paired on a laser disc. Remember laser disc? Like vampires, the stuff of horror movies is undead. Anything you haven't seen before is new. Take your pick. Throw a Halloween screening. Use hollowed-out turnips with candles in them instead of pumpkins.

If you want good movies, try Dreyer's *Vampyr* and neglected vampire movies such as *Martin*; or Ken Russell's *The Devils* (1971), based on Aldous Huxley's *The Devils of Loudon*. For light fare there is Veronica Lake in *I Married a Witch* (1942); or *The Witches of Eastwick* (1987), based on the novel by John Updike. Let us not forget the big-budget films such as the *Omen* series, etc. There are some entertaining films about love conquering death (*Ghost*, 1990), which I leave out of this book.

There are so many good and fine films I honestly cannot undertake to cope with them here. However, if you want trash of the "so bad it's good again" persuasion here is my personal, devil-may-care list of some superbly crude examples. None is a blockbuster. The Top 10 grossers in the U.S. have been: *Titanic* (1997), *Star Wars* (1977), *Star Wars: Episode One—The Phantom Menace* (1999), *E.T.* (1982), *Jurassic Park* (1993), *Forrest Gump* (1994), *Harry Potter and the Sorcerer's Stone* (2001), *The Lion King* (1994), *The Return of the Jedi* (1983), and *Independence Day* (1996), triumphs of special effects but hardly specially effective as works of art. Only *Harry Potter* really touches on the magical transformations that movies make so easy and that is still another "Kiddiema" hit, no sex.

Witchcraft through the Ages (1922).
A naked virgin is the altar.

I'd like to begin by mentioning a number of flix that were too bad to put in the extensive filmographies of *The Complete Book of Vampires* or *The Complete Book of Werewolves* or *The Complete Book of Ghosts and Poltergeists*—although I lowered standards for the poltergeist genre.

It is too bad about poltergeists because there does seem to be some evidence of such activity actually being connected with sex, in the historic belief that adolescent girls in the vicinity appear to bring it on. On the other hand there is no hard evidence that the dead or the undead come to get at us and I believe that demonic possession, though part of a number of modern faiths, is losing steam as a belief.

As you look at the whole subject of sex and magic in the context of this movie list, please bear in mind that fiction shadows fact, and that popular entertainment holds crucial clues to what people have been feeling, fearing, and hoping. Folklore and popular culture have exposed the emotional and intellectual underbelly of society, today and always.

As our high-culture writers and artists drift away from the common man, I say scan *TV Guide* and the not-very-comic comic books; listen to popular music and heed the lyrics if you can understand them—I have to omit this extremely significant manifestation of "where we're at" because I can't make out most of the lyrics—and lastly, see what's at the mall-typlex.

Americans are so puritanical at heart that they want to think of all diversion as recreation. Goofing off they are recreating themselves in order to return to work. They need to see entertainment as self-improvement. So here you go. You are going to learn about the heart and soul of Americans (and those who are educated to American values worldwide through cinema) as you indulge yourself in bad, bad movies. It's a good, good move. This, folks, is illuminating research.

The films that are briefly annotated stress to one degree or another sex, gore, and the supernatural. I'll leave out the losers with sex but no magic, and those with magic but no sex. Their titles can be misleading, such as *Devil Queen* (from Brazilian director Antonio Carlos Fontoura). It is not bad, but the queen is a black gay and the story is mostly about gangsters. You don't need *The Magic Christian* (1970), which is about neither Christianity nor magic, and you're not ready for Yul Brynner in drag. You don't need to bother with the promising sounding *High Priestess of Sexual Worship* in these serious researches on sexual magic. It is just Georgina Spelvin down to her old tricks: S&M but no SM (Sex Magic).

Foreign film English titles are often misleading, too. One example will suffice: the Swedish/Norwegian effort *Forfoelgelesen* is *The Witch Hunt* (1981, Anja Breien) in English. There's sex and an abortion but no witchcraft.

And now, here is the list with, I repeat, my own estimates of value or relevance.

Amazon Jail (1985). It's steamy in the Amazon so women wear very little, even when they escape from jail. This spins the plot when they encounter devil worshippers in the jungle.

The Antichrist (1974). Mel Ferrer in an Italian tale of Antichrist, bestiality, carnality, and so on down the alphabet at least as far as witchcraft. Also called *The Tempter*.

Asylum of Satan (1972). Dr. Spectre offers a virgin sacrifice to The Devil but she is not a virgin, so The Devil takes Dr. Spectre in her place. Always use the best materials.

The Beast of Morocco (1966). Seems that back in the 14th century a woman was buried alive. She's baaaaack, as a vampire, and chases after an architect.

The Believers (1987). Really a cop story, not sex, but I put it in because the *Santería* in New York is well done. For once a male (the cop's son) is threatened with becoming a human sacrifice.

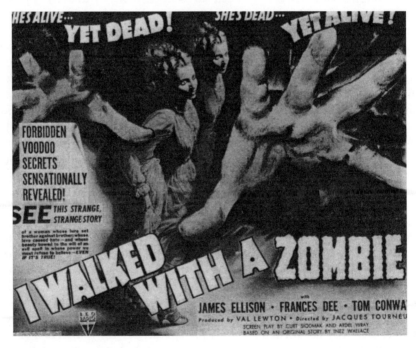

I Walked With a Zombie.
Frances Dee stars in this exposé of "forbidden voodoo secrets," confused about zombies but a horror masterpiece by Jacques Tourneur. Edith Barrett is a Christian missionary posing as a voodoo priestess.

Ingrid Pitt as the Countess Báthory.

Beverly Hills Vamp (1988). Britt Ekland runs an upscale whorehouse with vampire hostesses.

Beyond Evil (1980). As if the real Amityville and the bunch of movies it inspired were not kitschy enough, here's a rip-off on that craziness. Young couple moves into new real estate and the old unreal (a woman murdered hundreds of years before) returns: Lynda Day George gets possessed. John Saxon and other non-actors. Ridiculous but busy.

Beyond the Door (1975). Frisco femme finds herself pregnant and the daddy's a demon. Italian (dubbed into English) rip-off of *Rosemary's Baby* (1968). The bear-Satan-'s-kid plot continued with *To the Devil, A Daughter* (1976), *The Visitor* (1980), *The Seventh Sign* (1988), *Midnight Cabaret* (1990), etc.

The Black Cat (1981). Director Lucio Fulci (*Il Gato negro*) loose on an English village where the batty medium's spirits get into the animal of the title. Where's the sex? At least there's sexual jealousy as a vague motive for trying to kill the feline in Poe's *The Black Cat*.

Black Magic (1992). A made-for-cable effort with Judge Reinhold. His dead cousin appears in his dreams and the dead cousin's girlfriend he's taken up with may be a witch. Not to be confused with the 1949 film of the same obvious title, in which Orson Welles plays Cagliostro, directed, as much as one could direct Welles, by Gregory Ratoff.

Black Magic Terror (1979). A queen of black magic runs afoul of one of the men under her spell.

Macbeth (right, dressed as an early eighteenth-century Englishman) is shown by the three witches (left) the royal decendants of Banouo. From Nicholas Rowe's *William Shakespeare's Works* (1709).

of the Life and Death
of Doctor F A V S T V S.

With new Additions.

Written by *Ch. Mar.*

Nothing by Christopher Marlowe was published in his lifetime with his name on the title page. This quarto published long after his death has only *Ch. Mar.*, as you see. Dr. Faustus in the woodcut has called up a dragon-like deity (which he asks to come again in a more suitable shape, so the demon appears as a Catholic friar).

Black Magic Woman (1991). Mark Hamill is stuck in a script in which a young fellow has a voodoo spell cast on him by a beautiful but dangerous woman.

Blood and Roses (1960). Directed by Roger Vadim, so some will object to my listing it in this company, but in my view neither Vadim nor Elsa Martinelli could save this story of a lesbian vampire who hots on the bride-to-be.

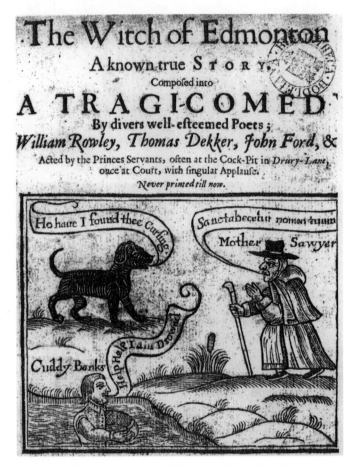

In the traditional system of illustrated medieval manu-
scripts on the lives of saints, more than one episode in
Mother Sawyer's story is depicted on this title page of
1658. The man in the water has been chasing a spirit he
thought was his beloved Katherine.

Blood Diner (1987). The meatloaf is tastier than usual. Two possessed diner
   owners not only kill women in their devilish rituals but also grind them
   up for the menu. That's not ketchup; that's blood.
The Blood Drinkers (1966). Also called *Vampire People*. A sterling example here
   of a specialty of the Filipino film industry: really awful vampire movies.
   Bloodsucking, heart transplantation, two hearts that beat as one. Directed
   by Gerry (Geraldo) de León.
Blood Orgy of the She-Devils (1974). Right up our alley. Get it for the title.

A genie asleep in the lap of a beautiful human. Arab literature has many exciting tales of sex magic involving these.

Bloodlust (Mosquito der Schander) (1976). This is a Swiss effort, of all things, with a non-supernatural vampire (there are such creatures). Werner Pochath plays a poor kid whose terrible childhood left him with defective speech and hearing, and a penchant for dolls and whores. He moves on to mortuaries where he drinks the blood of corpses (with a pipette) and steals eyes, etc., which he keeps in bottles. His only friend dies by accident and he exhumes and keeps the body. When he murders a couple he gets caught. Directed by Marijan Vajda. Unnatural sex drenches horror movies (and may be evident in a few of their devotées) but does not always have to be connected to the supernatural. Fritz Hartmann and Jeffrey Dahlmer were all too real.

The Blood-Spattered Bride (1974). A *Blood and Roses* kind of thing, another version of *Carmilla*. The lesbian and the seduced bride sleep on a coffin for two.

The Bloodsuckers (1970). From Simon Raven's novel *Doctors Wear Scarlet*. An Oxford don gets sucked into a vampire coven in Greece. The female vampire gets her sexual jollies from blood. Peter Cushing and the usual suspects.

The Bloody Pit of Horror (1965). Bodybuilder Mickey Hagitay (Mr. Jayne Mansfield) is possessed by a dead sadist and tortures a gaggle of sexy models who are visiting his castle for a photo shoot.

The Brainiac (1961). If *Blood Diner* didn't turn your stomach, what the sorcerer (executed way back) comes back to eat will.

The Bride with White Hair (1993). David Wu's film, available dubbed or (for purists) in Chinese with subtitles. Based on Leung Yu-sang's novel, this is a martial arts romp (with a 1993 sequel, if you want it) in which Siamese twins kill a witch, a young warrior brings her back from the dead, and the two battle evil twin rulers of the Mo Dynasty. Want mo'? The sequel features the same witch, as she can only be stopped by a man who loves her. Ain't that the truth?

The Brood (1979). Mama's demon children kill whenever she loses her temper. Samantha Eggar, Oliver Reed; good cast, weird David Cronenberg script.

The Burning Court (1962). Possession and a family curse. Maybe I'm stretching to get this John Dickson Carr story in but you have to admit that a family curse involves heredity and heredity involves sex. I just want to mention that the family curse operates in many horror plots. Think of *The Legacy* (1979, Sam Elliott and Katherine Ross) and as when gypsies in *El Returno de la Walpurgis* (Return of Walpurgis Night, 1973) put a werewolf curse on "Paul Naschy" because his ancestors killed their ancestors. *Cat People* (1942, remade 1982) involves a family curse, as does *Curse of the Cat People* (1944), *Cat Girl* (1957), etc.

See also *La Maledición de la llorena* (The Curse of the Crying Woman, 1961). For sibling rivalry see *Dead Men Walk* (1943). Many a horror-movie plot depends on sister or brother trying to find out what happened to a sibling.

Caged Virgins (1971). Also called *The Case of the Smiling Stiffs*. Harry Reems, the well-equipped porno star, appears alongside a female vampire who kills with oral sex. A Sean Cunningham film before he hit it big with *Friday the 13th*.

Cameron's Closet (1989). Reversing the old idea that you had to have some evil in you to call up demons, this movie says only a sexless, innocent child can call up the demon that takes up residence in his closet until it can gain strength enough to rampage.

Cantar al sol (Sing to the Sun, n.d.). Generally I omit documentaries (such as *Witchcraft through the Ages*) but this one about Haitian voodoo with some Santería in Eastern Cuba is remarkable.

Cast a Deadly Spell (1991). The hero, named Harry P. Lovecraft, is tracking down a stolen copy of the *Necronomicon* in magic-ridden, late forties LA. Sort of noir. Some people may say it is too good for this list, but I am expressing my subjective thumbs down.

Ceremonia sangrienta (Ceremony of Blood, 1972, also *The Female Butcher*). The Countess Báthory murdering many girls to bathe in their blood for her complexion. Oil of oy-vay.

Child of Darkness, Child of Light (1991). Kids in movie not too bright. Immaculate conception should have warned Mummy things are going to be odd.

One kid is the Messiah, the other is the Antichrist. Welcome *The Omen, Damian, The Chosen,* or any Antichrist but this one.

Countess Dracula (1970). This has nothing to do with vampires but deals with Countess Elizabeth Báthory, who bathed in virgin's blood (she turns up as a vampire in *The Devil's Wedding Night*).

The Crimson Cult (1968). This was not (as some claim) Boris Karloff's last movie. The one before this one ought to have had that distinction. Barbara Steele. S&M not MGM. At one point someone says it is "as though Boris Karloff is going to pop up at any minute," and then he does.

Curse of the Blue Lights (1988). See my book on curses for more flix such as these. This sample features necromancy and hanky-panky in Lovers' Lane.

Curse of the Queerwolf (1987). Humor or camp may save some of these selections for you. This one has a gay werewolf in Santa Barbara (CA), by the auteur of *A Polish Vampire in Burbank*.

Curtis's Charm (1996). In this treatment of a Jim Carroll story, a crack addict thinks his wife and mother-in-law are putting the voodoo kibosh on him. Winner of the Genie for the best screenplay adaptation of the year but no blue-ribbon achievement.

Dance of the Damned (1988). I suppose prostitutes often get clients who just want to talk. This one is a vampire who wants to know what daylight daily living is all about. Well, there's sex and the supernatural here, but not enough of either. There was a remake: *To Sleep with a Vampire* (1992), so someone saw more in the premise than I do. Favorite exchange: when the demon is reluctant the prostitute/exotic dancer asks, "Are you gay?" and he replies, "I'm not even human."

Daughters of Satan (1972). A young Tom Selleck and his wife get entangled with a coven. Couples are always doing that in Hollywood's view. See *American Scream* (1987) and *Because of the Cats* (1974), etc., and almost any bad movie involving Massachusetts, as in *City of the Dead* or *The Dark Secret of Harvest Home* or *Eye of the Demon* or *Gates of Hell*, and *Elvira, Mistress of the Dark,* etc. If we are to believe *The Sentinel* (1977), the entrance to hell is in a brownstone in my hometown—Brooklyn.

Deadtime Stories (1987). I shall omit many anthology films that combine stories but here is one sample: the first tale is of two witches to whom a lad is sold so they can revive a dead sister.

Demon Rage (1982). Also called *Satan's Mistress,* a title that is misleading because it's about a human's mistress, a *succubus.* Britt Ekland and that horror specialist, John Carradine, whose son David also played in the genre.

Demon Witch Child (1974). From Armando de Ossorio of *The Blind Dead* fame. A nine-year-old tot is possessed by a witch, and periodically turns her into an old hag who conducts satanic rituals.

Demoniacs (1973). Jean Rollin's French *Les Démoniaques, Tina, la naufrgeuse perverse* (Tina, The Perverse Shipwreck Woman), *Les Diablesses* (The Dia-

Love comes to a young man, *The Romaunt of the Rose.*

bolical Women) or *Deux Vierges pour Satan* (Two Virgins for Satan). This movie, whatever the title, sees two females (who don't look very virginal but do go diabolical) cast ashore on the coast of Belgium only to be raped by a gang of wreckers led by Tina (Joelle Coeur). The two unfortunate women make a pact with The Devil (Misha Zimovir) to get revenge and wind up crucified, nailed to wrecks as the waves engulf them.

Devil Doll (1964). Not the mad-scientist movie of 1936 (which is better) but the one with the soul of a dead man reincarnated in a ventriloquist's dummy who lusts after a pretty girl. He has a woody.

The Devil in Miss Jones (1973). Georgina Spelvin gets a second chance at life thanks to The Devil. Men, women, and snakes for the sex.

Devil Kiss (1977). Ever-wonderful *Videohound* says you can get this on Home Vision Cinema, and that it has "zombies, virgins, sorcery, and the inevitable living dead," but I have not seen it. Are the "zombies" the "living dead"?

The Devil Rides Out (1968). Christopher Lee complained that for U.S. release the title was changed to *The Devil's Bride* lest people think, "this film could only be a Western." It sports good production values and a professional cast of horror stars, but it isn't very good.

The Devil's Daughter (1939). An all-black cast (this was before the term *African-American*) and voodoo ceremonies. You want African-American? Try Eddie Murphy in *A Vampire in Brooklyn* (1995), just slightly better than this.

The Devil's Due (1973). Cindy West porn. She kills one fellow with poison on her nipples.

The Devil's Eye (1960). Early Ingmar Bergman, *Djävulens öga*. Bibi Anderssen is so chaste a girl (a parson's daughter) that it annoys The Devil no end and he sends Don Juan (Jarl Kulle) to deflower her. Based on the Danish radio drama *Return of Don Juan*. Very *Grand Guignol* (sadistic, melodramatic). Hell, it's a comedy.

The Devil's Hand (1961). Alan Alda's father (Robert) sees a doll in a curio shop that turns him on. Hey, the girl who looks like that (Bianca, played by Linda Christian) lives nearby, but she happens to be in a coven. Voodoo stuff of the great god Gamba. Alternate titles *Live to Love* and (unfortunately inaccurate) *The Naked Goddess*.

Merlin, the magician of King Arthur's Round Table, meeting Viviane in the Forest of Broceliande. Fifteenth century Limoges.

The Devil's Messenger (1962). Lon Chaney, Jr. as The Devil gives a woman who committed suicide a second chance at life so she can seduce more souls for him.

The Devil's Mistress (1966). Four cowboys rape a girl but she gets back at them. Orville Wanzer directed.

The Devil's Nightmare (1971). It's not The Devil who has a nightmare experience but seven people (representing the Seven Deadly Sins—look out for Lust and how it is punished) who run into a *succubus* in your standard creepy castle.

The Devil's Own (1966). Voodoo in Africa, Satanism in England, and Virgin Sacrifice narrowly averted. After this one, Joan Fontaine quit movies for good.

The Devil's Partner (1958). Sex and youth go together, so an over-the-hill man gets an over-the-Hell deal to make him young, get him a young wife, and launch him on a career of ritual magic replete with sacrifices, etc.

Devil's Rain (1975). Vivid rituals with Ernest Borgnine, though at one point this coven leader sprouts horns. Other horny things.

The Devil's Sisters (1966). Poor Sharon Saxon becomes a white slave, and is kept prisoner in a brothel, bound, and tortured. William Grefe directed. Good grief!

The Devil's Wedding Night (1973). Also known as *El Returno de la duquessa Dracula*, this features a vampiress who comes on strong to twin brothers.

Double, Double, Toil and Trouble (1994). The Olsen twins (Ashley and Mary Kate) face up to wicked Cloris Leachman with a magic gem, more fun than sexy, but still Halloween fare.

Dr. Faustus (1968). Christopher Marlowe's masterpiece is not so much about sex, but the silent appearance of Elizabeth Taylor in husband Richard Burton's boring rendition of this script says sex to me, anyway. Her face could indeed have "launched a thousand ships." This is the sells-soul-to-Devil *locus classicus*. Most Faustian attempts on screen are Goethe-inspired, more or less, not Marlovian.

Best movie on the topic may be *Faust* (1926) by F. W. Murnau in the German Expressionist style, of which Robert Weine's *The Cabinet of Dr. Caligari* (1919) and Murnau's own *Nosferatu* (1922) are the classics.

Dreamaniac (1987). A heavy-metal composer conjures up a succubus who goes wild at a sorority party. Directed by David DeCocteau. One cast member is Cynthia Crass.

The Dunwich Horror (1969). From H. P. Lovecraft's famous story in which a man (in the film Dean Stockwell) steals the *Necronomicon* and a virgin (in the film Sandra Dee) almost becomes a satanic sacrifice in a fertility rite.

976-Evil (1988). Robert Englund (who played the manicurelly-challenged Freddie in the various *Nightmares on Elm Street*) "directs" this tale of a lonely teenager who practices phone-sex with the Devil. In 1991, Jim Wynoski directed the sequel.

El Mundo de los vampiros (1962). The World of the Vampires. I suppose we have to have this seminal example of the many really terrible vampire movies out of Mexico. Directed by Henry G. Richards, with Edward B. Tucker and Lydia Larson.

El Vampiro (1957). Classic Mexican horror by the man who had just finished *El Ladrón de cadaveres* (The Thief of Corpses). Based not on the usual Bram Stoker material but on original sources such as *Nosferatu* and Tod Browning's 1931 *Dracula* (both

Ovid (43 BC–AD 17) appears in the Holkam Hall medieval manuscript in medieval clothes, reading his *Ars amatoria* (The Art of Love) to pairs of lovers in the dress of various medieval social strata.

of which you must see if you haven't already, featuring definitive performances from Max Schreck and Béla Lugosi). In this one, Dracula is Count Karol de Lavud, but he often turns up in horror movies under other names, Count Orlock, Count Yorga, Count Frankenhausen, even Alucard.

Embrace of the Vampire (1995). Alyssa Milano has two boyfriends, one for the day and one for the night. The vampire thinks she looks just like his love of centuries ago.

The Entity (1983). A supernatural entity repeatedly rapes the Barbara Hershey character.

Erotic House of Wax (1997). Vincent Price fans know all about wax museums, but unfortunately in this one Price is not there to liven things up. The wax figures come to life and (*Videohound* says) "act out their sexual fantasies."

Erotokill (1973). Also called *Jacula, The Bare-Breasted Countess*. Director Jesús Franco (here calling himself J. P. Franklin) did a less sexy version of this film as *La Comtesse Noire* (The Black Countess) and a more porno version

The Devil Rides Out (1967).
The magic circle.

he called *Les Aveleuses* (*The Loves of Irena*, for the English-language market). Victims lose semen, blood, and life simultaneously at orgasm.

Evil Dad (1982). Look! Here's an ancient book that has been used to summon demons. Samuel M. Taimi directed.

Evil Toons (1990). Four cute coeds undertake to clean a deserted mansion—it's not really difficult to get good help—and unfortunately have a dust-up with a lustful demon. Arte Johnson of *Laugh In* fame has a part. Some nudity is socked to us.

Exorcism's Daughter (1971). The trauma of seeing her mother die during an exorcism puts young Tania among the mad (hence the Spanish title, *Las Melancolicas*) in an asylum run by a martinet (symbolizing Spain itself?). A progressive psychiatrist is accused of sex and witchcraft.

Movies often accuse psychiatrists of being mad scientists, just part of the fear of science that pervaded the twentieth century. In fact, it has been around since Mrs. Shelley's *Frankenstein*.

Fear No Evil (1980). For the Archangel Gabriel is with us (disguised as a sexy young girl) to foil The Devil (disguised as a maniacal murdering teenage male). Thy rod and thy popcorn shall comfort thee.

Four Rooms (1995). Remember how "Doc" Simon foisted off short playlets as a movie called *Plaza Suite*? Here we have four rooms in a hotel in LA, courtesy of Quentin Tarantino. Each has its own drama. A coven resurrects a dead stripper, some demonic kiddies discover a body in their mattress, a movie scene featuring dismemberment is reenacted, and a married couple proves that not everyone need be Ozzie and Harriet. The star cast

includes Madonna, who won the Golden Raspberry for "worst supporting actress" of the year, hands down.

Ghosts Can't Do It (1990). Bo Derek wants her humpy husband back (he's dead). Recipient of a Golden Raspberry (Worst Film) award.

Grave of the Vampire (1972). A woman raped by a vampire (in a cemetery) gives birth to a baby who needs blood as well as mother's milk. The mother is drained dry. The baby grows up and is up to no good.

Grim Prairie Tales (1990). Western horror collection of tales. In one, a woman who looks pregnant but is not pregnant at all, seduces a passing cowboy, sucks him inside her, and goes off looking pregnant again.

The Guardian (1990). Watch out for babysitters! This one kidnaps babies to sacrifice in druidic ceremonies.

Habit (1997). Larry Fessenden, talented indie jack-of-all-trades (hampered by shoestring budget) is writer, director, and star of this morality tale of a guy who gets into the habit of sex in public places with a vampire named Anna (Meredith Snaider, who ought to come around more). Watch out whom you pick up in Manhattan.

Haunted Symphony (1994). Doug Wert, eighteenth-century composer, is caught writing a symphony for The Devil and killed. Much later, his niece finds the Unfinished Symphony and hires someone to complete it, setting off magic- and sex-capades.

The Haunting of Morella (1991). I mention the queerwolf so I suppose we must include the lesbian overtones of this one as a witch returns in the body of her sexy teenage daughter.

Hellraiser (1988). Clive Barker, the UK's Stephen King, offering "a love story from beyond the grave," with sadistic demons called cenobites, and more.

Hex (1973). A couple of nasty bikers get a comeuppance from the daughter of an Amerindian shaman. "Something awful is goin' on here; it ain't natural." It's the standard sex magic revenge for rape (or attempted rape). If you want to rent the video, it's called *The Shrieking*.

Evil Ed (Stephen Geoffreys) bears on his forehead the mark of an early run-in with a crucifix. *Fright Night* (1985).

The Horrible Dr. Hitchcock (1962). The doc killed his first wife in a sex game and remarries to get the new wife's blood to bring back the first wife. That's romantic! The sequel was *The Ghost* (1963), otherwise known as *Lo Spettro*—slightly more unsightly.

The Horrible Sexy Vampire (1973). Written and directed by Jim Delavena (actually, José Luis Madrid) this is a Spanish sex romp with nudity and vampires. Castles in Spain are okay to dream about, but if you inherit a real one, sell, don't visit.

Immoral Tales (1975). Written and directed by Walerian Borocyzk. One of the tales is of Countess Elizabeth Báthory.

Impure Thoughts (1986). I guess this qualifies because the discussion by four friends of their Catholic high school sex life takes place during the afterlife.

Incubus (1965). Here's a novelty: a movie in Esperanto (English subtitles). William Shatner (before *Star Trek*) is corrupted by a you-know-what.

Incubus (1982). John Cassavetes and trouble in sedate New England.

Infernal Idol (1974). Also called *Craze* and *Demon Master*, this is a UK Freddie Francis frenzy with Jack Palance and sexpot Diana Dors. A crazed antique dealer sacrifices women to an African idol called Chuku, not as scary as Chuckie.

Innocent Blood (1992). Anne Parillaud as a seductive vampire and Anthony LaPaglia as a policeman besotted with her. Combination vampire and crime movie. Very gory.

Jonathan (1970). Starting out as a political tract (evil count vampirizes tenants) this German movie had sex added to make it more commercial.

La Beauté du diable (1950). The beauty is Faust's Marguerite though The Devil's agent (Mephistopheles) is cute, too. He's Gérard

Faust (1909).

Phillipe (almost as pretty as in *Devil in the Flesh*, which is more a classic of older woman/teenage boy—Phillipe was 25 but played 17). Older Faust becomes young and attractive by selling his soul for sex and power (allegedly seeking knowledge). Of course if you are young and cute and powerful you do get to learn a lot if you should happen to want to.

La Tigra (The Tigress, 1990). A novel by José de la Cuadra is the basis for this film from Ecuador full of fact and fantasy, sex and witchcraft.

Lemora (The Lady Dracula) (1974). Richard Blackburn's movie of a female vampire attracted to an innocent young girl in Georgia (this was cast elsewhere) who introduces her to blood-sucking.

Lenor (1975). It's not Poe, people; it's the fourteenth century and a knight's lovely lady dies. Not content to sleep with a corpse (unlike Poe), he deals with The Devil to bring her back to life. She becomes a vampire and spreads the Black Plague. Directed by Juan Buñuel.

Les Sorcières de Salem (1957). This is Arthur Miller's *The Crucible*, at a time when Miller was blacklisted for communism, made in France. It starred Simon Signoret and Yves Montand in a script by Jean-Paul Sartre. The sex comes in because a servant (Mylène Demongeot) accuses her mistress of witchcraft to hide her guilt for having slept with the Yves Montand character. Of course, sexual repression also had a lot to do with the events in Salem back in 1692.

Little Witches (1996). This time girls in a Catholic school; nudity and sex.

Love at First Bite (1979). George Hamilton's career came back from the dead when he played the Count in this spoof of innumerable Dracula films, funnier than Roman Polanksi's gay vampire or Mel Brooks. The leads from TV's *The Jeffersons* show up.

Love Potion #9 (1992). The nerd's experiment has unexpected results. An effective if too brief appearance by Anne Bancroft (Mrs. Mel Brooks).

Lover's Knot (1996). This time Tim Curry (better known as a transsexual transvestite from Transylvania in *The Rocky Horror Picture Show*) is an angel,

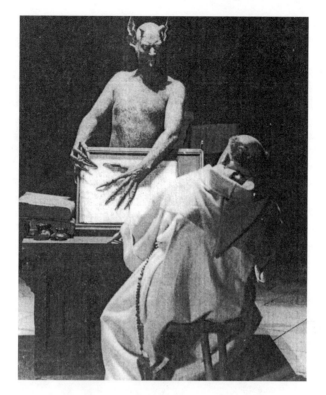

Häxan (Witchcraft, 1922).
The atrocities of the Inquisition are documented
in this Swedish production on "Witchcraft
through the Ages." A famous silent, it appeared in
a cut 1966 sound version narrated by William Bur-
roughs, the Beat guru. Director Benjamin Chris-
tiansen plays The Devil himself.

which may not be magic but is unquestionably supernatural. His job is to
get a pediatrician and an English professor (one pragmatic, one poetic)
to get together and stay together. It's harder than keeping them from jump-
ing off a bridge. Tim Curry is better here than in *The Worst Witch* (about
a witches' training school, 1986) but not as good as in the cult sensation
Rocky Horror.

The Magic Bubble (1993). Alfredo Ringel directs this tale of a woman who hits
40 going 60 and discovers a fountain of youth in a bottle of bubbles. The
Ponce de León theme is a natural for sex magic.

The Magic Hunter (1996). A police sharpshooter in Budapest makes a not so
sharp deal with The Devil for seven magic bullets that cannot miss. Not

really sex but useful here to underline the fact that many sexually motivated deals like this have a kicker (here The Devil gets to say whom the seventh bullet will hit).

Magic Wonderland (1985). Includes material from fairy tales involving sex such as *Beauty and the Beast* and *Sleeping Beauty*. Of course not on par with the Disney versions.

Mama Dracula (1980). In this comedy Countess Báthory is having trouble finding "wirgin blood" and turns to a substitute. Her two sons, vampires, want the real thing. Louise Fletcher (of *One Flew Over the Cuckoo's Nest*) is the countess.

Mark of the Devil (1969). Gory graphic torture scenes from "the burning time" with strong sexual overtones. This Austrian film is set in the Middle Ages. Also known as *Brenn, Hexe, Brenn* (Burn, Witch, Burn—also the name of

La Fée Carabosse (The Fairy Carabosse, 1906).
Film pioneer Georges Méliès shows the young knight Lothaire a magical vision of the woman he will marry. A wicked witch (angry because the knight gives her a purse of sand, not gold dust for a magical four-leaf clover), kindly druids, and the spirits of his ancestors (trick photography was common at this period), amazed audiences at the biograph.

a U.S. movie with Jane Blair, 1962, set in modern times). Herbert Lom, well-known in horror-dom. The sequel has more sadism.

Mary, Mary, Bloody Mary (1975). Mexican movie by Juan Moctezuma. Christina Ferrare is a bisexual bloodsucker who stabs lovers in the neck and drinks. Her father is John Carradine, another vampire. What's bred in the bone will come out in the blood.

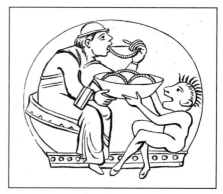

Mind, Body, and Soul (1992). Her boyfriend is, like, more or less connected to this satanic cult, right? With, you know, like, human sacrifices and stuff, so she naturally goes to the police who don't act right away or the movie would be over, you hear what I'm saying? Then the cult comes after her. Figures.

Mondo Magic (1976). One of those *Mondo* shock-you-mentaries following *Mondo Cane* and its sixties sequel. Tribal rituals.

Mother Joan of the Angels (1960). In Polish, *Matka Joanna od Aniólow*, a Jerzy Kawalerowicz film. The same subject as *The Devils of Loudon* by Aldous Huxley, *The Devils* by Ken Russell, the play by John Whiting *The Devils* (1961), the opera by Krzysztof Penderecki, and so on. This one helped to bring postwar Polish film to the west, Grotowski grunts to the theater, etc.

My Best Friend is a Vampire (1988). From the era of my mommy is a witch, my daddy is a werewolf, and so on. Teen comedy about a love bite that was more of a horror than a hickey.

My Demon Lover (1987). Some guys are demons when aroused. Scott Valentine is one. Comedy.

Near Dark (1987). A farm boy falls in with a passel of vampires roaming the west. I don't think the blood and goofs jibe, but a lot of people like it a lot better than I do. Directed by Katherine Bigelow.

Necromancer: Satan's Servant (1988). After rape, revenge. She goes to The Devil for help. At least he doesn't tell her she was asking for it. Russ Tamblyn appears.

Necropolis (1987). A witch is reincarnated as a motorcycle slut in New York. She has been out of the action so long (several hundred years) she doesn't realize the inner city is not the best place to look for a virgin sacrifice.

Netherworld (1990). A young man visiting his late father's home in the bayou discovers Dad had been dabbling in the black arts, and now two sexy witches are after him.

Night of the Death Cults (1975). The Knights Templar have had bad press (for the truth see specialized books on them or *Secret Societies*, edited by Norman MacKenzie, 1967, where David Annan gives a brief and reasoned history). They have also been much maligned in movies, one of which is this one. A couple at the seaside runs into a cult performing human sacrifices to appease some old fogeys who rise from the dead and are referred to as Templars. "Night" often signals sex magic.

Night of the Living Babes (1987). Two yuppies at a whorehouse are chased by female zombies. Actually, zombies are not supernatural. They are drugged humans. But they are popularly thought of as produced by magical appeals to the devilish Baron Samedi.

Night Strangler (1972). Every 21 years a spate of serial murders of women takes place in Seattle, which is making the city sleepless. Reporter Carl Kolchak

Mysterios de la magia negra.
(The Mysteries of Black Magic, 1958).
Nadia Haro Oliva is a reincarnated medieval witch who performs in the modern world as a stage magician. She falls in love with Aldo Monti and her warlock master returns from the grave in sexual jealousy.

Necronomicon.

(that's Darren McGavin and this is a sequel to his *Night Stalker*, 1971) is surprised to learn that over a century the murderer is reported as having the same appearance. Another hint: John Carradine is in the cast. His progression from Shakespeare to schlock was famous in horror circles.

Nightmare Castle (1965). Now stay with me on this. A mad scientist discovers his wife is unfaithful. He murders her and her lover. He takes the blood of the two corpses and rejuvenates an old servant. Probably got the idea from the old movie, *The Corpse Vanishes* (1942) or an even earlier one. The dead couple returns for revenge. They are not pleased that the mad scientist wants to marry the dead wife's sister. No sex magic, the reviving experiment is movie science not sorcery, but plenty of sex and the supernatural.

Nightmare Sisters (1987). David DeCocteau. Out of a crystal ball come sexy *succubi*. One of the *succubi* is Pia Snow alias porno star Michelle McClellan.

Nightstalker (1979). Here's The Concept: a brother and sister have been dead for thousands of years and they have to eat virgins to keep from decomposing. Starring Aldo Ray. Not the *Night Stalker* of Darren McGavin on TV. But see the next entry.

O Macabro Dr. Scivano. (Brazilian, The Macabre Dr. Scivano, 1971). The doctor dabbles in *macumba* and demons bring him money. He becomes a vampire. Though he sleeps with a store-window mannequin he goes after real women, to kill them. Raúl Calhado is all over this (touted as the first Brazilian sci-fi movie) and calls himself Edmundo Scivano in the cast list.

The Occultist (1989). Satan worshippers skin men alive in this one. If you go to an occultist, you need your eyes examined. If you go to *The Occultist*,

Max Schreck of *Nosferatu* is not the mesmerizing seducer one
would expect of a loveboat.

maybe you need your head examined. But if you like gore with the supernatural, grab your Raisinettes and get comfortable.

Omen 4: The Awakening (1991). We thought we had finally finished off diabolical Damian in *Omen 3: The Final Conflict* a decade before, but nooooo.
Along came this Antichrist for cable TV.

Once Bitten (1985). Jim Carrey, Lauren Hutton, good cast, but lacking substance. Ms. Hutton (a female vampire) has to bite a virgin before midnight
on Halloween or she will lose her model looks.

Onna kyuketsuki (Woman Vampire, 1959). Japanese shocker with Shigeru
Amachi in the title role, directed by Nobuo Nakagawa.

Orgy of the Dead (1965). Ed Wood, Jr. gets a lot of kidding for his low-bud-
get flix with paper plates for flying saucers and here (says *Videohound*) a
dozen nude spirits dance in a "cardboard graveyard," but just imagine what
he could have done with the budgets for *Ishtar* or *Waterworld*.

Other Hell (1985). The Devil in a convent. Italian, with Carlo de Mayo and
Francesca Carmeno. Nuns make some crazy people crazier; they want to
see virtue trashed.

The Playgirls and the Vampire (1960). Gee, just think what these bimbos look
like today! A busload of chorus girls arrives at the castle of Count Ker-
nassy. There's a vampire in the crypt where the Jacuzzi ought to be.

NIGHT of the SORCERERS

Bloodthirsty Bimbos. Sex and horror are a potent box office combo.

Prime Impulse (1974). I searched high and (very) low for the wildest male/female possession I could find and this is my choice: an astronaut lands on the moon and cannot get off. He lets out a terrific scream that possesses the mind of a woman on earth. It's not your usual demon-gets-in story.

The Pyx (1973). If you don't know that a pyx is the box in which they keep the wafers for Holy Communion you will get the idea from the alternate title of this story from John Buell, *The Hooker Cult Murders*. It's Canada, there's a hooker, and there's your basic satanic cult. Karen Black is excellent. I can't tolerate Christopher Plummer in this somehow, and so I call it bad. With different casting and bigger budgets many of the dogs I mention might have won best in show.

Quartier Mozart (The Mozart Neighborhood, or Mozart of The Quarter (?), 1992). In French with English subtitles. A witch in the African-American 'hood helps a young girl enter the body of a young man so she can understand the way boys think about sex.

Raging Angels (1995). "Alan Smithee" is the name Hollywood directors use when they don't want to put their own names on a work, much the way actors hide under "George Spelvin." (Remember Georgina Spelvin of porn?) There is reason for anonymity in a supernatural battle of Good vs. Evil that takes place in the skies over LA. Shelley Winters is in it and there is a cult called the Coalition for World Unity (which will sound ominous to those who think of the United Nations as satanic). For an NYC cult see Larry Cohen's *God Told Me To* (1976).

Repossessed (1990). Linda Blair parodies her hit with Leslie Nielsen as the exorcist. Golden Raspberry award for worst song of 1990: "He's [The Devil] Coming Back." Catchy.

Rest in Pieces (1987). A young woman inherits a mansion only to find that the estate has a satanic cult in residence. Location, location, location. Mayhem ensues.

Return of the Wolfman (1980). In the ninth (count them!) "Paul Naschy" outing, the wolfman and a vampiric countess (both executed for witchcraft centuries ago) appear in the modern world and battle each other. The wolfman wins, but then it's his show.

A Return to Salem's Lot (1987). You probably saw the theatrical release of Stephen King's *Salem Lot*, cut from a three-hour TV epic or as a TV film, with so many commercials at the wrong places it drove you insane. This is not really a sequel, because Larry Cohen took the name, a New England location, and vampires to do a new show with Michael Moriarity, June Havoc, Evelyn Keyes, and Samuel Fuller as maybe the worst Jewish actor in a blood-sucker movie after Mel Brooks.

Return of the Killer Tomatoes (1988) and *Sorority Babes* (1988). See that, coming up. Wouldn't it be fun to tell them at the office that you rented these titles last night? *S. Babes* and nerdy friends battle the demon somehow released from the bowling alley. The demon is not the sex here; it's the babelicious heroines.

Rockula (1990). Bo Diddley in a film about a vampire who has remained a virgin for 300 years and thinks it is time for a change. Consider what pop stars have added to sexual magic ideas as well as to sex, drugs, and rock 'n roll.

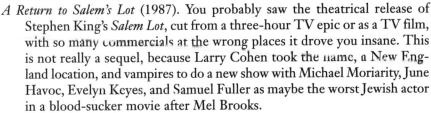

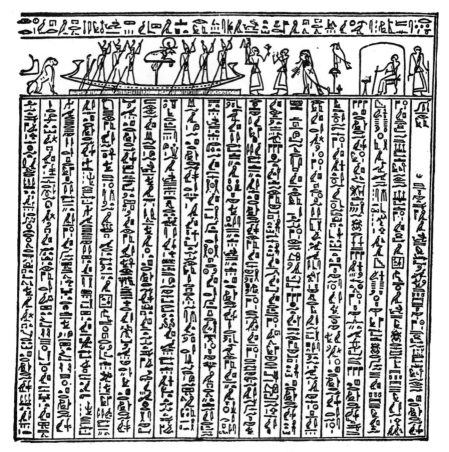

Egyptian Travel Guide.
Instructions for the spirit going to the land of the dead, a page from *The Book of the Dead.*

Rough Magic (1995). Magic Mayan potion, metamorphosis (man to sausage), a shaman, sexy Bridget Fonda—based on James Hadley Chase's novel *Miss Shumway Waves a Wand.*

Ruby (1992). It was being baptized in blood that started Ruby off wrong and here she is on a murderous rampage at the passion pit.

Satan's Cheerleaders (1977). The high-school janitor is a Satanist and wants to do something or other to a bevy of cheerleaders on his altar but they escape. Look for Yvonne de Carlo.

Satan's Mistress (1990). Bert I. Gordon film. The beautiful head of a modeling agency is 500 years old, a *succubus* who has ruined 1000 men and is starting on the son of a retired detective.

Satan's School for Girls (1973). Her sister has committed suicide and so our heroine looks at the circumstances and—guess what?—it's a satanic girls' school. Look for Cheryl Ladd.

Satanik (1969). Talk about makeovers: an old hag is turned into a knockout by a magic potion. But the effects don't last. Directed by Piero Vivarelli, Italian.

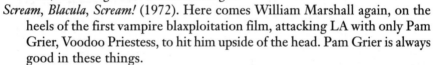

CUPIDS IN A BOWER.

Satanwar (1979). Various diabolical rites, including some with a sex angel.

Scream, Blacula, Scream! (1972). Here comes William Marshall again, on the heels of the first vampire blaxploitation film, attacking LA with only Pam Grier, Voodoo Priestess, to hit him upside of the head. Pam Grier is always good in these things.

The Seventh Victim (1943). The censors have taken out some of the sex, apparently, but Kim Hunter's search for a sister who has become involved with a satanic cult is clear enough.

Sex and the Vampire (1970). Jean Rollin has a honeymoon couple attacked by lusty vampires in an old castle. Doesn't anyone go to a hotel or motel any more? This was to be trumped by *The Nude Vampire and Caged Virgins*, which Rollin made soon after.

Sex is Crazy (1979). A mishmash of sex and magic directed by Jess Jesús Franco. Spanish with English subtitles.

The She-Beast (1965). You can't keep a bad woman down: burned at the stake in the eighteenth century, this witch returns as a young woman on her modern honeymoon in (where else?) Transylvania. Barbara Steele—but only briefly.

Shock 'em Dead (1990). A guy sells his soul to The Devil for fame as a rock 'n roll star. Traci Lords, Troy Donahue and Aldo Ray.

The Sins of Dorian Gray (1982). If we could have a Ms. Hyde we can have (for TV) a female Dorian Gray who stays young while her screen test ages. Belinda Bauer, Anthony Perkins.

Sisters of Satan (1975). Crazy nuns go to The Devil. Directed by Juan López Moctezuma. I don't believe that name or the script.

The Slaughter of the Vampires (1962). A honeymoon couple in an Austrian chalet and some "blood-ghouls." Eurotrash.

Sorceress (1988). Shouldn't that be plural, with Leigh Anne Harris and sister Lynette? One minor member of the cast is actress Anne de Sade.

Sorority Babes in the Slimebowl Bowl-a-Rama (1987). See it for the title alone.

Speak of the Devil (1990). A Southern evangelist sells his soul to The Devil.

Spectre (1996). Made for cable in Ireland, this movie deals with the ghost of a long-dead girl haunting a newly inherited house. The new owners find and re-inter the body but it doesn't help.

Stephen King's Thinner (1996). The novel first published under King's "Richard Bachman" pseudonym got to the screen solely because of King's fame. (He appears in a bit part as Dr. Bangor, presumably from Maine.) When Robert John Burke's car hits a gypsy he is cursed to lose weight much more noticeably than the Duchess of Kent on Weight Watchers, hence the title. Do you want to read AIDS decline into "thinner"?

The Student of Prague (1913). Pretty rickety treatment of a classic German story along Faustian lines: the student sells his soul for a beautiful woman. Just one example of a surprising amount of sex magic or magic in the silents.

Sugar Cookies (1977). You'd never guess from the title that what we have here is a satanic satyr and a lesbian and a bunch of cute females who are toyed with.

Sundown (1991). David Carradine, a reformed vampire, runs a clinic for others addicted to blood, a kind of bloody AA. Western and vampire genres don't mix. His father could have told him that.

Teen Witch (1989). She's after the high-school hunk. The most famous high-school teen is TV's *Buffy the Vampire Slayer*. (In one book I wrote *Buffy the Vampire Killer* and the mail came pouring in. Now there's an encyclopedia on *Buffy* and *Angel*. The public loves this stuff and it is gratifying to see teenage females fighting back rather than whimpering in the corners of horror flix.)

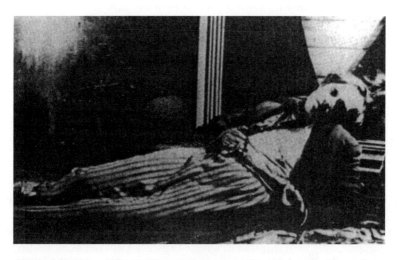

Conrad Veidt as *The Student of Prague* or *The Man who Cheated Life*, a film based on Poe's *William Wilson* via Hans Heinz Ewer's German novel, 1926.

Terror Creatures from the Grave (1966). Because the Black Plague wiped out a third or maybe as much as a half of the British population and changed all Europe too, the husband in this tale had no trouble recruiting the dead to terrorize his unfaithful wife. UK horror star Barbara Steele steals whatever show there is.

The Thirsty Dead (1974). Also known as *The Blood Cult of Shangri-La*, but the scene is but Filipino not Tibetan. Vampire seeks a wife who will go to bed during the day.

Tombs of the Blind Dead (1972). Also *La Noche de la muerta ciega* (Night of the Ditto). They are blind because they performed human sacrifices in the thirteenth century and crows picked out their eyes; they are dead but they come back in the twentieth century. Spanish. Popular. Sequels.

The Torture Chamber of Dr. Sadism (1969). Also called *Die Schlangengrube und das Pendel* because it has some connections to Poe's *The Pit and the Pendulum*. (A lot of Poe has been brought to the screen; most of it, if not camp, is the pits.) Count Regla sacrificed a dozen virgins; was caught, beheaded, drawn and quartered; but has been put back together again and is at it once more.

Troll (1986). I am omitting poltergeists here but maybe you ought to have one example of a teenage girl attracting chaos. Remember, female adolescents' sexuality seems to evoke "noisy spirits." Michael Moriarity, Shelley Hack in a John Buechler film. The family moves into an apartment building with a troll in the basement.

The Undead (1957). Here's one by Roger Corman, the Hitchcock of Second-Rate Horror. A botched scientific experiment (a horror film cliché) sends a prostitute back to the Middle Ages, where she is condemned to die as a witch. Other movies send a seventeenth-century warlock, about to be burned, into the twentieth, etc.

The Understudy (1988). You've heard of type-casting. Here a real vampire is cast as a vampire who is playing a vampire in a movie. It sucks.

The Unholy (1988). It's New Orleans; a demon becomes a beautiful woman that leads Roman Catholic priests astray. The ending was made more gruesome when critics said the film was not really a horror show. If Roman Catholic priests are going to break their vows of celibacy it is nice to see them doing it heterosexually.

The Unnamable (1988) and its sequel *The Unnamable II* (1992) are drawn from the eminent horror writer H. P. Lovecraft. Students at Miskatonic University get involved with a seventeenth-century half-woman/half-demon (not unnamable: she's named Alyda) who wants to return to earth. Screen treatment by Jean-Paul Ouellete.

Urusei Yatsura # 6: Always, My Darling (1991). A Japanese series starting in the eighties ends with this one in which Princess Lum (an alien visitor) has a boyfriend called Ataru and he is kidnapped in a plot to get the most potent love potion in the galaxy. Japanese with English subtitles but don't bother to read them. It is, like a lot of Japanese movies, just a kind of comic book for people who can't or won't read.

The Vamp (1986). Richard Wenk's wank about a couple of college kids who go to a vampire-infested *boîte* in the combat zone. Grace Jones is a vampire stripper, the movie's one saving grace. The part was written for Tina Turner, who refused it.

Vampire Doll (1970). A girl is raped by her father. He's a doctor, so he tries to make her well again, by hypnosis mostly, but it doesn't work. When she dies and becomes a vampire, watch out! A Japanese atrocity by Michuo Yamamoto.

Vampire Hookers (1978). John Carradine (suitably saturnine) uses prostitutes to lure victims to his fangy lair. The shills are best described by the alternate titles: *Cemetery Girls* and *Sensuous Vampires*.

The Vampire Lovers (1970). The first Hammer horror to sport nudity. This is the first of three Hammer films based on Joseph Sheridan LeFanu's *Carmilla*, the full text of which will come later in this book. The other Hammer ripoffs came the next year as *Lust for a Vampire* and *Twins of Evil* (title changed in production from *The Virgin Vampires*).

Vampyres, Daughters of Dracula (1975). Not to be confused with *Dracula's Daughter*, the sequel to the 1931 *Dracula*. Anulka and another vampire lure passersby into their old castle for sex and blood. One guy falls in love with one of them, which can happen when a female invites a male up for a drink.

Vampyros Lesbos (1970). The French and the Germans got together on this one. A girl *dreams* a lesbian vampire has seduced her. Does that count?

The Velvet Vampire (1971). Celeste Yarnell falls in love with another vampire woman while on her honeymoon. Politically correct, she kills a male chauvinist biker rapist. I mean he's a rapist and a motorcycle guy. Stephanie Rothman, director, is a feminist.

The Virgin of Nuremberg (1965). One of the many horror flix in which a young girl goes to a kooky kastle and is naturally subjected to the supernatural. Also known as *La Vergine de Norimberga* and directed by Anthony Dawson [Antonio Margheriti].

The Virgin Witch (1970). Also called *Lesbian Twins* and featuring twins Anne and Vicki Michelle. Is there life after the Playboy Mansion? There used to be: these two Bunnies (the first sister centerfolds in *Playboy*) got into this movie directed by Ray Austin and play, what else? . . . twins who go for a modeling job. They run into a coven of witches that wants to sacrifice one of them (what were you expecting?). Another pair of *Playboy* centerfolds (Mary and Madeleine Collinson) fall victim to a vampire in *Twins of Evil* (1971), directed by John Hough in the flamboyant Hammer Films horror style. Put both films on a twin bill and you would have lots of boobs in all senses of the word.

Warlock Moon (1973). At a secluded spa a young woman falls into the clutches of a coven. If you want a couple captured by a coven, try *Witches' Mountain* (1971).

The Werewolf vs. the Vampire Woman (1970). I listed many more werewolf and vampire films in my other books of this series. Here, as a sample, you get a kind of double feature. A Hispanic hirsute (the "Paul Naschy" character who keeps coming back like a bad dream) teams up with a couple of women to seek the tomb of a wicked witch. One of the women is possessed by the witch and we take it from there.

Werewolf Woman (1977). Gorgeous Daniella is a terror once she embarks on her hairy adventures. Many more wolf people in *The Complete Book of Werewolves*.

Wildest Dreams (1990). Chuck Vincent directed this comedy about a nerd whom a genie, released from his bottle, is determined to fix up with a girl. The nerd is overwhelmed by a bounty of bimbos. You wish!

Wishman (1993). It's Hollywood, and Hitch (a genie who has lost his bottle) helps an actor named Paul LeMat. LeMat is the Fool of the Tarot, so this must be a pseudonym. LeMat gets the girl he wants in exchange for recovering the magic bottle.

Witch Hunt (1994). Did you know that film studios in the fifties hired witches and wizards to cast spells? Dennis Hopper plays the PI who gets their ID.

The Witch (1966). Also called *La Strega in amore* (The Witch in Love), directed by Damiano Damiani.

Witchcraft (1988) and *Witchcraft 2* (1990) and *Witchcraft 3* (1990) and *Witchcraft 4* (1992) and *Witchcraft 5* (1992) and *Witchcraft 6* (1994) and *Witchcraft 7* (1995) and *Witchcraft 8* (1995) and *Witchcraft 9*—at which witchy point I gave up counting but for all I know this series could have run as long as the *Friday the 13th* stuff or Freddie's Follies on Elm Street. These *Witchcraft* movies are all the popular mixture of sex and horror, Satanism, seduction and spoof. Try #3, subtitled *The Kiss of Death*. It's about a young man seduced by a hottie into participation in hellish habits.

The Witches (1965). Italian *Le Streghe*, a French/Italian coproduction. It's really five separate stories. In one a woman uses witchcraft to gain revenge on a seducer.

Witching Time (1984). A seventeenth-century witch comes back to hit on a hubby whose wife is away and a triangle results when the wife comes home.

The Witching (1972). Even before Orson Welles needed a much wider widescreen than is available he made this loser, in which he is a big necromancer. Written and directed by Bert I. Gordon with Pamela Franklin as the love interest.

Witchmaker (1969). Also called *The Legend of Witch Hollow*, this one rather appeals to me because of its bayou setting and (as we say in Brooklyn) it may be okay by you. The witches are killing sexy girls in order to make themselves youthful.

The Wicker Man (1975).
Edward Woodward is a policeman lured to an island off
Scotland to be the virgin male sacrificed by being
burned alive in a giant "wicker man," an ancient pagan
witchcraft rite.

The Wizard of Gore (1970). Montag the Magician has an act in which he gets
   women from the audience and seems to inflict terrible mutilations on them.
   Later, at home, the women discover the mutilations are real.
Wizards of the Demon Sword (1994). As in the Merlin stories and in much sword-
   and-sorcery stuff, think of the sword as a phallic symbol. Why not? Here

The Witchfinder-General.
Brilliantly directed by Michael Reeves, this is a melodramatic but stunning treatment of a sadistic witch-hunter
(played by Vincent Price), Matthew Hopkins, who brought
many to their horrible deaths, accusing them of witchcraft
for profit and pleasure.

Russ Tamblyn, Lawrence Tierney, and friends battle over the sword that
can rule the world.

Wolf Blood (1925). Before sound and with an idea *avant la lettre*. When star
George Cheesbro (who also directed) is injured in an accident the doctor gives him wolf's blood instead of human blood. Uh-oh! Yes, you can
even buy films this old on videotape; this one is available at Grapevine
Video (PO Box 46161, Phoenix, AZ 85063) if it's still in operation. My
local Blockbuster just sold off all its tapes to go DVD, an ominous sign.
First the cinemas became bowling alleys, supermarkets, or multiplexes, and
now this. See the old movies while you still can!

The World of Vampires (1960). Directed by Alfonso Corona Blake. Dracula had
a trio of vampire girls (The Impalettes?); here the vampire has a horde of
female assistants (which he controls by playing a musical instrument made
of bones).

Yureiyasiki no kyofu: chi o su ningyo (Fear of the Ghost House: Blood-Sucking
Doll, 1971). Obviously, Japanese. *Doll* in many countries signals "horror."

QUOTATIONS

As a conclusion to this chapter of way-out ideas, I'd like to offer a bit of balance, in the form of the following thoughts from eminently sober individuals:

"I have often admired the mystical way of Pythagoras, and the secret magic of numbers."

—Sir Thomas Browne
Religio Medici [A Physician's Religion]

"Rationalism for the few, and magic for the many."

—Jakob Burckhardt
Nineteenth-Century Religion

"You have but to know an object by its proper name for it to lose its dangerous magic."

—Elias Canetti
Auto da Fé

"Alcohol is like love: the first kiss is magic, the second is intimate, the third is routine. After that you just take the girl's clothes off."

—Raymond Chandler
The Long Goodbye

"That old black magic's got me in its spell/That old black magic that you do so well. . . ."

—Johnny Mercer, songwriter

"If we were all given by magic the power to read each other's thoughts, I suppose the first effect would be to dissolve all friendships."

—Bertrand Russell, Earl Russell

"I will a round unvarnished tale deliver
Of my whole course of love; what drugs, what charms,
What conjuration, and what mighty magic,
For such proceeding I am charg'd withal,
I won his daughter."

—William Shakespeare, *Othello*

"But this rough magic I here abjure. . . .
I'll break my staff,
Bury it certain fathoms in the earth,
And, deeper than did ever plummet sound,
I'll drown my book."

—William Shakespeare, *The Tempest*

"Formerly, when religion was strong and science weak, men mistook magic for medicine; now, when science is strong and religion weak, men mistake medicine for magic."

—Thomas Szasz, *Science and Scientism*

In hell, demons torture those there because of the deadly sin of lust. From *Le grant kalendrier et compost des Bergiers* (1496).

7

The Literature of Sex and Magic

A LITTLE TREASURY

This is a feature that was suggested by readers of early books in this series, one that has been much commended in the most recent books of the series. I offer some selected stories and a few examples of poetry on the topic of the book, sex and the supernatural. This time there is a complete novella, too.

A CREATION LEGEND FROM SNORRI STURLSON'S *VOLUSPÁ*

Every culture has its story of how human beings came to be. Here is one with which you may not be familiar. It is from Old Norse.

> The first humans were Ask and Embla. They were created when logs—*Ask* is "Ash Tree" and *Embla* means "Little Elm"—washed ashore and the gods decided to make humans out of the wood. The great Odin breathed life into them. Heonir gave them the gift of sense. Loki gave them "life color" (red blood) and also the gift of speech.

> There are also many beautiful Amerindian creation stories right here in the U.S. They tell where the first humans came from and how sex was given to them so that the human race could spring forth. In *Genesis*, you may have noticed, tradition gives Adam a wife before Eve, named Lilith, a demon.

SOME BAWDY FROM APULEIUS' *THE GOLDEN ASS*

Meroe had a certain lover whom, by the utterance of a single word, she turned into a beaver because he loved another woman beside herself, and the reason she transformed him into such a beast is that it is his [a beaver's] nature, when he sees that the hunters and hounds are gaining on him, to bite off his genitals and leave them in the way so that the pursuers will stop when they find them. . . . Likewise she changed one of her neighbors, an old wine seller, because he was her competitor in business, into a frog, and now the poor wretch, swimming in one of his own barrels of wine, and well nigh drowned in the dregs, cries out and croaks continually. . . . Likewise she turned one of the lawyers of the court (because he pleaded and spoke against her) into a horned ram, so that now the poor ram must act as advocate. Moreover, she caused the wife of a certain lover of hers, because she criticized her and made jokes about her, not to be delivered of her child because her womb was permanently shut up, to be everlastingly pregnant, and, according to the calculations of all men, eight years have passed since the unfortunate woman first started to swell and now she has grown so big that it looks as if she is about to give birth to a great big elephant.

HOW AN ASCETIC LEARNED ABOUT SEX BY MAGICAL MEANS

The story is told about the ascetic Shri [Sir] Sankaracharya getting into a philosophical debate with a rival named Mandana. They made a bet that the loser of the argument would have to adopt the lifestyle of the winner, which meant that if Sankaracharya won Mandana would have to leave his wife Bharati and become a celibate mendicant monk and if Mandana won the monk would have to marry and settle down.

Sankaracharya had just got Mandana to admit defeat when Bharati came up with a clever argument: since "man and wife are one," the monk still had the "better half" to contend with—and she was going to go after the monk in an area where he had no expertise whatever, which is to say sex. Things looked bad for the reverend monk.

But just at that moment Rajah [King] Amarauka died. The monk learned this telepathically and hastened by astral projection to send his own soul into the monarch before his subjects could take the corpse and burn it on a funeral pyre. (The monk's own body, of course, went into a state of disuse and temporarily suspended animation).

In the court of the monarch everyone was delighted to see the ruler revive, especially all the ladies of his harem. They found their master much more attractive and energetic than ever before and romped with him delightedly. Others at court suspected that this new rajah must really be energized by a spirit from somewhere else and set out to find the body lying in suspended animation so that they could destroy it. But the disciples of the monk heard of the search and went to the palace of the rajah. They were able to convince the spirit of Sankarachaya to return to its own body so that his body would not be destroyed.

Thus it was that the monk's spirit left the rajah's body and returned to its own body. It did so with so much more information than it had ever had before that the monk was easily able to win an argument with Bharati on the subject of sex.

NICOLÒ MACCHIAVELLI'S STORY OF *THE DEVIL WHO TOOK A WIFE*

Here is a summary of an amusing tale of sex and the supernatural by a scholar better known as an historian of Florence and as the author of a classic of politics, *The Prince*. Unfortunately, I cannot give you any taste of the style, which makes the Italian original so charming, but I can tell you the clever plot, at least. I think it an amusing thing to include here even though a) it is about marriage rather than sex *per se*, and b) it involves exorcisms, yet there is no magic involved in them! Read on and see what I mean:

Hell was filling up with unfortunate men who attributed their fall to having taken wives. So it became a question of great interest in diabolical circles as to why, if that was true, exactly how that happened. Belfagor, who once had been an archangel and was now a leading light in the infernal regions, was chosen by lot—because none of the devils really wanted the assignment—to come to earth, pretend to be a human being, marry and live on earth ten years, and finally, pretending to die, report back what he was able to discover of the human institution of marriage and wives in general.

Accordingly he appeared with a lot of money in Florence, that being a fine place to function as a moneylender. He called himself Roderick of Castille and let it be known that he had come from Spain via Syria, where at Aleppo he had become wealthy.

Belfagor took on a handsome human appearance of a man of about thirty and this, as well as his money, made him attractive. A number of noble Florentines with more family than finances offered their daughters to him. He chose Onesta, a daughter of Amerigo Donati, who had seven children, four daughters and three grown sons, and not as much money as his position in society called for. There was an appropriately lavish wedding. Then the trouble began.

Having now some human emotions, Belfagor fell in love with Onesta, despite the fact that she was always wanting more money for this or that, complaining that clothes recently bought were utterly out of fashion and had to be replaced immediately at vast expense, and altogether causing him a great deal of woe if he ever dared to refuse her anything. Soon she was not only demanding more and more money for herself, for lavish parties and such, she likewise was pressing her husband to put up dowries for her three unmarried sisters and to finance her three brothers in what might become moneymaking schemes. One brother had to be given a big stake to go to the east with woollen textiles, one to the west with silks, and one set up as a goldsmith in Florence.

Belfagor had a hell of a time, because one of the brothers gambled away all the money that was given to him, one had been drowned when his merchant ship was lost at sea, and the minor devils who had come to earth with Belfagor as his familiars and servants said they would rather live in Hell than in Florence and went back down below. Belfagor could not meet the promissory notes he had distributed all over town. Eventually he had to flee the city, his creditors in hot pursuit.

At one point he left his horse in the road and fled across the fields, and that is when he met a peasant named Gianmatteo del Bricca, a worker for the landowner Giovanni del Bene.

This Gianmatteo may have been a lowly peasant but he was a godsend for Belfagor. Belfagor made him an offer he could not refuse: if he would hide him from the pursuers he would make the peasant rich and if he escaped them then this very day he would give proof of his power to do that. Delighted, the peasant concealed Belfagor in a huge pile of manure, which he had in the front yard of his house at Peretola, and when the pursuers came along he swore up and down he had seen no one. Belfagor's creditors and the accompanying angry mob had to make their way back to Florence empty-handed.

Now it was time for Belfagor to make good on his promise. So he made a clean breast of it all to the peasant. He told who he was and why he had come from Hell and married the beautiful Onesta in Florence. How he had spent all his money and was fleeing those who would jail him, or worse, because he owed them so much money. Of course this did not sound to Gianmatteo as if he was going to get the promised reward. But here was Belfagor's plan: He would possess a woman of some wealthy family and not leave her until Gianmatteo, pretending to be capable of exorcism, came along. Then Belfagor would exit the woman's body and Gianmatteo would get the credit and collect a fat fee.

Very soon after that the news spread all over Florence that the daughter of the rich merchant Ambrogio Amidei, whom he had married off to Bonaiuto Tebalducci, was possessed by a demon. Relatives tried everything, including the head of St. Zenobius and the cloak of St. Giovanni Gualberto. Belfagor secretly laughed them to scorn. Far from departing the poor woman, Belfagor spoke through her in frightening Latin, discoursed on philosophy as she herself never would have been able to do, and took the opportunity to reveal the secret sins of a number of Florentines, including a friar who had kept a woman (dressed as a male novice) in his cell for four years. When the truth of all the accusations was determined, people were more than a little impressed, not to say a trifle worried that further revelations might be on the way.

Then on the scene came the happy Gianmatteo, asking for 500 florins to buy a farm of his own at Peretola and absolutely guaranteeing that he could exorcise the demon. Gianmatteo dictated that a few Masses be said and made some mumbo jumbo of his own device, then whispered in the woman's ear, "Roderick, it's me."

Belfagor replied, "Fine, I'll leave her now as I promised you and you can collect your 500 florins. But that is not enough to make you really rich. I am going now to enter into the daughter of King Charles of Naples. I will never leave her except for you. Go to Naples and ask for a much bigger recompense for your exorcism and I will not leave her until you come."

Then Belfagor departed from the daughter of Ambrogio Amidei, and Gianmatteo was paid and all Florence rejoiced at the woman's escape from demonic possession.

Meanwhile, in Naples, Belfagor possessed the daughter of the king. Soon the news spread all over Italy. The king sought every means to relieve the situation and when he heard of the events in Florence he immediately sent for Gianmatteo.

For that case Gianmatteo asked for and got more than 50,000 ducats. But he also got this message from Belfagor: "You see, Gianmatteo, I have kept my promise to make you rich. Therefore, having discharged my debt, I am no longer obliged to you in any way. Therefore please do not appear before me ever again because, though I have been good to you thus far, I should then harm you dreadfully."

So Gianmatteo returned to Florence with all those ducats and looked forward to a happy retirement from the exorcist business. What should happen then, but the daughter of Louis VII, King of France, was suddenly possessed of a demon. The king heard of the success of Gianmatteo and sent representatives to him to request his presence in Paris. Gianmatteo, mindful of what Belfagor had threatened, pleaded indisposition. When the French government appealed to the officials of Florence, Gianmatteo reluctantly had to go to the French king.

In his first audience Gianmatteo pointed out to His Majesty that some demons are a lot trickier than others and that past performance was no guarantee of future results. His Majesty took the point but in reply said that he certainly expected that Gianmatteo would do his level best and that, should Gianmatteo fail, it would unfortunately be necessary for him to be hanged.

Gianmatteo had the bewitched girl brought to him and whispered in her ear, begging Belfagor to cooperate. Belfagor was furious. He said in no uncertain terms that he was sick and tired of hearing the boasts that Gianmatteo could drive out demons and that he had done quite enough for Gianmatteo, and that if Gianmatteo persisted in bothering him at work he would see to it that he met a very sticky end.

There was nothing for Gianmatteo to do but to go back to the king and say that this was an extremely difficult demon. Success perhaps should not be expected. If His Majesty was ready to supply what was needed, however, Gianmatteo was prepared to give it once last try. For that he said he would need a large platform erected in front of the church of Notre Dame and stands around it large enough to hold all the nobles and notables of the city of Paris. The stands were to be decorated in crimson and gold. On the platform His Majesty and principal officials would be arranged around an altar on which a solemn High Mass would be celebrated and after that the poor bewitched girl be brought forward. At one side of the square, around which the population of

Paris would be assembled, there would have to be at least 20 musicians: drums and trumpets, bagpipes and clarinets, cymbals and all sorts of noisemakers.

At a signal from Gianmatteo the bewitched girl would slowly come forward and the band would play as loudly as possible, marching toward the platform. This, Gianmatteo said, might just work. If it did not, he was prepared to go with the hangman, for what else could he do?

Accordingly all the preparations were made and the honored guests and curious crowd assembled in front of Notre Dame. The High Mass was celebrated and the bewitched girl was escorted to the platform by bishops and other dignitaries. Gianmatteo whispered a plea in her ear for Belfagor to leave, but he was furious and said that if Gianmatteo thought that he, a leading light of the infernal kingdom, well acquainted with the pomp of hell, was at all impressed by this attempt at splendor then he was sadly mistaken. Belfagor was staying and Gianmatteo could that very day go to the scaffold, not the platform, as far as Belfagor was concerned.

Then Gianmatteo raised his hat in signal and with a fearful burst of sound the band began to march to the platform. Belfagor wanted to know what the hell that was all about. Gianmatteo said, "It is Onesta, your wife, who has come to see you."

At that, dazed by the din, Belfagor did not stop to think about the logic of the remark. He fled in dismay from the bewitched girl and flew straight to Hell as fast as he could. He preferred to go to Hell rather than to suffer anymore of the spitefulness and danger of a wife, the acrimony of matrimony.

Thus it was that Belfagor went back home to testify to the denizens of Hell what trouble a wife brings to a home, and thus it was that Gianmatteo, who was cleverer than the devil, pulled off his third non-magical exorcism and earned the money and the fame that enabled him to live rich and content the rest of his life.

GOING A-NUTTING

The Devil, as Common People say,
Doth go a-nutting Holyrood Day,
And sure as lechery in cloth doth lurk
Going a-nutting does the Devil's work.

SEX AND MAGIC IN THE OLD BALLADS

There is a lot of sex magic reported in the old ballads. Here is a folk ballad by "Thomas the Rhymer" whose subject is very much like that of the art ballad by John Keats, which you know as *La Belle Dame sans Merci*. In Keats' case, the beautiful Lady without Mercy was tuberculosis; her grip was to be his death.

In Thomas' case a connection with the Queen of the Fairies was not fatal, but it did make him an indentured servant for the standard seven years. I'll modernize the language a little because words like *ferlie* (wonder) and even *mirk* (dark) of the old dialect might baffle you. For the rhyme I have had to retain *leven*, which is a sort of level field. I have cut some stanzas out. Folk ballads tend to have many, many of those. We come into this old ballad at the point where Thomas has encountered the Queen of the fairies and kissed her, whereupon:

Now you must go with me, she said,
True Thomas, you must go with me;
And you must serve me seven years
Through weal or woe, as chance may be.

She mounted on her milk-white steed,
She's taken True Thomas up behind;
And aye whenever her bridle rung
The steed flew swifter than the wind.

On they rode, and farther on—
The steed went swifter than the wind—
Until they reached a desert wide
And living land was left behind.

Alight, alight, True Thomas, now
And lean your head upon my knee;
Abide and rest a little space
And I will show you wonders three.

Oh see you not yon narrow road
So thick beset with thorns and briars?
That is the path of righteousness
Though after it but few inquires.

And see you not that broad, broad road
That lies across that lily leven?
That is the path of wickedness,
Though some call it the road to heaven.

And see ye not the bonny road
That winds about the ferny brae?
That is the road to fair Elfland
The road that we shall take today.

But, Thomas, you must hold your tongue,
Whatever you may hear or see.
If you speak a word in Elfin Land
You'll ne'er get back to your own country.

On they rode, and farther on,
And waded in rivers above the knee,
And they saw neither sun nor moon
But heard the roaring of the sea.

It was dark, dark night and no starlight,
They waded through red blood to the knee,
For all the blood's that shed on earth
Runs through the springs of that country.

In time they came to a garden green
An apple she pulled from a tree nearby

Take this for thy wages, True Thomas,
It will give you a tongue that cannot lie.

My tongue is my own, True Thomas said,
A goodly gift you would give to me.
I'd never dare to buy or sell
At fair or tryst where I might be.

I'd dare not speak to prince or peer
Nor ask for grace from fair lady.
Now hold your peace, the lady said,
For as I say so must it be.

He's gotten a coat of the even cloth
And a pair of shoes of velvet green;
And 'til seven years were gone and past
True Thomas on earth was never seen.

FROM ROBERT BURTON'S *THE ANATOMY OF MELANCHOLY*

One more [tale] I will relate out of Florilegus, *ad annum* [from the year] 1058, an honest historian of our nation, because he telleth it so confidently, as a thing in those days talked of all over Europe. A young gentleman of Rome, the same day that he was married, after dinner with the bride and his friends went a-walking into the fields, and towards evening to the tennis-court to recreate himself; whilst he played, he put his ring upon the finger of Venus' statue, which was thereby, made in brass; after he had sufficiently played . . . he came to fetch his ring, but Venus had bowed her finger in, and he could not get it off; whereupon, loath to make his company tardy, at the present there left it, intending to fetch it the next day or at some more convenient time, went to bed. In the night, when he should come to perform those nuptial rites, Venus steps between him and his wife (unseen or felt by her), and told her that she was his wife, that he had betrothed himself unto her by that ring which he put on her finger: she troubled him for some following nights. He, not knowing how to help himself, made his moan to one Palumbus, a learned magician in those days, who gave him a letter, and bid him at such a time of the night, in such a cross-way, at the town's end, where old Saturn would pass by with his associates, as commonly he did, deliver that script with his own hands to Saturn himself; the young man, of a bold spirit, accordingly did it; and when the old fiend had read it, he called Venus to him, who rode before him, and commanded her to deliver his ring, which forthwith she did, and so the gentleman was freed.

A RETELLING OF AN INCIDENT REPORTED IN HENRICUS INSTITORIS & JAKOB SPENGER'S *MALLEUS MALEFICARUM*

In the town of Ratisbon [Regensberg] a certain young man who had an affair with a girl, wishing to drop her, lost his male member, that is to say a glamour was cast over it so that he could see or touch nothing but his smooth body. Anxious about this he went to a tavern to drink some wine, and after a while he fell into conversation with a woman who was there and he told her the cause of his unhappiness. She was a shrewd woman and immediately asked him if there was anyone he suspected and, when he had told the name and the whole story, she said to him: "If talking to her is not enough we are going to have to turn to violence to make her restore you to health." So that evening the young man kept an eye open on the route that the  witch usually took and when he found her he beseeched her to restore the health of his body. When she claimed that she didn't know anything about all this he assaulted her, wrapped a towel around her neck, and choked her, saying: "Unless you give me back what I have lost I am going to kill you." At first she was unable to reply and her face began to turn dark but she managed to say, "Let me go and I will heal you." The young man thereupon loosened the towel and the witch touched him in the groin saying, "Now you have what you wanted." The young man (as he afterwards reported) immediately sensed, before he checked by looking or feeling, that his member had been restored to him by one touch of the witch.

THE AUTHOR OF THE TALE YOU ARE ABOUT TO READ

Despite his surname, Joseph Sheridan LeFanu (1814–1873) was Irish, his middle name underlying his connection with the family that produced the famous playwright Richard Brinsley Sheridan, whose sister Alice (herself a playwright) Joseph married. Joseph attended Trinity College, Dublin, and became a noted journalist, editing Dublin's *Evening Mail* and the *Dublin University Magazine*, but he is most famous for 13 novels (1863–1875), of which the haunting *The House by the Churchyard* and *Uncle Silas* were early examples. Of them all, *Carmilla* is the most noted, having been a great hit in the nineteenth-century long before Bram Stoker, another Irishman, penned the most deathless of vampire novels, *Dracula*, and, like *Dracula*, the basis for a number of films in modern times. Qualified as a lawyer,

LeFanu really made his mark as owner of several newspapers and ranks as second only to Charles James Lever among Irish nineteenth-century writers of fiction.

Like Wilkie Collins in *The Woman in White* (1860), in *Carmilla* there is the confusion of identity of mysterious women who look alike, but whereas Collins was laying the foundation of the mystery novel LeFanu specialized in the sensationalism that could be wrung out of the ominous and the occult. Where *The Vampyre* (once attributed to Lord Byron but actually written by his doctor, John Polidori) and the *Varney the Vampire* both featured males, *Carmilla* centers on a female vampire and has overtones of lesbianism. Sex and the occult are combined in the vampire legend. If the characters in the story
are slower on the uptake than you are, remember that LeFanu is writing well before Stoker's *Dracula* made everyone a vampire expert. LeFanu was one of the pioneers with *Carmilla*.

CARMILLA BY JOSEPH SHERIDAN LE FANU

Chapter I
An Early Fright

In Styria, we, though by no means magnificent people, inhabit a castle, or schloss. A small income, in that part of the world, goes a great way. Eight or nine hundred a year does wonders. Scantily enough ours would have answered among wealthy people at home. My father is English, and I bear an English name, although I never saw England. But here, in this lonely and primitive place, where everything is so marvellously cheap, I really don't see how ever so much more money would at all materially add to our comforts, or even luxuries.

My father was in the Austrian service, and retired upon a pension and his patrimony, and purchased this feudal residence, and the small estate on which it stands, a bargain.

Nothing can be more picturesque or solitary. It stands on a slight eminence in a forest. The road, very old and narrow, passes in front of its drawbridge, never raised in my time, and its moat, stocked with perch, and sailed over by many swans, and floating on its surface white fleets of water-lilies.

Over all this the schloss shows its many-windowed front; its towers, and its Gothic chapel.

The forest opens in an irregular and very picturesque glade before its gate, and at the right a steep Gothic bridge carries the road over a stream that winds in deep shadow through the wood.

I have said that this is a very lonely place. Judge whether I say truth. Looking from the hall door towards the road, the forest in which our castle stands extends fifteen miles to the right, and twelve to the left. The nearest inhabited village is about seven of your English miles to the left. The nearest inhabited schloss of any historic associations, is that of old General Spielsdorf, nearly twenty miles away to the right.

I have said "the nearest *inhabited* village," because there is, only three miles westward, that is to say in the direction of General Spielsdorf's schloss, a ruined village, with its quaint little church, now roofless, in the aisle of which are the mouldering tombs of the proud family of Karnstein, now extinct, who once owned the equally desolate château which, in the thick of the forest, overlooks the silent ruins of the town.

Respecting the cause of the desertion of this striking and melancholy spot, there is a legend which I shall relate to you another time.

I must tell you now, how very small is the party who constitute the inhabitants of our castle. I don't include servants, or those dependants who occupy rooms in the buildings attached to the schloss. Listen, and wonder! My father, who is the kindest man on earth, but growing old; and I, at the date of my story, only nineteen. Eight years have passed since then. I and my father constituted the family at the schloss. My mother, a Styrian lady, died in my infancy, but I had a good-natured governess, who had been with me from, I might almost say, my infancy. I could not remember the time when her fat, benignant face was not a familiar picture in my memory. This was Madame Perrodon, a native of Berne, whose care and good nature in part supplied to me the loss of my mother, whom I do not even remember, so early I lost her. She made a third at our little dinner party. There was a fourth, Mademoiselle De Lafontaine, a lady such as you term, I believe, a "finishing governess." She spoke French and German, Madame Perrodon French and broken English, to which my father and I added English, which, partly to prevent its becoming a lost language among us, and partly from patriotic motives, we spoke every day. The consequence was a Babel, at which strangers used to laugh, and which I shall make no attempt to reproduce in this narrative. And there

HOW SIR TRISTRAM DRANK OF THE LOVE DRINK

were two or three young lady friends besides, pretty nearly of my own age, who were occasional visitors, for longer or shorter terms; and these visits I sometimes returned.

These were our regular social resources; but of course there were chance visits from "neighbours" of only five or six leagues distance. My life was, notwithstanding, rather a solitary one, I can assure you.

My gouvernantes had just so much control over me as you might conjecture such sage persons would have in the case of a rather spoiled girl, whose only parent allowed her pretty nearly her own way in everything.

The first occurrence in my existence, which produced a terrible impression upon my mind, which, in fact, never has been effaced, was one of the very earliest incidents of my life which I can recollect. Some people will think it so trifling that it should not be recorded here. You will see, however, by-and-bye, why I mention it. The nursery, as it was called, though I had it all to myself, was a large room in the upper story of the castle, with a steep oak roof. I can't have been more than six years old, when one night I awoke, and looking round the room from my bed, failed to see the nursery-maid. Neither was my nurse there; and I thought myself alone. I was not frightened, for I was one of those happy children who are studiously kept in ignorance of ghost stories, of fairy tales, and of all such lore as makes us cover up our heads when the door creaks suddenly, or the flicker of an expiring candle makes the shadow of a bed-post dance upon the wall, nearer to our faces. I was vexed and insulted at finding myself, as I conceived, neglected, and I began to whimper, preparatory to a hearty bout of roaring; when to my surprise, I saw a solemn, but very pretty face looking at me from the side of the bed. It was that of a young lady who was kneeling, with her hands under the coverlet. I looked at her with a kind of pleased wonder, and ceased whimpering. She caressed me with her hands, and lay down beside me on the bed, and drew me towards her, smiling; I felt immediately delightfully soothed, and fell asleep again. I was wakened by a sensation as if two needles ran into my breast very deep at the same moment, and I cried loudly. The lady started back, with her eyes fixed on me, and then slipped down upon the floor, and, as I thought, hid herself under the bed.

I was now for the first time frightened, and I yelled with all my might and main. Nurse, nursery-maid, housekeeper, all came running in, and hearing my story, they made light of it, soothing me all they could meanwhile. But, child as I was, I could perceive that their faces were pale with an unwonted look of anxiety, and I saw them look under the bed, and about the room, and peep under tables and pluck open cupboards; and the housekeeper whispered to the

nurse: "Lay your hand along that hollow in the bed; some one *did* lie there, so sure as you did not; the place is still warm."

I remember the nursery-maid petting me, and all three examining my chest, where I told them I felt the puncture, and pronouncing that there was no sign visible that any such thing had happened to me.

The housekeeper and the two other servants who were in charge of the nursery, remained sitting up all night; and from that time a servant always sat up in the nursery until I was about fourteen.

Do you see PATER NOSTER in this?

I was very nervous for a long time after this. A doctor was called in, he was pallid and elderly. How well I remember his long saturnine face, slightly pitted with small-pox, and his chestnut wig. For a good while, every second day, he came and gave me medicine, which of course I hated.

The morning after I saw this apparition I was in a state of terror, and could not bear to be left alone, daylight though it was, for a moment.

I remember my father coming up and standing at the bedside, and talking cheerfully, and asking the nurse a number of questions, and laughing very heartily at one of the answers; and patting me on the shoulder, and kissing me, and telling me not to be frightened, that it was nothing but a dream and could not hurt me.

But I was not comforted, for I knew the visit of the strange woman was not a dream; and I was *awfully* frightened.

I was a little consoled by the nursery-maid's assuring me that it was she who had come and looked at me, and lain down beside me in the bed, and that I must have been half-dreaming not to have known her face. But this, though supported by the nurse, did not quite satisfy me.

I remember, in the course of that day, a venerable old man, in a black cassock, coming into the room with the nurse and housekeeper, and talking a little to them, and very kindly to me; his face was very sweet and gentle, and he told me they were going to pray, and joined my hands together, and desired me to say, softly, while they were praying, "Lord hear all good prayers for us, for Jesus' sake." I think these were the very words, for I often repeated them to myself, and my nurse used for years to make me say them in my prayers.

I remember so well the thoughtful sweet face of that white-haired old man, in his black cassock, as he stood in that rude, lofty, brown room, with the clumsy furniture of a fashion three hundred years old, about him, and the scanty light entering its shadowy atmosphere through the small lattice. He kneeled, and the three women with him, and he prayed aloud with an earnest quavering voice for, what appeared to me, a long time. I forget all my life preceding that event, and for some time after it is all obscure also, but the scenes I have just described stand out vivid as the isolated pictures of the phantasmagoria surrounded by darkness.

Chapter II
A Guest

I am now going to tell you something so strange that it will require all your faith in my veracity to believe my story. It not only true, nevertheless, but truth of which I have been an eye-witness.

It was a sweet summer evening, and my father asked me, as he sometimes did, to take a little ramble with him along that beautiful forest vista which I have mentioned as lying in front of the schloss.

"General Spielsdorf cannot come to us so soon as I had hoped," said my father, as we pursued our walk.

He was to have paid us a visit of some weeks, and we had expected his arrival next day. He was to have brought with him a young lady, his niece and ward, Mademoiselle Rheinfeldt, whom I had never seen, but whom I had heard described as a very charming girl, and in whose society I had promised myself many happy days. I was more disappointed than a young lady living in a town, or a bustling neighbourhood can possibly imagine. This visit, and the new acquaintance it promised, had furnished my day dream for many weeks.

"And how soon does he come?" I asked.

"Not till autumn. Not for two months, I dare say," he answered. "And I am very glad now, dear, that you never knew Mademoiselle Rheinfeldt."

"And why?" I asked, both mortified and curious.

"Because the poor young lady is dead," he replied. "I quite forgot I had not told you, but you were not in the room when I received the General's letter this evening."

I was very much shocked. General Spielsdorf had mentioned in his first letter, six or seven weeks before, that she was not so well as he would wish her, but there was nothing to suggest the remotest suspicion of danger.

"Here is the General's letter," he said, handing it to me. "I am afraid he is in great affliction; the letter appears to me to have been written very nearly in distraction."

We sat down on a rude bench, under a group of magnificent lime-trees. The sun was setting with all its melancholy splendour behind the sylvan horizon, and the stream that flows beside our home, and passes under the steep old bridge I have mentioned, wound through many a group of noble trees, almost at our feet, reflecting in its current the fading crimson of the sky. General Spieldorf's letter was so extraordinary, so vehement, and in some places so self-contradictory, that I read it twice over—the second time aloud to my father—and was still unable to account for it, except by supposing that grief had unsettled his mind.

It said, "I have lost my darling daughter, for as such I loved her. During the last days of dear Bertha's illness I was not able to write to you. Before then I had no idea of her danger. I have lost her, and now learn *all*, too late. She died in the peace of innocence, and in the glorious hope of a blessed futurity. The fiend who betrayed our infatuated hospitality has done it all. I thought I was receiving into my house innocence, gaiety, a charming companion for my lost Bertha. Heavens! What a fool have I been! I thank God my child died without a suspicion of the cause of her sufferings. She is gone without so much as conjecturing the nature of her illness, and the accursed passion of the agent of all this misery. I devote my remaining days to tracking and extinguishing a monster. I am told I may hope to accomplish my righteous and merciful purpose. At present there is scarcely a gleam of light to guide me. I curse my conceited incredulity, my despicable affectation of superiority, my blindness, my obstinacy—all—too late. I cannot write or talk collectedly now. I am distracted. So soon as I shall have a little recovered, I mean to devote myself for a time to enquiry, which may possibly lead me as far as Vienna. Some time in the autumn, two months hence, or earlier if I live, I will see you—that is, if you permit me; I will then tell you all that I scarce dare put upon paper now. Farewell. Pray for me, dear friend."

In these terms ended this strange letter. Though I had never seen Bertha Rheinfeldt my eyes filled with tears at the sudden intelligence; I was startled, as well as profoundly disappointed.

The sun had now set, and it was twilight by the time I had returned the General's letter to my father.

It was a soft clear evening, and we loitered, speculating upon the possible meanings of the violent and incoherent sentences which I had just been reading. We had nearly a mile to walk before reaching the road that passes the schloss in front, and by that time the moon was shining brilliantly. At the drawbridge we met Madame Perrodon and Mademoiselle De Lafontaine, who had come out, without their bonnets, to enjoy the exquisite moonlight.

We heard their voices gabbling in animated dialogue as we approached. We joined them at the drawbridge, and turned about to admire with them the beautiful scene.

The glade through which we had just walked lay before us. At our left the narrow road wound away under clumps of lordly trees, and was lost to sight amid the thickening forest. At the right the same road crosses the steep and

picturesque bridge, near which stands a ruined tower which once guarded that pass; and beyond the bridge an abrupt eminence rises, covered with trees, and showing in the shadows some grey ivy-clustered rocks.

Over the sward and low grounds a thin film of mist was stealing, like smoke, marking the distances with a transparent veil; and here and there we could see the river faintly flashing in the moonlight.

No softer, sweeter scene could be imagined. The news I had just heard made it melancholy; but nothing could disturb its character of profound serenity, and the enchanted glory and vagueness of the prospect.

My father, who enjoyed the picturesque, and I, stood looking in silence over the expanse beneath us. The two good governesses, standing a little way behind us, discoursed upon the scene, and were eloquent upon the moon.

Madame Perrodon was fat, middle-aged, and romantic, and talked and sighed poetically. Mademoiselle De Lafontaine—in right of her father, who was a German, assumed to be psychological, metaphysical, and something of a mystic— now declared that when the moon shone with a light so intense it was well known that it indicated a special spiritual activity. The effect of the full moon in such a state of brilliancy was manifold. It acted on dreams, it acted on lunacy, it acted on nervous people;  it had marvellous physical influences connected with life. Mademoiselle related that her cousin, who was mate of a merchant ship, having taken a nap on deck on such a night, lying on his back, with his face full in the light of the moon, had wakened, after a dream of an old woman clawing him by the cheek, with his features horribly drawn to one side; and his countenance had never quite recovered its equilibrium.

"The moon, this night," she said, "is full of idylic and magnetic influence— and see, when you look behind you at the front of the schloss, how all its windows flash and twinkle with that silvery splendour, as if unseen hands had lighted up the rooms to receive fairy guests."

There are indolent states of the spirits in which, indisposed to talk ourselves, the talk of others is pleasant to our listless ears; and I gazed on, pleased with the tinkle of the ladies' conversation.

"I have got into one of my moping moods to-night," said my father, after a silence, and quoting Shakespeare, whom, by way of keeping up our English, he used to read aloud, he said:

"'In truth I know not why I am so sad: It wearies me; you say it wearies you; But how I got it—came by it.'... I forget the rest. But I feel as if some great misfortune were hanging over us. I suppose the poor General's afflicted letter has had something to do with it."

At this moment the unwonted sound of carriage wheels and many hoofs upon the road, arrested our attention.

They seemed to be approaching from the high ground overlooking the bridge, and very soon the equipage emerged from that point. Two horsemen first crossed the bridge, then came a carriage drawn by four horses, and two men rode behind.

It seemed to be the travelling carriage of a person of rank; and we were all immediately absorbed in watching that unusual spectacle. It became, in a few moments, greatly more interesting, for just as the carriage had passed the summit of the steep bridge, one of the leaders, taking fright, communicated his panic to the rest, and after a plunge or two, the whole team broke into a wild gallop together, and dashing between the horsemen who rode in front, came thundering along the road towards us with the speed of a hurricane.

The excitement of the scene was made more painful by the clear, long-drawn screams of a female voice from the carriage window.

We all advanced in curiosity and horror; my father in silence, the rest with various ejaculations of terror.

Our suspense did not last long. Just before you reach the castle drawbridge, on the route they were coming, there stands by the roadside a magnificent lime-tree, on the other side stands an ancient stone cross, at sight of which the horses, now going at a pace that was perfectly frightful, swerved so as to bring the wheel over the projecting roots of the tree.

I knew what was coming. I covered my eyes, unable to see it out, and turned my head away; at the same moment I heard a cry from my lady-friends, who had gone on a little.

Curiosity opened my eyes, and I saw a scene of utter confusion. Two of the horses were on the ground, the carriage lay upon its side with two wheels in the air; the men were busy removing the traces, and a lady, with a commanding air and figure had got out, and stood with clasped hands, raising the handkerchief that was in them every now and then to her eyes. Through the carriage door was now lifted a young lady, who appeared to be lifeless. My dear old father was already beside the elder lady, with his hat in his hand, evidently tendering his aid and the resources of his schloss. The lady did not appear to hear him, or to have eyes for anything but the slender girl who was being placed against the slope of the bank.

I approached; the young lady was apparently stunned, but she was certainly not dead. My father, who piqued himself on being something of a physician, had just had his fingers to her wrist and assured the lady, who declared herself her mother, that her pulse, though faint and irregular, was undoubtedly still distinguishable. The lady clasped her hands and looked upward, as if in a momentary transport of gratitude; but immediately she broke out again in that theatrical way which is, I believe, natural to some people.

She was what is called a fine-looking woman for her time of life, and must have been handsome; she was tall, but not thin, and dressed in black velvet, and looked rather pale, but with a proud and commanding countenance, though now agitated strangely.

"Was ever any being so born to calamity?" I heard her say, with clasped hands, as I came up. "Here am I, on a journey of life and death, in prosecuting which to lose an hour is possibly to lose all. My child will not have recovered sufficiently to resume her route for who can say how long. I must leave her; I cannot, dare not, delay. How far on, sir, can you tell, is the nearest village? I must leave her there; and shall not see my darling, or even hear of her till my return, three months hence."

I plucked my father by the coat, and whispered earnestly in his ear: "Oh! papa, pray ask her to let her stay with us—it would be so delightful. Do, pray."

"If Madame will entrust her child to the care of my daughter, and of her good gouvernante, Madame Perrodon, and permit her to remain as our guest, under my charge, until her return, it will confer a distinction and an obligation upon us, and we shall treat her with all the care and devotion which so sacred a trust deserves."

"I cannot do that, sir, it would be to task your kindness and chivalry too cruelly," said the lady, distractedly.

"It would, on the contrary, be to confer on us a very great kindness at the moment when we most need it. My daughter has just been disappointed by a cruel misfortune, in a visit from which she had long anticipated a great deal of happiness. If you confide this young lady to our care it will be her best consolation. The nearest village on your route is distant, and affords no such inn as you could think of placing your daughter at; you cannot allow her to continue her journey for any considerable distance without danger. If, as you say, you cannot suspend your journey, you must part with her to-night, and nowhere could you do so with more honest assurances of care and tenderness than here."

There was something in this lady's air and appearance so distinguished, and even imposing, and in her manner so engaging, as to impress one, quite apart from the dignity of her equipage, with a conviction that she was a person of consequence.

By this time the carriage was replaced in its upright position, and the horses, quite tractable, in the traces again.

The lady threw on her daughter a glance which I fancied was not quite so affectionate as one might have anticipated from the beginning of the scene; then she beckoned slightly to my father, and withdrew two or three steps with him out of hearing; and talked to him with a fixed and stern countenance, not at all like that with which she had hitherto spoken.

I was filled with wonder that my father did not seem to perceive the change, and also unspeakably curious to learn what it could be that she was speaking, almost in his ear, with so much earnestness and rapidity. Two or three minutes at most I think she remained thus employed, then she turned, and a few steps brought her to where her daughter lay, supported by Madame Perrodon. She kneeled beside her for a moment and whispered, as Madame supposed, a little benediction in her ear; then hastily kissing her she stepped into her carriage, the door was closed, the footmen in stately liveries jumped up behind, the outriders spurred on, the postillions cracked their whips, the horses plunged and broke suddenly into a furious canter that threatened soon again to become a gallop, and the carriage whirled away, followed at the same rapid pace by the two horsemen in the rear.

Chapter III
We Compare Notes

We followed the *cortège* with our eyes until it was swiftly lost to sight in the misty wood; and the very sound of the hoofs and the wheels died away in the silent night air.

Nothing remained to assure us that the adventure had not been an illusion of a moment but the young lady, who just at that moment opened her eyes. I could not see, for her face was turned from me, but she raised her head, evidently looking about her, and I heard a very sweet voice ask complainingly, "Where is mamma?"

Our good Madame Perrodon answered tenderly, and added some comfortable assurances. I then heard her ask: "Where am I? What is this place?" and after that she said, "I don't see the carriage; and Matska, where is she?"

Madame answered all her questions in so far as she understood them; and gradually the young lady remembered how the misadventure came about, and was glad to hear that no one in, or in attendance on, the carriage was hurt; and on learning that her mamma had left her here, till her return in about three months, she wept.

I was going to add my consolations to those of Madame Perrodon when Mademoiselle De Lafontaine placed her hand on my arm, saying:

"Don't approach, one at a time is as much as she can at present converse with; a very little excitement would possibly overpower her now."

As soon as she is comfortably in bed, I thought, I will run up to her room and see her.

My father in the meantime had sent a servant on horseback for the physician, who lived about two leagues away; and a bedroom was being prepared for the young lady's reception.

The stranger now rose, and leaning on Madame's arm, walked slowly over the drawbridge and into the castle gate.

In the hall, servants waited to receive her, and she was conducted forthwith to her room.

The room we usually sat in as our drawing-room is long, having four windows, that looked over the moat and drawbridge, upon the forest scene I have just described.

It is furnished in old carved oak, with large carved cabinets, and the chairs are cushioned with crimson Utrecht velvet. The walls are covered with tapestry, and surrounded with great gold frames, the figures being as large as life, in ancient and very curious costume, and the subjects represented are hunting, hawking, and generally festive. It is not too stately to be extremely comfortable; and here we had our tea, for father with his usual patriotic leanings he insisted that the beverage should make its appearance regularly with our coffee and chocolate.

We sat here this night, and, with candles lighted, were talking over the adventure of the evening.

Madame Perrodon and Mademoiselle De Lafontaine were both of our party. The young stranger had hardly lain down in her bed when she sank into a deep sleep; and those ladies had left her in the care of a servant.

"How do you like our guest?" I asked, as soon as Madame entered. "Tell me all about her?"

"I like her extremely," answered Madame, "she is, I almost think, the prettiest creature I ever saw; about your age, and so gentle and nice."

"She is absolutely beautiful," threw in Mademoiselle, who had peeped for a moment into the stranger's room.

"And such a sweet voice!" added Madame Perrodon.

"Did you remark a woman in the carriage, after it was set up again, who did not get out," inquired Mademoiselle, "but only looked from the window?"

"No, we had not seen her."

Then she described a hideous black woman, with a sort of coloured turban on her head, who was gazing all the time from the carriage window, nodding and grinning derisively towards the ladies, with gleaming eyes and large white eye-balls, and her teeth set as if in fury.

"Did you remark what an ill-looking pack of men the servants were?" asked Madame.

"Yes," said my father, who had just come in, "ugly, hang-dog looking fellows, as ever I beheld in my life. I hope they mayn't rob the poor lady in the forest. They are clever rogues, however; they got everything to rights in a minute."

"I dare say they are worn out with too long travelling," said Madame. "Besides looking wicked, their faces were so strangely lean, and dark, and sullen. I am very curious, I own; but I dare say the young lady will tell us all about it to-morrow, if she is sufficiently recovered."

"I don't think she will," said my father, with a mysterious smile, and a lit-

tle nod of his head, as if he knew more about it than he cared to tell us.

This made me all the more inquisitive as to what had passed between him and the lady in the black velvet, in the brief but earnest interview that had immediately preceded her departure.

We were scarcely alone, when I entreated him to tell me. He did not need much pressing.

"There is no particular reason why I should not tell you. She expressed a reluctance to trouble us with the care of her daughter, saying she was in delicate health, and nervous, but not subject to any kind of seizure—she volunteered that—nor to any illusion; being, in fact, perfectly sane."

"How very odd to say all that?" I interpolated. "It was so unnecessary."

"At all events it *was* said," he laughed, "and as you wish to know all that passed, which was indeed very little, I tell you. She then said, 'I am making a long journey of *vital* importance'—she emphasized the word—rapid and secret; 'I shall return for my child in three months; in the meantime, she will be silent as to who we are, whence we come, and whither we are travelling.' That is all she said. She spoke very pure French. When she said the word 'secret,' she paused for a few seconds, looking sternly, her eyes fixed on mine. I fancy she makes a great point of that. You saw how quickly she was gone. I hope I have not done a very foolish thing, in taking charge of the young lady."

For my part, I was delighted. I was longing to see and talk to her; and only waiting till the doctor should give me leave. You, who live in towns, can have no idea how great an event the introduction of a new friend is, in such a solitude as surrounded us.

The doctor did not arrive till nearly one o'clock; but I could no more have gone to my bed and slept, than I could have overtaken, on foot, the carriage in which the princess in black velvet had driven away.

When the physician came down to the drawing-room, it was to report very favourably upon his patient. She was now sitting up, her pulse quite regular, apparently perfectly well. She sustained no injury, and the little shock to her nerves had passed away quite harmlessly. There could be no harm certainly in my seeing her, if we both wished it; and, with this permission, I sent, forthwith, to know whether she would allow me to visit her for a few minutes in her room.

The servant returned immediately to say that she desired nothing more.

You may be sure I was not long in availing myself of this permission.

Our visitor lay in one of the handsomest rooms in the schloss. It was, perhaps, a little stately. There was a sombre piece of tapestry opposite the foot of the bed, representing Cleopatra with the asp to her bosom; and other solemn classic scenes were displayed, a little faded, upon the other walls. But there was gold carving, and rich and varied colour enough in the other decorations of the room, to more than redeem the gloom of the old tapestry.

There were candles at the bed-side. She was sitting up; her slender pretty figure enveloped in the soft silk dressing gown, embroidered with flowers, and lined with thick quilted silk, which her mother had thrown over her feet as she lay upon the ground.

What was it that, as I reached the bed-side and had just begun my little greeting, struck me dumb in a moment, and made me recoil a step or two from before her? I will tell you.

I saw the very face which had visited me in my childhood at night, which remained so fixed in my memory, and on which I had for so many years so often ruminated with horror, when no one suspected of what I was thinking.

It was pretty, even beautiful; and when I first beheld it, wore the same melancholy expression.

But this almost instantly lighted into a strange fixed smile of recognition.

There was a silence of fully a minute, and then at length *she* spoke; I could not.

"How wonderful!" she exclaimed, "Twelve years ago, I saw your face in a dream, and it has haunted me ever since."

"Wonderful indeed!" I repeated, overcoming with an effort the horror that had for a time suspended my utterances. "Twelve years ago, in vision or reality, *I* certainly saw you. I could not forget your face. It has remained before my eyes ever since."

Her smile had softened. Whatever I had fancied strange in it, was gone, and it and her dimpling cheeks were now delightfully pretty and intelligent.

I felt reassured, and continued more in the vein which hospitality indicated, to bid her welcome, and to tell her how much pleasure her accidental arrival had given us all, and especially what a happiness it was to me.

I took her hand as I spoke. I was a little shy, as lonely people are, but the situation made me eloquent, and even bold. She pressed my hand, she laid hers upon it, and her eyes glowed, as, looking hastily into mine, she smiled again, and blushed.

She answered my welcome very prettily. I sat down beside her, still wondering; and she said:

"I must tell you my vision about you; it is so very strange that you and I should have had, each of the other so vivid a dream, that each should have seen, I you and you me, looking as we do now, when of course we both were mere children. I was a child, about six years old, and I awoke from a confused and troubled dream, and found myself in a room, unlike my nursery, wainscoted clumsily in some dark wood, and with cupboards and bedsteads, and chairs, and benches placed about it. The beds were, I thought, all empty, and the room itself without anyone but myself in it; and I, after looking about me for some time, and admiring especially an iron candlestick, with two branches, which I should certainly know again, crept under one of the beds to reach the window; but as I got from under the bed, I heard some one crying; and looking, up, while I was still upon my knees, *you*—most assuredly you—as I see you now; a beautiful young lady, with hair and large blue eyes, and lips—your lips—you, as you here. Your looks won me; I climbed on the bed and put my arms about you, and I think we both fell asleep. I was aroused by a scream; you were sitting up screaming. I was frightened, and slipped down upon the ground, and, it seemed to me, lost consciousness for a moment; and when I came to myself, I was again in my nursery at home. Your face I have never forgotten since. I could not be misled by mere resemblance. You are the lady whom I then saw."

It was now my turn to relate my corresponding vision, which I did, to the undisguised wonder of my new acquaintance.

"I don't know which should be most afraid of the other," she said, again smiling—"If you were less pretty I think I should be very much afraid of you, but being as you are, and you and I both so young, I feel only that I have made your acquaintance twelve years ago, and have already a right to intimacy; at all events it does seem as if we were destined, from our earliest childhood, to be friends. I wonder whether you feel as strangely drawn towards me as I do to you; I never had a friend—shall I find one now?" She sighed, and fine dark eyes gazed passionately on me.

Now the truth is, I felt rather unaccountably towards the beautiful stranger. I did feel, as she said, "drawn towards her," but there was also something of repulsion. In this ambiguous feeling, however, the sense of attraction immensely prevailed. She interested and won me; she was so beautiful and so indescribably engaging.

I perceived now something of langour and exhaustion stealing over her, and hastened to bid her good night.

"The doctor thinks," I added, "that you ought to have a maid to sit up with you to-night; one of ours is waiting, and you will find her a very useful and quiet creature."

"How kind of you, but I could not sleep, I never could with an attendant in the room. I shan't require any assistance—and, shall I confess my weakness, I am haunted with a terror of robbers. Our house was robbed once, and two servants murdered, so I always lock my door. It has become a habit—and you look so kind I know you will forgive me. I see there is a key in the lock."

She held me close in her pretty arms for a moment and whispered in my ear, "Good night, darling, it is very hard to part with you, but good-night; to-morrow, but not early, I shall see you again."

She sank back on the pillow with a sigh, and her fine eyes followed me with a fond and melancholy gaze, and she murmured again "Good-night, dear friend."

Young people like, and even love, on impulse. I was flattered by the evident, though as yet undeserved, fondness she showed me. I liked the confidence with which she at once received me. She was determined that we should be very near friends.

Next day came and we met again. I was delighted with my companion; that is to say, in many respects.

Her looks lost nothing in daylight—she was certainly the most beautiful creature I had ever seen, and the unpleasant remembrance of the face presented in my early dream had lost the effect of the first unexpected recognition.

She confessed that she had experienced a similar shock on seeing me, and precisely the same faint antipathy that had mingled with my admiration of her. We now laughed together over our momentary horrors.

Chapter IV
Her Habits—a Saunter

I told you that I was charmed with her in most particulars. There were some that did not please me so well.

She was above the middle height of women. I shall begin by describing her. She was slender, and wonderfully graceful. Except that her movements were languid—*very* languid—indeed, there was nothing in her appearance to indicate an invalid. Her complexion was rich and brilliant; her features were small and beautifully formed; her eyes large, dark, and lustrous; her hair was

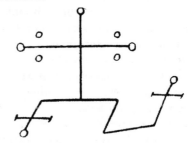

The *Sigil* of Dantalian, Duke of Hell, who kindles love and produces, in visions, anyone you wish.

quite wonderful, I never saw hair so magnificently thick and long when it was down about her shoulders; I have often placed my hands under it, and laughed with wonder at its weight. It was exquisitely fine and soft, and in colour a rich very dark brown, with something of gold. I loved to let it down, tumbling with its own weight, as, in her room, she lay back in her chair talking in her sweet low voice, I used to fold and braid it, and spread it out and play with it. Heavens! If I had but known all!

I said there were particulars which did not please me. I have told you that her confidence won me the first night I saw her; but I found that she exercised with respect to herself, her mother, her history, everything in fact connected with her life, plans, and people, an ever wakeful reserve. I dare say I was unreasonable, perhaps I was wrong; I dare say I ought to have respected the solemn injunction laid upon my father by the stately lady in black velvet. But curiosity is a restless and unscrupulous passion, and no one girl can endure, with patience, that hers should be baffled by another. What harm could it do anyone to tell me what I so ardently desired to know? Had she no trust in my good sense or honour? Why would she not believe me when I assured her, so solemnly, that I would not divulge one syllable of what she told me to any mortal breathing.

There was a coldness, it seemed to me, beyond her years, in her smiling melancholy persistent refusal to afford me the least ray of light.

I cannot say we quarrelled upon this point, for she would not quarrel upon any. It was, of course, very unfair of me to press her, very ill-bred, but I really could not help it; and I might just as well have let it alone.

What she did tell me amounted, in my unconscionable estimation—to nothing.

It was all summed up in three very vague disclosures:

First.—Her name was Carmilla.

Second.—Her family was very ancient and noble.

Third.—Her home lay in the direction of the west.

She would not tell me the name of her family, nor their armorial bearings, nor the name of their estate, nor even that of the country they lived in.

You are not to suppose that I worried her incessantly on these subjects. I watched for opportunity, and rather insinuated than urged my inquiries. Once or twice, indeed, I did attack her more directly. But no matter what my tactics, utter failure was invariably the result. Reproaches and caresses were all lost upon her. But I must add this, that her evasion was conducted with so pretty a melancholy and deprecation, with so many, and even passionate declarations of her liking for me, and trust in my honour, and with so many promises that I should at last know all, that I could not find it in my heart long to be offended with her.

She used to place her pretty arms about my neck, draw me to her, and laying her cheek to mine, murmur with her lips near my ear, "Dearest, your little heart is wounded; think me not cruel because I obey the irresistible law of my strength and weakness; if your dear heart is wounded, my wild heart bleeds with yours. In the rapture of my enormous humiliation I live in your warm life, and you shall die—die, sweetly die—into mine. I cannot help it; as I draw near to you, you, in your turn, will draw near to others, and learn the rapture of that cruelty, which yet is love; so, for a while, seek to know no more of me and mine, but trust me with all your loving spirit."

And when she had spoken such a rhapsody, she would press me more closely in her trembling embrace, and her lips in soft kisses gently glow upon my cheek.

Her agitations and her language were unintelligible to me.

From these foolish embraces, which were not of very frequent occurrence, I must allow, I used to wish to extricate myself; but my energies seemed to fail me. Her murmured words sounded like a lullaby in my ear, and soothed my resistance into a trance, from which I only seemed to recover myself when she

withdrew her arms.

In these mysterious moods I did not like her. I experienced a strange tumultuous excitement that was pleasurable, ever and anon, mingled with a vague sense of fear and disgust. I had no distinct thoughts about her while such scenes lasted, but I was conscious of a love growing into adoration, and also of abhorrence. This I know is paradox, but I can make no other attempt to explain the feeling.

I now write, after an interval of more than ten years, with a trembling hand, with a confused and horrible recollection of certain occurrences and situations, in the ordeal through which I was unconsciously passing; though with a vivid and very sharp remembrance of the main current of my story. But, I suspect, in all lives there are certain emotional scenes, those in which our passions have been most wildly and terribly roused, that are of all others the most vaguely and dimly remembered.

Sometimes after an hour of apathy, my strange and beautiful companion would take my hand and hold it with a fond pressure, renewed again and again; blushing softly, gazing in my face with languid and burning eyes, and breathing so fast that her dress rose and fell with the tumultuous respiration. It was like the ardour of a lover; it embarrassed me; it was hateful and yet overpowering; and with gloating eyes she drew me to her, and her hot lips travelled along my cheek in kisses; and she would whisper,  almost in sobs, "You are mine, you *shall* be mine, you and I are one for ever." Then she had thrown herself back in her chair, with her small hands over her eyes, leaving me trembling.

"Are we related," I used to ask; "what can you mean by all this? I remind you perhaps of some one whom you love; but you must not, I hate it; I don't know you—I don't know myself when you look so and talk so."

She used to sigh at my vehemence, then turn away and drop my hand.

Respecting these very extraordinary manifestations I strove in vain to form any satisfactory theory—I could not refer them to affectation or trick. It was unmistakably the momentary breaking out of suppressed instinct and emotion. Was she, notwithstanding her mother's volunteered denial, subject to brief visitations of insanity; or was there here a disguise and a romance? I had read in old story books of such things. What if a boyish lover had found his way into the house, and sought to persecute his suit in masquerade, with the assistance of a clever old adventuress? But there were many things against this hypothesis, highly interesting as it was to my vanity.

I could boast of no little attentions such as masculine gallantry delights to offer. Between these passionate moments there were long intervals of common-place, of gaiety, of brooding melancholy, during which, except that I detected her eyes so full of melancholy fire, following me, at times I might have been as nothing to her. Except in these brief periods of mysterious excitement her ways were girlish; and there was always a langour about her, quite incompatible with a masculine system in a state of health.

In some respects her habits were odd. Perhaps not so singular in the opinion of a town lady like you, as they appeared to us rustic people. She used to come down very late, generally not till one o'clock. She would then take a cup of chocolate, but eat nothing; we then went out for a walk, which was a mere saunter, and she seemed, almost immediately, exhausted, and either returned to the schloss or sat on one of benches that were placed, here and there, among the trees. This was a bodily langour in which her mind did not sympathise. She was always an animated talker, and very intelligent.

She sometimes alluded for a moment to her own home, or mentioned an adventure or situation, or an early recollection, which indicated a people of strange manners, and described customs of which we knew nothing. I gathered from these chance hints that her native country was much more remote than I had at first fancied.

As we sat thus one afternoon under the trees a funeral passed us by. It was that of a pretty young girl, whom I had often seen, the daughter of one of the rangers of the forest. The poor man was walking behind the coffin of his darling; she was his only child, and he looked quite heartbroken. Peasants walking two-and-two came behind, they were singing a funeral hymn.

I rose to mark my respect as they passed, and joined in the hymn they were very sweetly singing.

My companion shook me a little roughly, and I turned surprised.

She said brusquely, "Don't you perceive how discordant that is?"

"I think it very sweet, on the contrary," I answered, vexed at the interruption, and very uncomfortable, lest the people who composed the little procession should observe and resent what was passing.

I resumed, therefore, instantly, and was again interrupted. "You pierce my ears," said Carmilla, almost angrily, and stopping her ears with her tiny fingers. "Besides, how can you tell that your religion and mine are the same; your forms wound me, and I hate funerals. What a fuss! Why *you* must die—*everyone* must die; and all are happier when they do. Come home."

"My father has gone on with the clergyman to the churchyard. I thought you knew she was to be buried to day."

"*She?* I don't trouble my head about peasants. I don't know who she is," answered Carmilla, with a flash from her fine eyes.

"She is the poor girl who fancied she saw a ghost a fortnight ago, and has been dying ever since, till yesterday, when she expired."

"Tell me nothing about ghosts. I shan't sleep to-night if you do."

"I hope there is no plague or fever coming; all this looks very like it," I continued. "The swineherd's young wife died only a week ago, and she thought something seized her by the throat as she lay in her bed, and nearly strangled her. Papa says such horrible fancies do accompany some forms of fever. She was quite well the day before. She sank afterwards, and died before a week."

"Well, *her* funeral is over, I hope, and *her* hymn sung; and our ears shan't be tortured with that discord and jargon. It has made me nervous. Sit down here, beside me; sit close; hold my hand; press it hard—hard—harder."

We had moved a little back, and had come to another seat.

She sat down. Her face underwent a change that alarmed and even terrified me for a moment. It darkened, and became horribly livid; her teeth and hands were clenched, and she frowned and compressed her lips, while she stared down upon the ground at her feet, and trembled all over with a continued shudder as irrepressible as ague. All her energies seemed strained to suppress a fit, with which she was then breathlessly tugging; and at length a low convulsive cry of suffering broke from her, and gradually the hysteria subsided. "There! That comes of strangling people with hymns!" she said at last. "Hold me, hold me still. It is passing away."

And so gradually it did; and perhaps to dissipate the sombre impression which the spectacle had left upon me, she became unusually animated and chatty; and so we got home.

This was the first time I had seen her exhibit any definable symptoms of that delicacy of health which her mother had spoken of. It was the first time, also, I had seen her exhibit anything like temper.

Both passed away like a summer cloud; and never but once afterwards did I witness on her part a momentary sign of anger. I will tell you how it happened.

She and I were looking out of one of the long drawing-room windows, when there entered the court-yard, over the drawbridge, a figure of a wanderer whom I knew very well. He used to visit the schloss generally twice a year.

It was the figure of a hunchback, with the sharp lean features that generally accompany deformity. He wore a pointed black beard, and he was smiling from ear to ear, showing his white fangs. He was dressed in buff, black, and scarlet, and crossed with more straps and belts than I could count, from which hung all manner of things. Behind, he carried a magic-lantern, and two boxes, which I well knew, in one of which was a salamander, and in the other a mandrake. These monsters used to make my father laugh. They were compounded of parts of monkeys, parrots, squirrels, fish, and hedgehogs, dried and stitched together with great neatness and startling effect. He had a fiddle, a box of conjuring apparatus, a pair of foils and masks attached to his belt, several other mysterious cases dangling about him, and a black staff with copper ferrules in his hand. His companion was a rough spare dog, that followed at his heels, but stopped short, suspiciously at the drawbridge, and in a little while began to howl dismally.

In the meantime, the mountebank, standing in the midst of the court-yard, raised his grotesque hat, and made us a very ceremonious bow, paying his compliments very volubly in execrable French, and German not much better. Then, disengaging his fiddle, he began to scrape a lively air, to which he sang with a merry discord, dancing with ludicrous airs and activity, that made me laugh, in spite of the dog's howling.

Then he advanced to the window with many smiles and salutations, and his hat in his left hand, his fiddle under his arm, and with a fluency that never took breath, he gabbled a long advertisement of all his accomplishments, and the resources of the various arts which he placed at our service, and the curiosities and entertainments which it was in his power, at our bidding, to display.

"Will your ladyships be pleased to buy an amulet against the oupire, which is going like the wolf, I hear, through these woods," he said, dropping his hat on the pavement. "They are dying of it right and left, and here is a charm that never fails; only pinned to the pillow, and you may laugh in his face."

These charms consisted of oblong slips of vellum, with cabalistic ciphers and diagrams upon them.

Carmilla instantly purchased one, and so did I.

He was looking up, and we were smiling down upon him, amused; at least, I can answer for myself. His piercing black eye, as he looked up in our faces, seemed to detect something that fixed for a moment his curiosity.

In an instant he unrolled a leather case, full of all manner of odd little steel instruments.

"See here, my lady," he said, displaying it, and addressing me, "I profess, among other things less useful, the art of dentistry. Plague take the dog!" he interpolated. "Silence, beast! He howls so that your ladyships can scarcely hear a word. Your noble friend, the young lady at your right, has the sharpest tooth,—long, thin, pointed, like an awl, like a needle; ha, ha! With my sharp and long sight, as I look up, I have seen it distinctly; now if it happens to hurt the young lady, and I think it must, here am I, here are my file, my punch, my nippers; I will make it round and blunt, if her ladyship pleases; no longer the tooth of a fish, but of a beautiful young lady as she is. Hey? Is the young lady displeased? Have I been too bold? Have I offended her?"

The young lady, indeed, looked very angry as she drew back from the window.

"How dare that mountebank insult us so? Where is your father? I shall demand redress from him. My father would have had the wretch tied up to the pump, and flogged with a cart-whip, and burnt to the bones with the castle brand!"

She retired from the window a step or two, and sat down, and had hardly lost sight of the offender, when her wrath subsided as suddenly as it had risen, and she gradually recovered her usual tone, and seemed to forget the little hunchback and his follies.

My father was out of spirits that evening. On coming in he told us that there had been another case very similar to the two fatal ones which had lately occurred. The sister of a young peasant on his estate, only a mile away, was very ill, had been, as she described it, attacked very nearly in the same way, and was now slowly but steadily sinking.

"All this," said my father, "is strictly referable to natural causes. These poor people infect one another with their superstitions, and so repeat in imagination the images of terror that have infested their neighbours."

"But that very circumstance frightens one horribly," said Carmilla.

"How so?" inquired my father.

"I am so afraid of fancying I see such things; I think it would be as bad as reality."

"We are in God's hands; nothing can happen without his permission, and all will end well for those who love him. He is our faithful creator; He has made us all, and will take care of us."

"Creator! *Nature*!" said the young lady in answer to my gentle father. "And this disease that invades the country is natural. Nature. All things proceed from Nature—don't they? All things in the heaven, on the earth, and under the earth, act and live as Nature ordains? I think so."

"The doctor said he would come here to-day," said my father, after a silence. "I want to know what he thinks about it, and what he thinks we had better do."

"Doctors never did me any good," said Carmilla.

"Then you have been ill?" I asked.

"More ill than ever you were," she answered.

"Long ago?"

"Yes, a long time. I suffered from this very illness; but I forget all but my pain and weakness, and they were not so bad as are suffered in other diseases."

"You were very young then?"

"I dare say; let us talk no more of it. You would not wound a friend?" She looked languidly in my eyes, and passed her arm round my waist lovingly, and led me out of the room. My father was busy over some papers near the window.

"Why does your papa like to frighten us?" said the pretty girl, with a sigh and a little shudder.

"He doesn't, dear Carmilla, it is the very furthest thing from his mind."

"Are you afraid, dearest?"

"I should be very much if I fancied there was any real danger of my being attacked as those poor people were."

"You are afraid to die?"

"Yes, everyone is."

"But to die as lovers may—to die together, so that they may live together. Girls are caterpillars while they live in the world, to be finally butterflies when the summer comes; but in the meantime there are grubs and larvae, don't you see—each with their peculiar propensities, necessities and structure. So says

Monsieur Buffon, in his big book, in the next room."

Later in the day the doctor came and was closeted with papa for some time. He was a skilful man, of sixty and upwards, he wore powder, and shaved his pale face as smooth as a pumpkin. He and papa emerged from the room together, and heard papa laugh, and say as they came out:

"Well, I do wonder at a wise man like you. What do you say to hippogriffs and dragons?"

The doctor was smiling, and made answer, shaking his head—

"Nevertheless life and death are mysterious states, and we know little of the resources of either."

And so they walked on, and I heard no more. I did not then know what the doctor had been broaching, but I think I guess it now.

Chapter V
A Wonderful Likeness

This evening there arrived from Gratz the grave, dark-faced son of the picture cleaner, with a horse and cart laden with two large packing cases, having many pictures in each. It was a journey of ten leagues, and whenever a messenger arrived at the schloss from our little capital of Gratz, we used to crowd about him in the hall, to hear the news.

This arrival created in our secluded quarters quite a sensation. The cases remained in the hall, and the messenger was taken charge of by the servants till he had eaten his supper. Then with assistants, and armed with hammer, ripping-chisel, and turnscrew, he met us in the hall, where we had assembled to witness the unpacking of the cases.

Carmilla sat looking listlessly on, while one after the other the old pictures, nearly all portraits, which had undergone the process of renovation, were brought to light. My mother was of an old Hungarian family, and most of these pictures, which were about to be restored to their places, had come to us through her.

My father had a list in his hand, from which he read, as the artist rummaged out the corresponding numbers. I don't know that the pictures were very good, but they were, undoubtedly, very old, and some of them very curious also. They had, for the most part, the merit of being now seen by me, I may say, for the first time; for the smoke and dust of time had all but obliterated them.

"There is a picture that I have not seen yet," said my father. "In one corner, at the top of it, is the name, as well as I could read, 'Marcia Karnstein,' and the date '1698'; and I am curious to see how it has turned out."

I remembered it; it was a small picture, about a foot and a half high, and nearly square, without a frame; but it was so blackened by age that I could not make it out.

The artist now produced it, with evident pride. It was quite beautiful; it was startling; it seemed to live. It was the effigy of Carmilla!

"Carmilla, dear, here is an absolute miracle. Here you are, living, smiling, ready to speak, in this picture. Isn't it beautiful, papa? And see, even the little mole on her throat."

My father laughed, and said, "Certainly it is a wonderful likeness," but he looked away, and to my surprise seemed but little struck by it, and went on talking to the picture cleaner, who was also something of an artist, and discoursed with intelligence about the portraits or other works, which his art had just brought into light and colour, while *I* was more and more lost in wonder the more I looked at the picture.

"Will you let me hang this picture in my room, papa?" I asked.

"Certainly, dear," said he, smiling, "I'm very glad you think it so like. It must be prettier even than I thought it, if it is."

The young lady did not acknowledge this pretty speech, did not seem to hear it. She was leaning back in her seat, her fine eyes under their long lashes gazing on me in contemplation, and she smiled in a kind of rapture.

"And now you can read quite plainly the name that is written in the corner. It is not Marcia; it looks as if it was done in gold. The name is Mircalla, Countess Karnstein, and this is a little coronet over it, and underneath AD 1698. I am descended from the Karnsteins; that is, mamma was."

"Ah?" said the lady, languidly, "so am I, I think, a very long descent, very ancient. Are there any Karnsteins living now?"

"None who bear the name, I believe. The family were ruined, I believe, in some civil wars, long ago, but the ruins of the castle are only about three miles away."

"How interesting," she said, languidly. "But see what beautiful moonlight!" She glanced through the hall-door, which stood a little open. "Suppose you take a little ramble round the court, and look down at the road and river."

"It is so like the night you came to us," I said.

She sighed, smiling.

She rose, and each with her arm about the other's waist, we walked out upon the pavement.

In silence, slowly we walked down to the drawbridge, where the beautiful landscape opened before us.

"And so you were thinking of the night I came here?" she almost whispered. "Are you glad I came?"

"Delighted, dear Carmilla," I answered.

"And you asked for the picture you think like me, to hang in your room," she murmured with a sigh, as she drew her arm closer about my waist, and let her pretty head sink upon my shoulder.

"How romantic you are, Carmilla," I said. "Whenever you tell me your story, it will be made up chiefly of some one great romance."

She kissed me silently.

"I am sure, Carmilla, you have been in love; that there is, at this moment, an affair of the heart going on."

"I have been in love with no one, and never shall," she whispered, "unless it should be with you."

How beautiful she looked in the moonlight!

Shy and strange was the look with which she quickly hid her face in my neck and hair, with tumultuous sighs, that seemed almost to sob, and pressed in mine a hand that trembled.

Her soft cheek was glowing against mine. "Darling, darling," she murmured, "I live in you; and you would die for me, I love you so."

I started from her.

She was gazing on me with eyes from which all fire, all meaning had flown, and a face colourless and apathetic.

"Is there a chill in the air, dear?" she said drowsily. "I almost shiver; have I been dreaming? Let us come in. Come; come; Come in."

"You look ill, Carmilla; a little faint. You certainly must take some wine," I said.

"Yes, I will. I'm better now. I shall be quite well in a few minutes. Yes, do give me a little wine," answered Carmilla, we approached the door. "Let us look again for a moment; it the last time, perhaps, I shall see the moonlight with you."

"How do you feel now, dear Carmilla? Are you really better?" I asked.

I was beginning to take alarm, lest she should have been stricken with the strange epidemic that they said had invaded the country about us.

"Papa would be grieved beyond measure," I added, "if he thought you were ever so little ill, without immediately letting us know. We have a very skilful doctor near this, the physician who was with papa to-day."

"I'm sure he is. I know how kind you all are; but, dear child, I am quite well again. There is nothing ever wrong with me, but a little weakness. People say I am languid; I am incapable of exertion; I can scarcely walk as far as a child of three years old; and every now and then the little strength I have falters, and I become as you have just seen me. But after all I am very easily set up again; in a moment I am perfectly myself. See how I have recovered."

So, indeed, she had; and she and I talked a great deal, and very animated she was; and the remainder of that evening passed without any recurrence of what I called her infatuations. I mean her crazy talk and looks, which embarrassed, and even frightened me.

But there occurred that night an event which gave my thoughts quite a new turn, and seemed to startle even Carmilla's languid nature into momentary energy.

Chapter VI
A Very Strange Agony

When we got into the drawing-room, and had sat down to our coffee and chocolate, although Carmilla did not take any, she seemed quite herself again, and Madame, and Mademoiselle De Lafontaine, joined us, and made a little card party, in the course of which papa came in for what he called his "dish of tea."

When the game was over he sat down beside Carmilla on the sofa, and asked her, a little anxiously, whether she had heard from her mother since her arrival.

She answered "No."

He then asked whether she knew where a letter would reach her at present.

"I cannot tell," she answered ambiguously, "but I have been thinking of leaving you; you have been already too hospitable and too kind to me. I have given you an infinity of trouble, and I should wish to take a carriage to-morrow, and post in pursuit of her; I know where I shall ultimately find her, although I dare not yet tell you."

"But you must not dream of any such thing," exclaimed my father, to my great relief. "We can't afford to lose you so, and I won't consent to your leaving us, except under the care of your mother, who was so good as to consent to your remaining with us till she should herself return. I should be quite happy if I knew that you heard from her; but this evening the accounts of the progress of the mysterious disease that has invaded our neighbourhood, grow even more alarming; and my beautiful guest, I do feel the responsibility, unaided by advice from your mother, very much. But I shall do my best; and one thing is certain, that you must not think of leaving us without her distinct direction to that effect. We should suffer too much in parting from you to consent to it easily."

"Thank you, sir, a thousand times for your hospitality," she answered, smiling bashfully. "You have all been too kind to me; I have seldom been so happy in all my life before, as in your beautiful château, under your care, and in the society of your dear daughter."

So he gallantly, in his old-fashioned way, kissed her hand, smiling and pleased at her little speech.

I accompanied Carmilla as usual to her room, and sat and chatted with her while she was preparing for bed.

"Do you think," I said at length, "that you will ever confide fully in me?"

She turned round smiling, but made no answer, only continued to smile on me.

"You won't answer that?" I said. "You can't answer pleasantly; I ought not to have asked you."

"You were quite right to ask me that, or anything. You not know how dear you are to me, or you could not think confidence too great to look for. But I am under vows, no nun half so awfully, and I dare not tell my story yet, even to you. The time is very near when you shall know everything. You will think me cruel, very selfish, but love is always selfish; the more ardent the more selfish. How jealous I am you cannot know. You must come with me, loving me, to death; or else hate me and still come with me, and *hating* me through death and after. There is no such word as indifference in my apathetic nature."

"Now, Carmilla, you are going to talk your wild nonsense again," I said hastily.

"Not I, silly little fool as I am, and full of whims and fancies; for your sake I'll talk like a sage. Were you ever at a ball?"

"No; how you do run on. What is it like? How charming it must be."

"I almost forget, it is years ago," I laughed.

"You are not so old. Your first ball can hardly be yet."

"I remember everything about it—with an effort. I see it all, as divers see what is going on above them, through a medium, dense, rippling, but transparent. There occurred that night what has confused the picture, and made its colours faint. I was all but assassinated in my bed, wounded *here*," she touched her breast, "and never was the same since."

"Were you near dying?"

"Yes, very—a cruel love—strange love, that would have taken my life. Love will have its sacrifices. No sacrifice without blood. Let us go to sleep now; I feel so lazy. How can I get up just now and lock my door?"

She was lying with her tiny hands buried in her rich wavy hair, under her cheek, her little head upon the pillow, and her glittering eyes followed me wherever I moved, with a kind of shy smile that I could not decipher.

I bid her good-night, and crept from the room with an uncomfortable sensation.

I often wondered whether our pretty guest ever said her prayers. *I* certainly had never seen her upon her knees. In the morning she never came down until long after our family prayers were over, and at night she never left the drawing-room to attend our brief evening prayers in the hall.

If it had not been that it had casually come out in one of our careless talks that she had been baptised, I should have doubted her being a Christian. Religion was a subject on which I had never heard her speak a word. If I had known the world better, this particular neglect or antipathy would not have so much surprised me.

The precautions of nervous people are infectious, and persons of a like temperament are pretty sure, after a time, to imitate them. I had adopted Carmilla's habit of locking her bed-room door, having taken into my head all her whimsical alarms about midnight invaders and prowling assassins. I had also adopted her precaution of making a brief search through her room, to satisfy herself that no lurking assassin or robber was "ensconced."

These wise measures taken, I got into my bed and fell asleep. A light was burning in my room. This was an old habit, of very early date, and which nothing could have tempted me to dispense with.

Thus fortified I might take my rest in peace. But dreams come through stone walls, light up dark rooms, or darken light ones, and their persons make their exits and their entrances as they please, and laugh at locksmiths. I had a dream that night that was the beginning of a very strange agony.

I cannot call it a nightmare, for I was quite conscious of being asleep. But I was equally conscious of being in my room, and lying in bed, precisely as I actually was. I saw, or fancied I saw, the room and its furniture just as I had seen it last, except that it was very dark, and I saw something moving round the foot of the bed, which at first I could not accurately distinguish. But I soon saw that it was a sooty-black animal that resembled a monstrous cat. It appeared to me about four or five feet long, for it measured fully the length of the hearth-rug as it passed over it; and it continued toing and froing with the lithe sinister restlessness of a beast in a cage. I could not cry out, although as you may suppose, I was terrified. Its pace was growing faster, and the room rapidly darker and darker, and at length so dark that I could no longer see anything of it but its eyes. I felt it spring lightly on the bed. The two broad eyes approached my face, and suddenly I felt a stinging pain as if two large needles darted, an inch or two apart, deep into my breast. I waked with a scream. The room was lighted by the candle that burnt there all through the night, and I saw a female figure standing at the foot of the bed, a little at the right side. It was in a dark loose dress, and its hair was down and covered its shoulders. A block of stone could not have been more still. There was not the slightest stir of respiration. As I stared at it, the figure appeared to have changed its place, and was now nearer the door; then, close to it, the door opened, and it passed out.

I was now relieved, and able to breathe and move. My first thought was that Carmilla had been playing me a trick, and that I had forgotten to secure my door. I hastened to it, and found it locked as usual on the inside. I was afraid to open it—I was horrified. I sprang into my bed and covered my head up in the bed-clothes, and lay there more dead than alive till morning.

Chapter VII
Descending

It would be vain my attempting to tell you the horror with which, even now, I recall the occurrence of that night. It was no such transitory terror as a dream leaves behind it. It seemed to deepen by time, and communicated itself to the room and the very furniture that had encompassed the apparition.

I could not bear next day to be alone for a moment. I should have told papa, but for two opposite reasons. At one time I thought he would laugh at my story, and I could not bear its being treated as a jest; and at another, I thought he might fancy that I had been attacked by the mysterious complaint which had invaded our neighbourhood. I had myself no misgivings of the kind, and as he had been rather an invalid for some time, I was afraid of alarming him.

I was comfortable enough with my good-natured companions, Madame Paradon, and the vivacious Mademoiselle De Lafontaine. They both perceived that I was out of spirits and nervous, and at length I told them what lay so heavy at my heart.

Mademoiselle laughed, but I fancied that Madame Paradon looked anxious.

"By-the-bye," said Mademoiselle, laughing, "the long lime-tree walk, behind Carmilla's bedroom-window, is haunted!"

"Nonsense!" exclaimed Madame, who probably thought the theme rather inopportune, "and who tells that story, my dear?"

"Martin says that he came up twice, when the old yard-gate was being repaired, before sunrise, and twice saw the same female figure walking down the lime-tree avenue."

"So he well might, as long as there are cows to milk in the river fields," said Madame.

"I daresay; but Martin chooses to be frightened, and never did I see fool *more* frightened."

"You must not say a word about it to Carmilla, because she can see down that walk from her room window," I interposed, "and she is, if possible, a greater coward than I."

Carmilla came down rather later than usual that day.

"I was so frightened last night," she said, so soon as were together, "and I am sure I should have seen something dreadful if it had not been for that charm I bought from the poor little hunchback whom I called such hard names. I had a dream of something black coming round my bed, and I awoke in a perfect horror, and I really thought, for some seconds, I saw a dark figure near the chimney-piece, but I felt under my pillow for my charm, and the moment my fingers touched it, the figure disappeared, and I felt quite certain, only that I had it by me, that something frightful would have made its appearance, and, perhaps, throttled me, as it did those poor people we heard of."

"Well, listen to me," I began, and recounted my adventure, at the recital of which she appeared horrified.

"And had you the charm near you?" she asked, earnestly.

"No, I had dropped it into a china vase in the drawing-room, but I shall certainly take it with me to-night, as you have so much faith in it."

At this distance of time I cannot tell you, or even understand, how I overcame my horror so effectually as to lie alone in my room that night. I remember distinctly that I pinned the charm to my pillow. I fell asleep almost immediately, and slept even more soundly than usual all night.

Next night I passed as well. My sleep was delightfully deep and dreamless. But I wakened with a sense of lassitude and melancholy, which, however, did not exceed a degree that was almost luxurious.

"Well, I told you so," said Carmilla, when I described my quiet sleep, "I had such delightful sleep myself last night; I pinned the charm to the breast of my night-dress. It was too far away the night before. I am quite sure it was all fancy, except the dreams. I used to think that evil spirits made dreams, but our doctor told me it is no such thing. Only a fever passing by, or some other malady, as they often do, he said, knocks at the door, and not being able to get in, passes on, with that alarm."

"And what do you think the charm is?" said I.

"It has been fumigated or immersed in some drug, and is an antidote against the malaria," she answered. "Then it acts only on the body?"

"Certainly; you don't suppose that evil spirits are frightened by bits of ribbon, or the perfumes of a druggist's shop? No, these complaints, wandering in the air, begin by trying the nerves, and so infect the brain, but before they

can seize upon you, the antidote repels them. That I am sure is what the charm has done for us. It is nothing magical, it is simply natural."

I should have been happier if I could have quite agreed with Carmilla, but I did my best, and the impression was a little losing its force.

For some nights I slept profoundly; but still every morning I felt the same lassitude, and a languor weighed upon me all day. I felt myself a changed girl. A strange melancholy was stealing over me, a melancholy that I would not have interrupted. Dim thoughts of death began to open, and an idea that I was slowly sinking took gentle, and, somehow, not unwelcome, possession of me. If it was sad, the tone of mind which this induced was also sweet. Whatever it might be, my soul acquiesced in it.

I would not admit that I was ill, I would not consent to tell my papa, or to have the doctor sent for.

Carmilla became more devoted to me than ever, and her strange paroxysms of languid adoration more frequent. She used to gloat on me with increasing ardour the more my strength and spirits waned. This always shocked me like a momentary glare of insanity.

Without knowing it, I was now in a pretty advanced stage of the strangest illness under which mortal ever suffered. There was an unaccountable fascination in its earlier symptoms that more than reconciled me to the incapacitating effect of that stage of the malady. This fascination increased for a time, until it reached a certain point, when gradually a sense of the horrible mingled itself with it, deepening, as you shall hear, until it discoloured and perverted the whole state of my life.

The first change I experienced was rather agreeable. It was very near the turning point from which began the descent to Avernus.

Certain vague and strange sensations visited me in my sleep. The prevailing one was of that pleasant, peculiar cold thrill which we feel in bathing, when we move against the current of a river. This was soon accompanied by dreams that seemed interminable, and were so vague that I could never recollect their scenery and persons, or any one connected portion of their action. But they left an awful impression, and a sense of exhaustion, as if I had passed through a long period of great mental exertion and danger. After all these dreams there remained on waking a remembrance of having been in a place very nearly dark, and of having spoken to people whom I could not see; and especially of one clear voice, of a female, very deep, that spoke as if at a distance, slowly, and producing always the same sensation of indescribable solemnity and fear. Sometimes there came a sensation as if a hand was drawn softly along my cheek and neck. Sometimes it was as if warm lips kissed me, and longer and more lovingly as they reached my throat, but there the caress fixed itself. My heart beat faster, my breathing rose and fell rapidly and full drawn; a sobbing, that rose into a sense of strangulation, supervened, and turned into a dreadful convulsion, in which my senses left me and I became unconscious.

It was now three weeks since the commencement of this unaccountable state. My sufferings had, during the last week, told upon my appearance. I had grown pale, my eyes were dilated and darkened underneath, and the languor which I had long felt began to display itself in my countenance.

My father asked me often whether I was ill; but, with an obstinacy which now seems to me unaccountable, I persisted in assuring him that I was quite well.

In a sense this was true. I had no pain, I could complain of no bodily derangement. My complaint seemed to be one of the imagination, or the nerves, and, horrible as my sufferings were, I kept them, with a morbid reserve, very nearly to myself.

It could not be that terrible complaint which the peasants called the oupire, for I had now been suffering for three weeks, and they were seldom ill for much more than three days, when death put an end to their miseries.

Carmilla complained of dreams and feverish sensations, but by no means of so alarming a kind as mine. I say that mine were extremely alarming. Had I been capable of comprehending my condition, I would have invoked aid and advice on my knees. The narcotic of an unsuspected influence was acting upon me, and my perceptions were benumbed.

I am going to tell you now of a dream that led immediately to an odd discovery.

One night, instead of the voice I was accustomed to hear in the dark, I heard one, sweet and tender, and at the same time terrible, which said, "Your mother warns you to beware of the assassin." At the same time a light unexpectedly sprang up, and I saw Carmilla, standing, near the foot of my bed, in her white nightdress, bathed from her chin to her feet, in one great stain of blood.

I wakened with a shriek, possessed with the one idea that Carmilla was being murdered. I remember springing from my bed, and my next recollection is that of standing in the lobby, crying for help.

Madame and Mademoiselle came scurrying out of their rooms in alarm; a lamp burned always in the lobby, and seeing me, they soon learned the cause of my terror.

I insisted on our knocking at Carmilla's door. Our knocking was unanswered. It soon became a pounding and an uproar. We shrieked her name, but all was vain.

We all grew frightened, for the door was locked. We hurried back, in panic, to my room. There we rang the bell long and furiously. If my father's room had been at that side of the house, we would have called him up at once to our aid. But, alas! he was quite out of hearing, and to reach him involved an excursion for which none of us had courage.

Servants, however, soon came running up the stairs; I had got on my dressing-gown and slippers meanwhile, and my companions were already similarly furnished. Recognizing the voices of the servants on the lobby, we sallied out together; and having renewed, as fruitlessly, our summons at Carmilla's door, I ordered the men to force the lock. They did so, and we stood, holding our lights aloft, in the doorway, and so stared into the room.

We called her by name; but there was still no reply. We looked round the room. Everything was undisturbed. It was exactly in the state in which I had left it on bidding her goodnight. But Carmilla was gone.

Chapter VIII
Search

At sight of the room, perfectly undisturbed except for our violent entrance, we began to cool a little, and soon recovered our senses sufficiently to dismiss the men. It had struck Mademoiselle that possibly Carmilla had been wakened by the uproar at her door, and in her first panic had jumped from her bed, and hid herself in a press, or behind a curtain, from which she could not, of course, emerge until the majordomo and his myrmidons had withdrawn. We now recommenced our search, and began to call her by name again.

It was all to no purpose. Our perplexity and agitation increased. We examined the windows, but they were secured. I implored of Carmilla, if she had concealed herself, to play this cruel trick no longer—to come out, and to end our anxieties. It was all useless. I was by this time convinced that she was not in the room, nor in the dressing-room, the door of which was still locked on this side. She could not have passed it. I was utterly puzzled. Had Carmilla discovered one of those secret passages which the old housekeeper said were known to exist in the schloss, although the tradition of their exact situation had been lost. A little time would, no doubt, explain all—utterly perplexed as, for the present, we were.

It was past four o'clock, and I preferred passing the remaining hours of darkness in Madame's room. Daylight brought no solution of the difficulty.

The whole household, with my father at its head, was in a state of agitation next morning. Every part of the château was searched. The grounds were explored. Not a trace of the missing lady could be discovered. The stream was about to be dragged; my father was in distraction; what a tale to have to tell the poor girl's mother on her return. I, too, was almost beside myself, though my grief was quite of a different kind.

The morning was passed in alarm and excitement. It was now one o'clock, and still no tidings. I ran up to Carmilla's room, and found her standing at her dressing table. I was astounded. I could not believe my eyes. She beckoned me with her with her pretty finger, in silence. Her face expressed extreme fear.

I ran to her in an ecstasy of joy; I kissed and embraced her again and again. I ran to the bell and rang it vehemently, to bring others to the spot, who might at once relieve my father's anxiety.

"Dear Carmilla, what has become of you all this time? We have been in agonies of anxiety about you," I exclaimed. "Where have you been? How did you come back?"

"Last night has been a night of wonders," she said.

"For mercy's sake, explain all you can."

"It was past two last night," she said, "when I went to sleep as usual in my bed, with my doors locked, that of the dressing-room, and that opening upon the gallery. My sleep was uninterrupted, and, so far as I know, dreamless; but I awoke just now on the sofa in the dressing-room there, and I found the door between the rooms open, and the other door forced. How could all this have happened without my being wakened? It must have been accompanied with a great deal of noise, and I am particularly easily wakened; and how could I have been carried out of my bed without my sleep having been interrupted, I whom the slightest stir startles?"

By this time, Madame, Mademoiselle, my father, and a number of the servants were in the room. Carmilla was, of course, overwhelmed with inquiries, congratulations, and welcomes. She had but one story to tell, and seemed the least able of all the party to suggest any way of accounting for what had happened.

My father took a turn up and down the room, thinking. I saw Carmilla's eye follow him for a moment with a sly, dark glance.

When my father had sent the servants away, Mademoiselle having gone in search of a little bottle of valerian and sal-volatile, and there being no one now in the room with Carmilla, except my father, Madame, and myself, he came to her thoughtfully, took her hand very kindly, led her to the sofa, and sat down beside her.

"Will you forgive me, my dear, if I risk a conjecture, and ask a question?"

"Who can have a better right?' she said. "Ask what you please, and I will tell you everything. But my story is simply one of bewilderment and darkness. I know absolutely nothing. Put any question you please. But you know, of course, the limitations mamma has placed me under."

"Perfectly, my dear child. I need not approach the topics on which she desires our silence. Now, the marvel of last night consists in your having been removed from your bed and your room, without being wakened, and this removal having occurred apparently while the windows were still secured, and the two doors locked upon the inside. I will tell you my theory, and first ask you a question."

Carmilla was leaning on her hand dejectedly; Madame and I were listening breathlessly.

"Now, my question is this. Have you ever been walking in your sleep?"

"Never, since I was very young indeed."

"But you did walk in your sleep when you were young?"

"Yes; I know I did. I have been told so often by my nurse." My father smiled and nodded.

"Well, what has happened is this. You got up in your sleep, unlocked the door, not leaving the key, as usual, in the lock, but taking it out and locking it on the outside; you again took the key out, and carried it away with you to some one of the five-and-twenty rooms on this floor, or perhaps up-stairs or down-stairs. There are so many rooms and closets, so much heavy furniture, and such accumulations of lumber, that it would require a week to search this old house thoroughly. Do you see, now, what I mean?"

"I do, but not all," she answered.

"And how, papa, do you account for her finding herself on the sofa in the dressing-room, which we had searched so carefully?"

"She came there after you had searched it, still in her sleep, and at last awoke spontaneously, and was as much surprised to find herself where she was as any one else. I wish all mysteries were as easily and innocently explained as yours, Carmilla," he said, laughing. "And so we may congratulate ourselves on the certainty that the most natural explanation of the occurrence is one that involves no drugging, no tampering with locks, no burglars, or poisoners, or witches—nothing that need alarm Carmilla, or any one else, for our safety."

Carmilla was looking charmingly. Nothing could be more beautiful than her tints. Her beauty was, I think, enhanced by that graceful languor that was peculiar to her. I think my father was silently contrasting her looks with mine, for he said:

"I wish my poor Laura was looking more like herself" and he sighed.

So our alarms were happily ended, and Carmilla restored to her friends.

Chapter IX
The Doctor

As Carmilla would not hear of an attendant sleeping in her room, my father arranged that a servant should sleep outside her door, so that she could not attempt to make another such excursion without being arrested at her own door.

That night passed quietly; and next morning early, the doctor, whom my father had sent for without telling me a word about it, arrived to see me. Madame accompanied me to the library; and there the grave little doctor, with white hair and spectacles, whom I mentioned before, was waiting to receive me.

I told him my story, and as I proceeded he grew graver and graver. We were standing, he and I, in the recess of one of the windows, facing one another. When my statement was over, he leaned with his shoulders against the wall, and with his eyes fixed on me earnestly, with an interest in which was a dash of horror.

After a minute's reflection, he asked Madame if he could see my father.

He was sent for accordingly, and as he entered, smiling, he said:

"I dare say, doctor, you are going to tell me that I am an old fool for having brought you here; I hope I am."

But his smile faded into shadow as the doctor, with a very grave face, beckoned him to him.

He and the doctor talked for some time in the same recess where I had just conferred with the physician. It seemed an earnest and argumentative conversation. The room is very large, and I and Madame stood together, burning with curiosity, at the further end. Not a word could we hear, however, for they spoke in a very low tone, and the deep recess of the window quite concealed the doctor from view, and very nearly my father, whose foot, arm, and shoulder only could we see; and the voices were, I suppose, all the less audible for the sort of closet which the thick wall and window formed.

After a time my father's face looked into the room; it was pale, thoughtful, and, I fancied, agitated.

"Laura, dear, come here for a moment. Madame, we shan't trouble you, the doctor says, at present."

Accordingly I approached, for the first time a little alarmed; for, although I felt very weak, I did not feel ill; and strength, one always fancies, is a thing that may be picked up when we please.

My father held out his hand to me, as I drew near, but he was looking at the doctor, and he said:

"It certainly *is* very odd; I don't understand it quite. Laura, come here, dear; now attend to Doctor Spielsberg, and recollect yourself."

"You mentioned a sensation like that of two needles piercing the skin, somewhere about your neck, on the night when you experienced your first horrible dream. Is there still any soreness?"

"None at all," I answered.

"Can you indicate with your finger about the point at which you think this occurred?"

"Very little below my throat—here," I answered.

I wore a morning dress, which covered the place I pointed to.

"Now you can satisfy yourself," said the doctor. "You won't mind your papa's lowering your dress a very little. It is necessary, to detect a symptom of the complaint under which you have been suffering."

I acquiesced. It was only an inch or two below the edge of my collar.

"God bless me!—so it is," exclaimed my father, growing pale.

"You see it now with your own eyes," said the doctor, with a gloomy triumph.

"What is it?" I exclaimed, beginning to be frightened.

"Nothing, my dear young lady, but a small blue spot, about the size of the tip of your little finger; and now," he continued, turning to papa, "the question is, what is best to be done?"

"Is there any danger?" I urged, in great trepidation.

"I trust not, my dear," answered the doctor. "I don't see why you should not recover. I don't see why you should not begin immediately to get better. That is the point at which the sense of strangulation begins?"

"Yes," I answered. "And—recollect as well as you can—the same point was a kind of centre of that thrill which you described just now, like the current of a cold stream running against you?"

"It may have been; I think it was."

"Ay, you see?" he added, turning to my father. "Shall I say a word to Madame?"

"Certainly," said my father.

He called Madame to him, and said:

"I find my young friend here far from well. It won't be of any great consequence, I hope; but it will be necessary that some steps be taken, which I will explain by-and-bye; but in the meantime, Madame, you will be so good as not to let Miss Laura be alone for one moment. That is the only direction I need give for the present. It is indispensable."

"We may rely upon your kindness, Madame, I know," added my father. Madame satisfied him eagerly.

"And you, dear Laura, I know you will observe the doctor's direction."

"I shall have to ask your opinion upon another patient, whose symptoms slightly resemble those of my daughter, that have just been detailed to you—very much milder in degree, but I believe quite of the same sort. She is a young lady—our guest; but as you say you will be passing this way again this evening, you can't do better than take your supper here, and. you can then see her. She does not come down till the afternoon."

"I thank you," said the doctor. "I shall be with you, then, at about seven this evening."

And then they repeated their directions to me and to Madame, and with this parting charge my father left us, and walked out with the doctor; and I saw them pacing together up and down between the road and the moat, on the grassy platform in front of the castle, evidently absorbed in earnest conversation.

The doctor did not return. I saw him mount his horse there, take his leave, and ride away eastward through the forest.

Nearly at the same time I saw the man arrive from Dranfeld with the letters, and dismount and hand the bag to my father.

In the meantime, Madame and I were both busy, lost in conjecture as to the reasons of the singular and earnest direction which  the doctor and my father had concurred in imposing. Madame, as she afterwards told me, was afraid the doctor apprehended a sudden seizure, and that, without prompt assistance, I might either lose my life in a fit, or at least be seriously hurt.

This interpretation did not strike me; and I fancied, perhaps luckily for my nerves, that the arrangement was prescribed simply to secure a companion, who would prevent my taking too much exercise, or eating unripe fruit, or doing any of the fifty foolish things to which young people are supposed to be prone.

About half-an-hour after my father came in—he had a letter in his hand—and said:

"This letter has been delayed; it is from General Spielsdorf. He might have been here yesterday, he may not come till tomorrow, or he may be here to-day."

He put the open letter into my hand; but he did not look pleased, as he used when a guest, especially one so much loved as the General, was coming. On the contrary, he looked as if he wished him at the bottom of the Red Sea. There was plainly something on his mind which he did not choose to divulge.

"Papa, darling, will you tell me this?" said I, suddenly laying my hand on his arm, and looking, I am sure, imploringly in his face.

"Perhaps," he answered, smoothing my hair caressingly over my eyes.

"Does the doctor think me very ill?"

"No, dear; he thinks, if right steps are taken, you will be quite well again, at least, on the high road to a complete recovery, in a day or two," he answered, a little drily. I wish our good friend, the General, had chosen any other time; that is, I wish you had been perfectly well to receive him."

"But do tell me, papa," I insisted, "what does he think is the matter with me?"

"Nothing; you must not plague me with questions," he answered, with more irritation than I ever remember him to have displayed before; and seeing that I looked wounded, I suppose, he kissed me, and added, "You shall know all about it in a day or two; that is, all that I know. In the meantime you are not to trouble your head about it."

He turned and left the room, but came back before I had done wondering and puzzling over the oddity of all this; it was merely to say that he was going to Karnstein, and had ordered the carriage to be ready at twelve, and that I and Madame should accompany him; he was going to see the priest who lived near those picturesque grounds, upon business, and as Carmilla had never seen them, she could follow, when she came down, with Mademoiselle, who would bring materials for what you call a picnic, which might be laid for us in the ruined castle.

At twelve o'clock, accordingly, I was ready, and not long after, my father, Madame and I set out upon our projected drive.

Passing the drawbridge we turn to the right, and follow the road over the steep Gothic bridge, westward, to reach the deserted village and ruined castle of Karnstein.

No sylvan drive can be fancied prettier. The ground breaks into gentle hills and hollows, all clothed with beautiful woods, totally destitute of the comparative formality which artificial planting and early culture and pruning impart.

The irregularities of the ground often lead the road out of its course, and cause it to wind beautifully round the sides of broken hollows and the steeper sides of the hills, among varieties of ground almost inexhaustible.

Turning one of these points, we suddenly encountered our old friend, the General, riding towards us, attended by a mounted servant. His portmanteaus were following in a hired waggon, such as we term a cart.

The General dismounted as we pulled up, and, after the usual greetings, was easily persuaded to accept the vacant seat in the carriage, and send his horse on with his servant to the schloss.

Chapter X
Bereaved

It was about ten months since we had last seen him; but that time had sufficed to make an alteration of years in his appearance. He had grown thinner; something of gloom and anxiety had taken the place of that cordial serenity which used to characterize his features. His dark blue eyes, always penetrating, now gleamed with a sterner light from under his shaggy grey eyebrows. It was not such a change as grief alone usually induces, and angrier passions seemed to have had their share in bringing it about.

We had not long resumed our drive, when the General began to talk, with his usual soldierly directness, of the bereavement, as he termed it, which he had sustained in the death of his beloved niece and ward; and he then broke out in a tone of intense bitterness and fury, inveighing against the "hellish arts" to which she had fallen a victim, and expressing, with more exasperation than piety, his wonder that Heaven should tolerate so monstrous an indulgence of the lusts and malignity of hell.

My father, who saw at once that something very extraordinary had befallen, asked him, if not too painful to him, to detail the circumstances which he thought justified the strong terms in which he expressed himself.

"I should tell you all with pleasure," said the General, "but you would not believe me."

"Why should I not?" he asked.

"Because," he answered testily, "you believe in nothing but what consists with your own prejudices and illusions. I remember when I was like you, but I have learned better."

"Try me," said my father; "I am not such a dogmatist as you suppose. Besides which, I very well know that you generally require proof for what you believe, and am, therefore, very strongly pre-disposed to respect your conclusions."

"You are right in supposing that I have not been led lightly into a belief in the marvellous—for what I have experienced *is* marvellous—and I have been forced by extraordinary evidence to credit that which ran counter, diametrically, to all my theories. I have been made the dupe of a preternatural conspiracy."

Notwithstanding his professions of confidence in the General's penetration, I saw my father, at this point, glance at the General, with, as I thought, a marked suspicion of his sanity.

The General did not see it, luckily. He was looking gloomily and curiously into the glades and vistas of the woods that were opening before us.

"You are going to the ruins of Karnstein?" he said. "Yes, it is a lucky coincidence; do you know I was going to ask you to bring me there to inspect them. I have a special object in exploring. There is a ruined chapel, ain't there, with a great many tombs of that extinct family?"

"So there are—highly interesting," said my father. "I hope you are thinking of claiming the title and estates?"

My father said this gaily, but the General did not recollect the laugh, or even the smile, which courtesy exacts for a friend's joke; on the contrary, he looked grave and even fierce, ruminating on a matter that stirred his anger and horror.

"Something very different," he said, gruffly. "I mean to unearth some of those fine people. I hope, by God's blessing, to accomplish a pious sacrilege here, which will relieve our earth of certain monsters, and enable honest people to sleep in their beds without being assailed by murderers. I have strange things to tell you, my dear friend, such as I myself would have scorned as incredible a few months since."

My father looked at him again, but this time not with a glance of suspicion—with an eye, rather, of keen intelligence and alarm.

"The house of Karnstein," he said, "has been long extinct a hundred years at least. My dear wife was maternally descended from the Karnsteins. But the name and title have long ceased to exist. The castle is a ruin; the very village is deserted; it is fifty years since the smoke of a chimney was seen there; not a roof left."

"Quite true. I have heard a great deal about that since I last saw you; a great deal that will astonish you. But I had better relate everything in the order in which it occurred," said the General.

"You saw my dear ward—my child, I may call her. No creature could have been more beautiful, and only three months ago none more blooming."

"Yes, poor thing! When I saw her last she certainly was quite lovely," said my father. "I was grieved and shocked more than I can tell you, my dear friend; I knew what a blow it was to you."

He took the General's hand, and they exchanged a kind pressure. Tears gathered in the old soldier's eyes. He did not seek to conceal them. He said:

"We have been very old friends; I knew you would feel for me, childless as I am. She had become an object of very near interest to me, and repaid my care by an affection that cheered my home and made my life happy. That is all gone. The years that remain to me on earth may not be very long; but by God's mercy I hope to accomplish a service to mankind before I die, and to subserve the vengeance of Heaven upon the fiends who have murdered my poor child in the spring of her hopes and beauty!"

"You said, just now, that you intended relating everything as it occurred," said my father. "Pray do; I assure you that it is not mere curiosity that prompts me."

By this time we had reached the point at which the Drunstall road, by which the General had come, diverges from the road which we were travelling to Karnstein.

"How far is it to the ruins?" inquired the General, looking anxiously forward.

"About half a league," answered my father. "Pray let us hear the story you were so good as to promise."

Chapter XI
The Story

"With all my heart," said the General, with an effort; and after a short pause in which to arrange his subject, he commenced one of the strangest narratives I ever heard.

"My dear child was looking forward with great pleasure to the visit you had been so good as to arrange for her to your charming daughter." Here he made me a gallant but melancholy bow. "In the meantime we had an invitation to my old friend the Count Carlsfeld, whose schloss is about six leagues to the other side of Karnstein. It was to attend the series of fêtes which, you remember, were given by him in honour of his illustrious visitor, the Grand Duke Charles."

"Yes; and very splendid, I believe, they were," said my father.

"Princely! But then his hospitalities are quite regal. He has Aladdin's lamp. The night from which my sorrow dates was devoted to a magnificent masquerade. The grounds were thrown open, the trees hung with coloured lamps. There was such a display of fireworks as Paris itself had never witnessed. And such music—music, you know, is my weakness—such ravishing music! The finest instrumental band, perhaps, in the world, and the finest singers who could be collected from all the great operas in Europe. As you wandered through these fantastically illuminated grounds, the moon-lighted château throwing a rosy light from its long rows of windows, you would suddenly hear these ravishing voices stealing from the silence of some grove, or rising from boats upon the lake. I felt myself, as I looked and listened, carried back into the romance and poetry of my early youth.

"When the fireworks were ended, and the ball beginning, we returned to the noble suite of rooms that were thrown open to the dancers. A masked ball, you know, is a beautiful sight; but so brilliant a spectacle of the kind I never saw before.

"It was a very aristocratic assembly. I was myself almost the only 'nobody' present.

"My dear child was looking quite beautiful. She wore no mask. Her excitement and delight added an unspeakable charm to her features, always lovely. I remarked a young lady, dressed magnificently, but wearing a mask, who appeared to me to be observing my ward with extraordinary interest. I had seen her, earlier in the evening, in the great hall, and again, for a few minutes, walking near us, on the terrace under the castle windows, similarly employed. A lady, also masked, richly and gravely dressed, and with a stately air, like a person of rank, accompanied her as a chaperon. Had the young lady not worn a mask, I could, of course, have been much more certain upon the question whether she was really watching my poor darling. I am now well assured that she was.

"We were now in one of the *salons*. My poor dear child had been dancing, and was resting a little in one of the chairs near the door; I was standing near. The two ladies I have mentioned had approached, and the younger took the chair next my ward; while her companion stood beside me, and for a little time addressed herself, in a low tone, to her charge.

"Availing herself of the privilege of her mask, she turned to me, and in the tone of an old friend, and calling me by my name, opened a conversation with me, which piqued my curiosity a good deal. She referred to many scenes where she had met me—at Court, and at distinguished houses. She alluded to little incidents which I had long ceased to think of, but which, I found, had only lain in abeyance in my memory, for they instantly started into life at her touch.

"I became more and more curious to ascertain who she was, every moment. She parried my attempts to discover very adroitly and pleasantly. The knowledge she showed of many passages in my life seemed to me all but unaccountable; and she appeared to take a not unnatural pleasure in foiling my curiosity, and in seeing me flounder, in my eager perplexity, from one conjecture to another.

"In the meantime the young lady, whom her mother called by the odd name of Millarca, when she once or twice addressed her, had, with the same ease and grace, got into conversation with my ward.

"She introduced herself by saying that her mother was a very old acquaintance of mine. She spoke of the agreeable audacity which a mask rendered practicable; she talked like a friend; she admired her dress, and insinuated very prettily her admiration of her beauty. She amused her with laughing criticisms

upon the people who crowded the ballroom, and laughed at my poor child's fun. She was very witty and lively when she pleased, and after a time they had grown very good friends, and the young stranger lowered her mask, displaying a remarkably beautiful face. I had never seen it before, neither had my dear child. But though it was new to us, the features were so engaging, as well as lovely, that it was impossible not to feel the attraction powerfully. My poor girl did so. I never saw anyone more taken with another at first sight, unless, indeed, it was the stranger herself, who seemed quite to have lost her heart to her.

"In the meantime, availing myself of the licence of a masquerade, I put not a few questions to the elder lady.

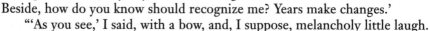

"'You have puzzled me utterly,' I said, laughing. 'Is that not enough? Won't you, now, consent to stand on equal term, and do me the kindness to remove your mask?'

"'Can any request be more unreasonable? she replied. 'Ask a lady to yield an advantage! Beside, how do you know should recognize me? Years make changes.'

"'As you see,' I said, with a bow, and, I suppose, melancholy little laugh.

"'As philosophers tell us,' she said; 'and how do you think that a sight of my face would help you?'

"'I should take chance for that,' I answered. 'It is trying to make yourself out an old woman; your figure belies you.'

"'Years, nevertheless, have passed since I saw you, since you saw me, for that is what I am considering. The young lady there, is my daughter; I cannot then be young, even in opinion of people whom time has taught to be indulgent, I may not like to be compared with what you remember me. You have no mask to remove. You can offer me nothing in exchange.'

"'My petition is to your pity, to remove it.'

"'And mine to yours, to let it stay where it is,' she replied.

"'Well, then, at least you will tell me whether you are French or German; you speak both languages so perfectly.'

"'I don't think I shall tell you that, General; you intend a surprise, and are meditating the particular point of attack.'

"'At all events, you won't deny this,' I said, 'that being honoured by your permission to converse, I ought to know how to address you. Shall I say Madame la Comtesse?'

"She laughed, and she would, no doubt, have met me with another evasion—if, indeed, I can treat any occurrence in an interview every circumstance of which was pre-arranged, as I now believe, with the profoundest cunning, as liable to be modified by accident.

"'As to that,' she began; but she was interrupted, almost as she opened her lips, by a gentleman, dressed in black, who looked particularly elegant and distinguished, with this drawback, that his face was the most deadly pale I ever saw, except in death. He was in no masquerade—in the plain evening dress of a gentleman; and he said, without a smile, but with a courtly and unusually low bow:—

"'Will Madame la Comtesse permit me to say a very few words which may interest her?'

"The lady turned quickly to him, and touched her lip in token of silence; she then said to me, 'Keep my place for me, General; I shall return when I have said a few words.'

"And with this injunction, playfully given, she walked a little aside with the gentleman in black, and talked for some minutes, apparently very earnestly. They then walked away slowly together in the crowd, and I lost them for some minutes.

"I spent the interval in cudgelling my brains for a conjecture as to the identity of the lady who seemed to remember me so kindly, and I was thinking of turning about and joining in the conversation between my pretty ward and the Countess's daughter, and trying whether, by the time she returned, I might not have a surprise in store for her, by having her name, title, château, and estates at my fingers' ends. But at this moment she returned, accompanied by the pale man in black, who said:

"'I shall return and inform Madame la Comtesse when her carriage is at the door.'

"He withdrew with a bow."

Chapter XII
A Petition

"'Then we are to lose Madame la Comtesse, but I hope only for a few hours,' I said, with a low bow.

"It may be that only, or it may be a few weeks. It was very unlucky his speaking to me just now as he did. Do you now know me?'

"I assured her I did not.

"'You shall know me,' she said, 'but not at present. We are older and better friends than, perhaps, you suspect. I cannot yet declare myself. I shall in three weeks pass your beautiful schloss, about which I have been making enquiries. I shall then look in upon you for an hour or two, and renew a friendship which I never think of without a thousand pleasant recollections. This moment a piece of news has reached me like a thunderbolt. I must set out now, and travel by a devious route, nearly a hundred miles, with all the dispatch I can possibly make. My

perplexities multiply. I am only deterred by the compulsory reserve I practise as to my name from making a very singular request of you. My poor child has not quite recovered her strength. Her horse fell with her, at a hunt which she had ridden out to witness, her nerves have not yet recovered the shock, and our physician says that she must on no account exert herself for some time to come. We came here, in consequence, by very easy stages—hardly six leagues a day. I must now travel day and night, on a mission of life and death—a mission the critical and momentous nature of which I shall be able to explain to you when we meet, as I hope we shall, in a few weeks, without the necessity of any concealment.'

"She went on to make her petition, and it was in the tone of a person from whom such a request amounted to conferring, rather than seeking a favour. This was only in manner, and, as it seemed, quite unconsciously. Than the terms in which it was expressed, nothing could be more deprecatory. It was simply that I would consent to take charge of her daughter during her absence.

"This was, all things considered, a strange, not to say, an audacious request. She in some sort disarmed me, by stating and admitting everything that could be urged against it, and throwing herself entirely upon my chivalry. At the same moment, by a fatality that seems to have predetermined all that happened, my poor child came to my side, and, in an undertone, besought me to invite her new friend, Millarca, to pay us a visit. She had just been sounding her, and thought, if her mamma would allow her, she would like it extremely.

"At another time I should have told her to wait a little, until, at least, we knew who they were. But I had not a moment to think in. The two ladies assailed me together, and I must confess the refined and beautiful face of the young lady, about which there was something extremely engaging, as well as the elegance and fire of high birth, determined me; and, quite overpowered, I submitted, and undertook, too easily, the care of the young lady, whom her mother called Millarca.

"The Countess beckoned to her daughter, who listened with grave attention while she told her, in general terms, how suddenly and peremptorily she had been summoned, and also of the arrangement she had made for her under my care, adding that I was one of her earliest and most valued friends.

"I made, of course, such speeches as the case seemed to call for, and found myself, on reflection, in a position which I did not half like.

"The gentleman in black returned, and very ceremoniously conducted the lady from the room.

"The demeanour of this gentleman was such as to impress me with the conviction that the Countess was a lady of very much more importance than

her modest title alone might have led me to assume.

"Her last charge to me was that no attempt was to be made to learn more about her than I might have already guessed, until her return. Our distinguished host, whose guest she was, knew her reasons.

"'But here,' she said, 'neither I nor my daughter could safely remain for more than a day. I removed my mask imprudently for a moment, about an hour ago, and, too late, I fancied you saw me. So I resolved to seek an opportunity of talking a little to you. Had I found that you had seen me, I should have thrown myself on your high sense of honour to keep my secret for some weeks. As it is, I am satisfied that you did not see me; but if you now *suspect*, or, on reflection, *should* suspect, who I am, I commit myself, in like manner, entirely to your honour. My daughter will observe the same secrecy, and I well know that you will, from time to time, remind her, lest she should thoughtlessly disclose it.'

"She whispered a few words to her daughter, kissed her hurriedly twice, and went away, accompanied by the pale gentleman in black, and disappeared in the crowd.

"'In the next room,' said Millarca, 'there is a window that looks upon the hall door. I should like to see the last of mamma, and to kiss my hand to her.'

"We assented, of course, and accompanied her to the window. We looked out, and saw a handsome old-fashioned carriage, with a troop of couriers and footmen. We saw the slim figure of the pale gentleman in black, as he held a thick velvet cloak, and placed it about her shoulders and threw the hood over her head. She nodded to him, and just touched his hand with hers. He bowed low repeatedly as the door closed, and the carriage began to move.

"'She is gone,' said Millarca, with a sigh.

"'She is gone,' I repeated to myself, for the first time—in the hurried moments that had elapsed since my consent—reflecting upon the folly of my act.

"'She did not look up,' said the young lady, plaintively.

"'The Countess had taken off her mask, perhaps, and did not care to show her face,' I said; 'and she could not know that you were in the window.'

"She sighed, and looked in my face. She was so beautiful that I relented. I was sorry I had for a moment repented of my hospitality, and I determined to make her amends for the unavowed churlishness of my reception.

"The young lady, replacing her mask, joined my ward in persuading me to return to the grounds, where the concert was soon to be renewed. We did so, and walked up and down the terrace that lies under the castle windows. Millarca became very intimate with us, and amused us with lively descriptions and stories of most of the great people whom we saw upon the terrace. I liked her more and more every minute. Her gossip, without being ill-natured, was extremely diverting to me, who had been so long out of the great world. I thought what life she would give to our sometimes lonely evenings at home.

"This ball was not over until the morning sun had almost reached the horizon. It pleased the Grand Duke to dance till then, so loyal people could not go away, or think of bed.

"We had just got through a crowded salon, when my ward asked me what had become of Millarca. I thought she had been by her side, and she fancied she was by mine. The fact was, we had lost her.

"All my efforts to find her were vain. I feared that she had mistaken, in the confusion of a momentary separation from us, other people for her new friends, and had, possibly, pursued and lost them in the extensive grounds which were thrown open to us.

"Now, in its full force, I recognised a new folly in my having undertaken the charge of a young lady without so much as knowing her name; and lettered as I was by promises, of the reasons for imposing which I knew nothing, I could not even point my inquiries by saying that the missing young lady was the daughter of the Countess who had taken her departure a few hours before.

"Morning broke. It was clear daylight before I gave up my search. It was not till near two o'clock next day that we heard anything of my missing charge.

"At about that time a servant knocked at my niece's door, to say that he had been earnestly requested by a young lady, who appeared to be in great distress, to make out where she could find the General Baron Spieldsdorf and the young lady his daughter, in whose charge she had been left by her mother.

"There could be no doubt, notwithstanding the slight inaccuracy, that our young friend had turned up; and so she had. Would to heaven we had lost her!

"She told my poor child a story to account for her having failed to recover us for so long. Very late, she said, she had got to the housekeeper's bedroom in despair of finding us, and had then fallen into a deep sleep which, long as it was, had hardly sufficed to recruit her strength after the fatigues of the ball.

"That day Millarca came home with us. I was only too happy, after all, to have secured so charming a companion for my dear girl.

Chapter XIII
The Woodman

"There soon, however, appeared some drawbacks. In the first place, Millarca complained of extreme languor—the weakness that remained after her late illness—and she never emerged from her room till the afternoon was pretty far advanced. In the next place, it was accidentally discovered, although she always locked her door on the inside, and never disturbed the key from its place till she admitted the maid to assist at her toilet, that she was undoubtedly sometimes absent from her room in the very early morning, and at various times

later in the day, before she wished it to be understood that she was stirring. She was repeatedly seen
from the windows of the schloss, in the first faint
grey of the morning, walking through the trees, in
an easterly direction, and looking like a person in
a trance. This convinced me that she walked in her
sleep. But this hypothesis did not solve the puzzle.
How did she pass out from her room, leaving the
door locked on the inside? How did she escape
from the house without unbarring door or win-
dow?

"In the midst of my perplexities, an anxiety of a far more urgent kind presented itself.

"My dear child began to lose her looks and health, and that in a manner
so mysterious, and even horrible, that I became thoroughly frightened.

"She was at first visited by appalling dreams; then, as she fancied, by a spectre, sometimes resembling Millarca, sometimes in the shape of a beast, indis-
tinctly seen, walking round the foot of her bed, from side to side. Lastly came
sensations. One, not unpleasant, but very peculiar, she said, resembled the flow
of an icy stream against her breast. At a later time, she felt something like a
pair of large needles pierce her, a little below the throat, with a very sharp pain.
A few nights after, followed a gradual and convulsive sense of strangulation;
then came unconsciousness."

I could hear distinctly every word the kind old General was saying, because
by this time we were driving upon the short grass that spreads on either side
of the road as you approach the roofless village which had not shown the smoke
of a chimney for more than half a century.

You may guess how strangely I felt as I heard my own symptoms so exactly
described in those which had been experienced by the poor girl who, but for
the catastrophe which followed, would have been at that moment a visitor at
my father's château. You may suppose, also, how I felt as I heard him detail
habits and mysterious peculiarities which were, in fact, those of our beautiful
guest, Carmilla!

A vista opened in the forest; we were on a sudden under the chimneys and
gables of the ruined village, and the towers and battlements of the disman-
tled castle, round which gigantic trees are grouped, overhung us from a slight
eminence.

In a frightened dream I got down from the carriage, and in silence, for
we had each abundant matter for thinking; we soon mounted the ascent, and
were among the spacious chambers, winding stairs, and dark corridors of the
castle.

"And this was once the palatial residence of the Karnsteins!" said the old
General at length, as from a great window he looked out across the village,

and saw the wide, undulating expanse of forest. "It was a bad family, and here its bloodstained annals were written," he continued. "It is hard that they should, after death, continue to plague the human race with their atrocious lusts. That is the chapel of the Karnsteins, down there."

He pointed down to the grey walls of the Gothic building, partly visible through the foliage, a little way down the steep. "And I hear the axe of a woodman," he added, "busy among the trees that surround it; he possibly may give us the information of which I am in search, and point out the grave of Mircalla, Countess of Karnstein. These rustics preserve the local traditions of great families, whose stories die out among the rich and titled so soon as the families themselves become extinct."

"We have a portrait, at home, of Mircalla, the Countess Karnstein; should you like to see it?" asked my father.

"Time enough, dear friend," replied the General. "I believe that I have seen the original; and one motive which has led me to you earlier than I at first intended, was to explore the chapel which we are now approaching."

"What! see the Countess Mircalla," exclaimed my father; "why, she has been dead more than a century!"

"Not so dead as you fancy, I am told," answered the General.

"I confess, General, you puzzle me utterly," replied my father, looking at him, I fancied, for a moment with a return of the suspicion I detected before. But although there was anger and detestation, at times, in the old General's manner, there was nothing flighty.

"There remains to me," he said, as we passed under the heavy arch of the Gothic church—for its dimensions would have justified its being so styled—"but one object which can interest me during the few years that remain to me on earth, and that is to wreak on her the vengeance which, I thank God, may still be accomplished by a mortal arm."

"What vengeance can you mean?" asked my father, increasing amazement.

"I mean, to decapitate the monster," he answered, with a fierce flush, and a stamp that echoed mournfully through the hollow ruin, and his clenched hand was at the same moment raised, as if it grasped the handle of an axe, while he shook it ferociously in the air.

"What?" exclaimed my father, more than ever bewildered.

"To strike her head off."

"Cut her head off!"

"Aye, with a hatchet, with a spade, or with anything that can cleave through her murderous throat. You shall hear," answered, trembling with rage. And

hurrying forward he said:

"That beam will answer for a seat; your dear child is fatigued; let her be seated, and I will, in a few sentences, close my dreadful story."

The squared block of wood, which lay on the grass-grown pavement of the chapel, formed a bench on which I was very glad to seat myself, and in the meantime the General called to the woodman, who had been removing some boughs which leaned upon the old walls; and, axe in hand, the hardy old fellow stood before us.

He could not tell us anything of these monuments; but there was an old man, he said, a ranger of this forest, at present sojourning in the house of the priest, about two miles away, who could point out every monument of the old Karnstein family; and, for a trifle, he undertook to bring him back with him, if we would lend him one of our horses, in little more than half-an-hour.

"Have you been long employed about this forest?" asked my father of the old man.

"I have been a woodman here," he answered in his *patois*, "under the forester, all my days; so has my father before me, and so on, as many generations as I can count up. I could show you the very house in the village here, in which my ancestors lived."

"How came the village to be deserted?" asked the General.

"It was troubled by *revenants*, sir; several were tracked to their graves, there detected by the usual tests, and extinguished in the usual way, by decapitation, by the stake, and by burning; but not until many of the villagers were killed.

"But after all these proceedings according to law," he continued—"so many graves opened, and so many vampires deprived of their horrible ani-

Magic circle attributed to Honorius.

mation—the village was not relieved. But a Moravian nobleman, who happened to be travelling this way, heard how matters were, and being skilled—as many people are in his country—in such affairs, he offered to deliver the village from its tormentor. He did so thus: There being a bright moon that night, he ascended, shortly after sunset, the tower of the chapel here, from whence he could distinctly see the churchyard beneath him; you can see it from that window. From this point he watched until he saw the vampire come out of his grave, and place near it the linen clothes in which he had been folded, and then glide away towards the village to plague its inhabitants.

"The stranger, having seen all this, came down from the steeple, took the linen wrappings of the vampire, and carried them up to the top of the tower, which he again mounted. When the vampire returned from his prowlings and missed his clothes, he cried furiously to the Moravian, whom he saw at the summit of the tower, and who, in reply, beckoned him to ascend and take them. Whereupon the vampire, accepting his invitation, began to climb the steeple, and so soon as he had reached the battlements, the Moravian, with a stroke of his sword, clove his skull in twain, hurling him down to the churchyard, whither, descending by the winding stairs, the stranger followed and cut his head off, and next day delivered it and the body to the villagers, who duly impaled and burnt them.

"This Moravian nobleman had authority from the then head of the family to remove the tomb of Mircalla, Countess Karnstein, which he did effectually, so that in a little while its site was quite forgotten."

"Can you point out where it stood?" asked the General, eagerly.

The forester shook his head and smiled.

"Not a soul living could tell you that now," he said; "besides, they say her body was removed; but no one is sure of that either."

Having thus spoken, as time pressed, he dropped his axe and departed, leaving us to hear the remainder of the General's strange story.

Chapter XIV
The Meeting

"My beloved child," he resumed, "was now growing rapidly worse. The physician who attended her had failed to produce the slightest impression upon her disease, for such I then supposed it to be. He saw my alarm, and suggested a consultation. I called in an abler physician, from Gratz. Several days elapsed before he arrived. He was a good and pious, as well as a learned man. Having seen my poor ward together, they withdrew to my library to confer and discuss. I, from the adjoining room, where I awaited their summons, heard these two gentlemen's voices raised in something sharper than a strictly philosophical discussion. I knocked at the door and entered. I found the old physician from Gratz maintaining his theory. His rival was combating it with undisguised ridicule, accompanied with bursts of laughter. This unseemly manifestation subsided and the altercation ended on my entrance.

"'Sir,' said my first physician, 'my learned brother seems to think that you want a conjuror, and not a doctor.'

"'Pardon me,' said the old physician from Gratz, looking displeased, 'I shall state my own view of the case in my own way another time. I grieve, Monsieur le Général, that by my skill and science I can be of no use. Before I go I shall do myself the honour to suggest something to you.'

"He seemed thoughtful, and sat down at a table and began to write. Profoundly disappointed, I made my bow, and as I turned to go, the other doctor pointed over his shoulder to his companion who was writing, and then, with a shrug, significantly touched his forehead.

"This consultation, then, left me precisely where I was. I walked out into the grounds, all but distracted. The doctor from Gratz, in ten or fifteen minutes, overtook me. He apologized for having followed me, but said that he could not conscientiously take his leave without a few words more. He told me that he could not be mistaken; no natural disease exhibited the same symptoms; and that death was already very near. There remained, however, a day, or possibly two, of life. If the fatal seizure were at once arrested, with great care and skill her strength might possibly return. But all hung now upon the confines of the irrevocable. One more assault might extinguish the last spark of vitality which is, every moment, ready to die.

"'And what is the nature of the seizure you speak of?' I entreated.

"'I have stated all fully in this note, which I place in your hands upon the distinct condition that you send for the nearest clergyman, and open my letter in his presence, and on no account read it till he is with you; you would despise it else, and it is a matter of life and death. Should the priest fail you, then, indeed, you may read it.'

"He asked me, before taking his leave finally, whether I would wish to see a man curiously learned upon the very subject, which, after I had read his letter, would probably interest me above all others, and he urged me earnestly to invite him to visit him there; and so took his leave.

"The ecclesiastic was absent, and I read the letter by myself. At another time, or in another case, it might have excited my ridicule. But into what quackeries will not people rush for a last chance, where all accustomed means have failed, and the life of a beloved object is at stake?

"Nothing, you will say, could be more absurd than the learned man's letter. It was monstrous enough to have consigned him to a madhouse. He said that the patient was suffering from the visits of a vampire! The punctures which she described as having occurred near the throat, were, he insisted, the insertion of those two long, thin, and sharp teeth which, it is well known, are peculiar to vampires; and there could be no doubt, he added, as to the well-defined presence of the small livid mark which all concurred in describing as that induced by the demon's lips, and every symptom described by the sufferer was in exact conformity with those recorded in every case of a similar visitation.

"Being myself wholly sceptical as to the existence of any such portent as the vampire, the supernatural of the good doctor furnished, in my opinion, but another learning and intelligence oddly associated with some one hallucination. I was so miserable, however, that, rather try nothing, I acted upon

the instructions of the letter.

"I concealed myself in the dark dressing-room, that upon the poor patient's room, in which a candle was burning, and watched there till she was fast asleep. I stood at the door, peeping through the small crevice, my sword laid on the table beside me, as my directions prescribed, until, a little after one, I saw a large black object, very ill-defined, crawl, as it seemed to me, over the foot of the bed, and swiftly spread itself up to the poor girl's throat, where it swelled, in a moment, into a great, palpitating mass.

"For a few moments I had stood petrified. I now sprang forward, with my sword in my hand. The black creature suddenly contracted toward the foot of the bed, glided over it, and, standing on the floor about a yard below the foot of the bed, with a glare of skulking ferocity and horror fixed on me, I saw Millarca. Speculating I know not what, I struck at her instantly with my sword; but I saw her standing near the door, unscathed. Horrified, I pursued, and struck again. She was gone; and my sword flew to shivers against the door.

"I can't describe to you all that passed on that horrible night. The whole house was up and stirring. The spectre Millarca was gone. But her victim was sinking fast, and before the morning dawned, she died."

The old General was agitated. We did not speak to him. My father walked to some little distance, and began reading the inscriptions on the tombstones; and thus occupied, he strolled into the door of a side-chapel to prosecute his researches. The General leaned against the wall, dried his eyes, and sighed heavily. I was relieved on hearing the voices  of Carmilla and Madame, who were at that moment approaching. The voices died away.

In this solitude, having just listened to so strange a story, connected, as it was, with the great and titled dead, whose monuments were mouldering among the dust and ivy round us, and every incident of which bore so awfully upon my own mysterious case—in this haunted spot, darkened by the towering foliage that rose on every side, dense and high above its noiseless walls—a horror began to steal over me, and my heart sank as I thought that my friends were, after all, not about to enter and disturb this triste and ominous scene.

The old General's eyes were fixed on the ground, as he leaned with his hand upon the basement of a shattered monument.

Under a narrow, arched doorway, surmounted by one of those demoniacal grotesques in which the cynical and ghastly fancy of old Gothic carving delights, I saw very gladly the beautiful face and figure of Carmilla enter the shadowy chapel.

I was just about to rise and speak, and nodded smiling, in answer to her peculiarly engaging smile; when with a cry, the old man by my side caught up the woodman's hatchet, and started forward. On seeing him a brutalized change came over her features. It was an instantaneous and horrible transformation, as she made a crouching step backwards. Before I could utter a scream, he struck at her with all his force, but she dived under his blow, and unscathed, caught him in her tiny grasp by the wrist. He struggled for a moment to release his arm, but his hand opened, the axe fell to the ground, and the girl was gone.

He staggered against the wall. His grey hair stood upon his head, and a moisture shone over his face, as if he were at the point of death.

The frightful scene had passed in a moment. The first thing I recollect after, is Madame standing before me, and impatiently repeating again and again, the question, 'Where is Mademoiselle Carmilla?'

I answered at length, "I don't know—I can't tell—she went there," and I pointed to the door through which Madame had just entered; "only a minute or two since."

"But I have been standing there, in the passage, ever since Mademoiselle Carmilla entered; and she did not return."

She then began to call "Carmilla," through every door and passage and from the windows, but no answer came.

"She called herself Carmilla?" asked the General, agitated.

"Carmilla, yes," I answered.

"Aye," he said; "that is Millarca. That is the same who long ago was called Mircalla, Countess Karnstein. Depart from this accursed ground, my poor child, as quickly as you can. Drive to the clergyman's house, and stay there till we come. Begone! May you never behold Carmilla more; you will not find her here."

Chapter XV
Ordeal and Execution

As he spoke one of the strangest-looking men I ever beheld, entered the chapel at the door through which Carmilla had made her entrance and her exit. He was tall, narrow-chested, stooping, with high shoulders, and dressed in black. His face was brown and dried in with deep furrows; he wore an oddly shaped hat with a broad leaf. His hair, long and grizzled, hung on his shoulders. He wore a pair of gold spectacles, and walked slowly, with an odd shambling gait, with his face sometimes turned up to the sky, and sometimes bowed down toward the ground, and seemed to wear a perpetual smile; his long thin arms were swinging, and his lank hands, in old black gloves ever so much too wide for them, waving and gesticulating in utter abstraction.

"The very man?" exclaimed the General, advancing with manifest delight. "My dear Baron, how happy I am to see you, I had no hope of meeting you so soon." He signed to my father, who had by this time returned, leading the fantastic old gentleman, whom he called the Baron, to meet him. He introduced him formally, and they at once entered into earnest conversation. The stranger took a roll of paper from his pocket, and spread it on the worn surface of a tomb that stood by. He had a pencil case in his fingers, with which he traced imaginary lines from point to point on the paper, which from their often glancing from it, together, at certain points of the building, I concluded to be a plan of the chapel. He accompanied, what I may term, his lecture, with occasional readings from a dirty little book, whose yellow leaves were closely written over.

They sauntered together down the side aisle, opposite to the spot where I was standing, conversing as they went; then they began measuring distances by paces, and finally they all stood together, facing a piece of the side-wall, which they began to examine with great minuteness; pulling off the ivy that clung over it, and rapping the plaster with the ends of their sticks, scraping here, and knocking there. At length they ascertained the existence of a broad marble tablet, with letters carved in relief upon it.

With the assistance of the woodman, who soon returned, a monumental inscription, and carved escutcheon, were disclosed. They proved to be those of the long lost monument of Mircalla, Countess Karnstein.

The old General, though not I fear given to the praying mood, raised his hands and eyes to heaven, in mute thanksgiving for some moments.

"To-morrow," I heard him say; "the commissioner will be here, and the Inquisition will be held according to law."

Then turning to the old man with the gold spectacles, whom I have described, he shook him warmly by both hands and said:

"Baron, how can I thank you? How can we all thank you? You will have delivered this region from a plague that has scourged its inhabitants for more than a century. The horrible enemy, thank God, is at last tracked."

My father led the stranger aside, and the General followed. I knew that he had led them out of hearing, that he might relate my case, and I saw them glance often quickly at me, and the discussion proceeded.

My father came to me, kissed me again and again, and leading me from the chapel, said:

"It is time to return, but before we go home, we must add to our party the good priest, who lives but a little way from this; and persuade him to accompany us to the schloss."

In this quest we were successful: and I was glad, being unspeakably fatigued

when we reached home. But my satisfaction was changed to dismay, on discovering that there were no tidings of Carmilla. Of the scene that had occurred in the ruined chapel, no explanation was offered to me, and it was clear that it was a secret which my father for the present determined to keep from me.

The sinister absence of Carmilla made the remembrance of the scene more horrible to me. The arrangements for that night were singular. Two servants, and Madame were to sit up in my room that night; and the ecclesiastic with my father kept watch in the adjoining dressing-room.

The priest had performed certain solemn rites that night, the purport of which I did not understand any more than I comprehended the reason of this extraordinary precaution taken for my safety during sleep.

I saw all clearly a few days later.

The disappearance of Carmilla was followed by the discontinuance of my nightly sufferings.

You have heard, no doubt, of the appalling superstition that prevails in Upper and Lower Styria, in Moravia, Silesia, in Turkish Servia, in Poland, even in Russia; the superstition, so we must call it, of the Vampire.

If human testimony, taken with every care and solemnity, judicially, before commissions innumerable, each consisting of many members, all chosen for integrity and intelligence, and constituting reports more voluminous perhaps than exist upon any one other class of cases, is worth anything, it is difficult to deny, or even to doubt the existence of such a phenomenon as the Vampire.

For my part I have heard no theory by which to explain what I myself have witnessed and experienced, other than that supplied by the ancient and well-attested belief of the country.

The next day the formal proceedings took place in the Chapel of Karnstein. The grave of the Countess Mircalla was opened; and the General and my father recognized each his perfidious and beautiful guest, in the face now disclosed to view. The features, though a hundred and fifty years had passed since her funeral, were tinted with the warmth of life. Her eyes were open; no cadaverous smell exhaled from the coffin. The two medical men, one officially present, the other on the part of the promoter of the inquiry, attested the marvellous fact, that there was a faint but appreciable respiration, and a corresponding action of the heart. The limbs were perfectly flexible, the flesh elastic; and the leaden coffin floated with blood, in which to a depth of seven inches, the body lay immersed. Here then, were all the admitted signs and proofs of vampirism. The body, therefore, in accordance with the ancient practice, was raised, and a sharp stake driven through the heart of the vampire, who uttered a piercing shriek at the moment, in all respects such as might escape from a living person in the last agony. Then the head was struck off, and a torrent of blood flowed from the severed neck. The body and head were next placed on a pile of wood, and reduced to ashes, which were thrown upon the river and borne away, and that territory has never since been plagued by the visits of a vampire.

My father has a copy of the report of the Imperial Commission, with the signatures of all who were present at these proceedings, attached in verification of the statement. It is from this official paper that I have summarized my account of this last shocking scene.

Chapter XVI
Conclusion

I write all this you suppose with composure. But far from it; I cannot think of it without agitation. Nothing but your earnest desire so repeatedly expressed, could have induced me to sit down to a task that has unstrung my nerves for months to come, and reinduced a shadow of the unspeakable horror which years after my deliverance continued to make my days and nights dreadful, and solitude insupportably terrific.

Let me add a word or two about that quaint Vordenburg, to whose curious lore we were indebted for discovery of the Countess Mircalla's grave.

He had taken up his abode in Gratz, where, living upon mere pittance, which was all that remained to him of princely estates of his family, in Upper Styria, he himself to the minute and laborious investigation of the marvellously authenticated tradition of Vampirism. He had at his fingers' ends all the great and little works upon the "Magia Posthuma," "Phlegon de Mirabilibus," "Augustinus cura pro Mortuis," "Philosophicae et Christianae Codex Vampiris," by John Christofer Harenberg; and a others, among which I remember only a few of those which he lent to my father. He had a voluminous digest of all the judicial cases, from which he had extracted a system of principles that appear to govern—some always, and others occasionally only—the condition of the vampire. I may mention, in passing, that the deadly pallor attributed to that sort of revenants, is a mere melodramatic fiction. They present, in the grave, and when they show themselves in human society, the appearance of healthy life. When disclosed to light in their coffins, they exhibit all the symptoms that are enumerated as those which proved the vampire-life of the long-dead Countess Karnstein.

How they escape from their graves and return to them for certain hours every day, without displacing the day or leaving any trace of disturbance in the state of the coffin or the cerements, has always been admitted to be utterly inexplicable. The amphibious existence of the vampire is sustained by daily renewed slumber in the grave. Its horrible lust for living blood supplies the vigour of its waking existence. The vampire is prone to be fascinated with an engrossing vehemence, resembling the passion of love, by particular persons. In pursuit of these it will exercise inexhaustible patience and stratagem, for access to a particular object may be obstructed in a hundred ways. It will never desist until it has satiated its passion, and drained the very life of its coveted victim. But it will, in these cases, husband and protract its murderous enjoyment with the refinement of an epicure, and heighten it by the gradual approaches of an artful courtship. In these cases it seems to yearn for something like sympathy and consent. In ordinary ones it goes direct to its object, overpowers with violence, and strangles and exhausts often at a single feast.

The vampire is, apparently, subject, in certain situations, to special conditions. In the particular instance of which I have given you a relation, Mircalla seemed to be limited to a name which, if not her real one, should at least reproduce, without the omission or addition of a single letter, those, as we say, anagrammatically, which compose it. Carmilla did this; so did Millarca.

My father related to the Baron Vordenburg, who remained with us for two or three weeks after the expulsion of Carmilla, the story about the Moravian nobleman and the vampire at Karnstein churchyard, and then he asked the Baron how he had discovered the exact position of the long-concealed tomb of the Countess Millarca. The Baron's grotesque features puckered up into a mysterious smile; he looked down, still smiling, on his worn spectacle-case and fumbled with it. Then looking up, he said:

"I have many journals, and other papers, written by that remarkable man; the most curious among them is one treating of the visit of which you speak, to Karnstein. The tradition, of course, discolours and distorts a little. He might have been termed a Moravian nobleman, for he had changed his abode to that territory, and was, beside, a noble. But he was, in truth, a native of Upper Styria. It is enough to say that in very early youth he had been a passionate and favoured lover of the beautiful Mircalla, Countess Karnstein. Her early death plunged him into inconsolable grief. It is the nature of vampires to increase and multiply, but according to an ascertained and ghostly law.

"Assume, at starting, a territory perfectly free from that pest. How does it begin, and how does it multiply itself? I will tell you. A person, more or less wicked, puts an end to himself. A suicide, under certain circumstances, becomes a vampire. That spectre visits living people in their slumbers; they die, and almost invariably, in the grave, develop into vampires. This happened in the case of the beautiful Mircalla, who was haunted by one of those demons. My ancestor, Vordenburg, whose title I still bear, soon discovered this, and in the course of the studies to which he devoted himself, learned a great deal more.

"Among other things, he concluded that suspicion of vampirism would probably fall, sooner or later, upon the dead Countess, who in life had been his idol. He conceived a horror, be she what she might, of her remains being profaned by the outrage of a posthumous execution. He has left a curious paper to prove that the vampire, on its expulsion from its amphibious existence, is projected into a far more horrible life; and he resolved to save his once beloved Mircalla from this.

"He adopted the stratagem of a journey here, a pretended removal of her remains, and a real obliteration of her monument. When age had stolen upon him, and from the vale of years he looked back on the scenes he was leaving, he considered, in a different spirit, what he had done, and a horror took possession of him. He made the tracings and notes which have guided me to the very spot, and drew up a confession of the deception that he had practised. If he had intended any further action in this matter, death prevented him; and the hand of a remote descendant has, too late for many, directed the pursuit to the lair of the beast."

We talked a little more, and among other things he said was this:

"One sign of the vampire is the power of the hand. The slender hand of Mircalla closed like a vice of steel on the General's wrist when he raised the hatchet to strike. But its power is not confined to its grasp; it leaves a numbness in the limb it seizes, which is slowly, if ever, recovered from."

The following Spring my father took me on a tour through Italy. We remained away for more than a year. It was long before the terror of recent events subsided; and to this hour the image of Carmilla returns to memory with ambiguous alternations—sometimes the playful, languid, beautiful girl; sometimes the writhing fiend I saw in the ruined church; and often from a reverie I have started, fancying I heard the light step of Carmilla at the drawing-room door.

THE END

COUNT LEO TOLSTOY'S *THE STORY OF YEMILAN AND THE EMPTY DRUM*

Lev Nikolaevich Tolstoi (1828–1910) was born an aristocrat and ended life as he wished, as a peasant, following a religious change and excommunication from the Russian Orthodox Church. In between he wrote such masterpieces of fiction as *War and Peace* (1863–1869) and *Anna Karenina* (1873–1877). This little story of the magic of a helpful wife deserves more fame. The translation is by Nathan Haskell Dole (1899). He left some words in Russian (such as *voyevode*, "vovoide" or "governor"), which I have translated to English.

Yemilyan lived out life as a day-laborer. Once upon a time he was on his way to the meadow where his work was, and lo and behold! A frog leaped out before him. He almost set his foot on it. But he stepped over it. Suddenly he heard someone calling to him from behind. He looked 'round and saw a beautiful girl standing there, and she said to him:—

"Yemilyan, why are you not married?"

"How could I be married, my pretty maid. Look at me; I have nothing at all. No one would take me."

"Well," said the girl, "take me for a wife."

The girl greatly pleased Yemilyan; said he:—

"I should like to; but where shall we live?"

"That is something to think about," said the girl. "Hard work and little sleep is all that is required; but we can find clothes and food anywhere."

"Very good, I'm agreed; let us get married. Where shall we go?"

"Let us go to the city."

Yemilyan and the girl went to the city. The girl took him to a little cottage at the farther end of the city, and they were married and lived there.

One time, the governor came to the city. He passed by Yemilyan's cottage, and Yemilyan's wife went out to look at him. When the governor saw her he was amazed.

"Where did such a beauty as that come from?"

He reined in his horse, and summoned Yemilyan's wife, and began to question her.

"Who are you?" he asked.

The legend of Mélusine has appeared in many forms since the Middle Ages. Perhaps identified with Mater Lucina, a goddess of childbirth, the fairy-tale character of Mélusine (half-fairy, half-human as the daughter of Elinas, king of Albania) married the all-human Raymondin de Poitiers and built for him some magic castles in Lusignan. When her fairy nature was discovered, she vanished. All along her nether extremities had turned reptilian every Saturday, which is why she would not let her husband see her on that day each week. Maybe, along with a night out each week with the boys, husbands ought to arrange to let wives do something of their own on Saturdays.

"The wife of the peasant Yemilyan," said she.

"How did it happen," said he, "that such a beautiful woman as you married a peasant? You ought to be a princess."

"Thank you," said she, "for your flattering remark, but I am satisfied with my husband."

The governor talked with her awhile, and then rode on his way. He reached his palace. But he could not help thinking of Yemilyan's wife. He lay awake all night long, planning how he might get her away from Yemilyan. He could not think of any way of doing it. He summoned his servants, and bade them devise some way. And the governor's servants said to him:—

A fifteenth-century French woodcut shows a scene from Jean d'Arras' *Chronique de Mélusine* (end of the previous century) in which a human mates with a fairy-like sea creature. Human and fairy romances could give magical powers to mortals.

"Take Yemilyan as your workman," said they. "We'll work him to death; his wife will be a widow, and then you can have her."

So the governor did; he sent for Yemilyan to come to him as a handyman, and offered [them] a house . . . the messengers came and told Yemilyan their story. But Yemilyan's wife said:—

"Very good," said she. "Go. Work there during the daytime but at night return to me."

Yemilyan went. When he reached the palace, the governor's steward said to him:—

"Why have you come here alone, without your wife?"

"Why should I bring her? Her place is at home."

In the governor's courtyard they gave him so much work to do that two men could not have accomplished it. Yemilyan took hold of the work, but it seemed hopeless for him to finish it. But lo and behold! When evening came it was all done. The steward saw that he had finished it and gave him four times as much for the next day. Yemilyan went home and found the house all neatly swept and in order; the fire was burning in the stove, the baking and boiling were under way. His wife was sitting at the table sewing and waiting for her husband. When he entered she met him, got supper ready, and, after he had had all he wanted to eat and drink, she began to ask him about his work.

"Well," said he, "it went badly. They gave me more than I had the strength to do. They are going to kill me with work."

"Now, then," said she, "don't you worry about your work, and don't look back and don't look forward to see if much has been done and much remains to be done. Only work. All will come out right."

Yemilyan went to bed. The next morning he went to his work again. He took hold of it, and not once did he look 'round. And lo and behold! It was all done by four o'clock, and while it was still light he went home for the night. And though they kept adding to his tasks, still Yemilyan always managed to finish it up and go home for the night.

Thus passed a week. The governor's servants perceived that they could not overcome the peasant by "black work." They began to impose handiwork upon him, but this also proved vain. Carpentry work and mason work and the art of thatching—whatever they imposed upon him, that Yemilyan got done in ample time

for him to go home and spend the night with his wife. Thus passed a second week. The governor summoned his servants, and said:—

"I should like to know if I feed you for doing nothing? Here two weeks have passed and I can't see that you have done anything at all. You were going to put Yemilyan out of the way for me, but from the window I see him going home every afternoon, singing songs. I should like to know if you are scheming to turn me into ridicule?"

The servants began to justify themselves:—

"We tried with all our might," said they, "to kill him off by 'black work,' but we could not do anything with him. Everything we gave him to work at he worked out, and we could not tire him. Then we gave him handiwork to do, thinking he would not have wit enough to do it, but in this too we failed to get him. It is like magic. As soon as he touches anything it is done. It must be that either he or his wife practices some witchcraft. We are tired to death of him. And now we are trying to think of something that he can't do. We have decided to make him build a new cathedral in one day. So will you summon Yemilyan and command him to build a new cathedral opposite your palace in one day? And if he does not have it done, then we will have his head cut off as punishment."

The governor sent for Yemilyan.

"Well," said he, "this is my command. Build me a new cathedral on the square opposite my palace, so that it shall be all done to-morrow evening. If you get it built, I will reward you; if you fail, I shall punish you."

Yemilyan heard the command, he turned 'round and went home.

"Well," he said to himself, "that's the end of me."

He went to his wife and said:—

"Get yourself ready, wife; we must make our escape somewhere or other, else we shall be ruined."

"Why," she said, "are you such a coward that you must run away?"

"How can I help being?" said he. "The governor has ordered me to come to-morrow and build a new cathedral all in one day. And if I don't get it built, he threatens to cut off my head. The only thing left to do is to escape while there is time."

But his wife would not hear this.

"The governor has many servants. They will catch us anywhere. You can't escape from him. But since you have the power, you must obey him."

"Yes, but how can one obey him, if one has not the power?"

"Listen, my dear fellow. Don't you worry. Eat your supper and go to bed. In the morning get up a little earlier than usual; you'll have it all done."

Yemilyan went to bed; his wife wakened him.

"Go," said she, "build your cathedral as quickly as possible. Here are nails and a hammer; there'll be work enough for you for the day."

Yemilyan went to the city; when he got there the new cathedral was already standing in the midst of the square, almost finished. Yemilyan went to work to finish it; by evening it was complete.

The governor woke up, he looked out of his palace window, and saw that the cathedral was already built. Yemilyan was walking up and down, here and there driving in nails. And the governor was not pleased to see the cathedral; he was vexed because he had nothing to punish Yemilyan for, and could not take away his wife. So he called his servants again.

"Yemilyan has accomplished his task; there is nothing to punish him for. This task," said he "was too small for him. Something craftier must be thought up. Put your wits to work, or else I will punish you instead of him."

And the governor's servants suggested that he should command Yemilyan to make a river which should flow round the palace, and that ships should be sailing on it. The governor summoned Yemilyan, and laid before him the new task.

"If you are able," said he, "in one night to build a cathedral, then you will be able to do this also. See to it that to-morrow everything be as I commanded. And if it is not ready, then I will cut off your head."

Yemilyan was more than ever discouraged, and he returned to his wife in a very gloomy frame of mind.

"Why," said his wife, "are you so discouraged? Have you some new task imposed on you?"

Yemilyan told her.

"We must make our escape," said he.

But his wife said:—

"You can't run away; they will catch you everywhere; you must obey."

"Yes, but how can I obey?"

"Well, my dear fellow, there is nothing to be discouraged about. Eat your supper and go to bed. But get up earlier than usual; everything will be in order."

Yemilyan went to bed and slept. Early in the morning his wife waked him.

"Go," said she, "go to the city, all is ready. You will find one mound only at the harbor. Take your spade and level it off."

Yemilyan started. He reached the city; round the palace was a river, ships were sailing on it. Yemilyan reached the harbor, he saw the uneven place and began to level it.

The governor woke up, he saw the river where no river had been; ships were sailing on it and Yemilyan was leveling a mound with his spade. The governor was horror-struck and was not rejoiced at the sight of the river and the ships; but he was vexed because he could not punish Yemilyan. He said to himself:—

"There is no task that he cannot accomplish it. What shall we try now?"

He summoned his servants and proceeded to consult with them.

"Think up some task," said he, "that will be above Yemilyan's powers. For whatever you have so far devised for him, he has done at once, and it is impossible to take his wife from him."

The servants cudgeled their brains, and at last had a bright idea. They came to the governor and said:—

"You must summon Yemilyan and say to him:—

"'Go somewhere, you know not where, and bring back something, you know not what.' He won't be able to escape from this. Wherever he goes you will say that he went to the wrong place, and whatever he brings back you will say that he brought back the wrong thing. Then you will be able to punish him and take away his wife."

This pleased the governor.

"This time," said he, "you have had a bright idea."

He sent for Yemilyan and said to him:—

"Go somewhere, you know not where, and bring back something, you know not what, and if you don't bring it, I will cut your head off."

Yemilyan went to his wife, and told her what the governor had said. His wife put on her thinking-cap.

"Well," said she, "they've been teaching the governor something to his own ruin. We must work now wisely."

She sat down, pondered for a while, and then said to her husband:—

"You will have to take a long journey—to our *babushka*, our grandmother—to the ancient peasant mother—and you must ask for her good will. And from her you will receive an object; then go straightway to the governor, and I shall be there. For now I shall not get out of their hands. They will take me by force, but not for long. If you do all the old *babushka* commands, you will speedily rescue me."

The wife got her husband ready; she gave him a wallet and gave him a spindle.

"Here, take this," said she, "and give it to her. By this she will know you're my husband."

She showed him the way. Yemilyan started; he went beyond the city, and he saw some bowmen drilling. Yemilyan stopped and watched them. After the bowmen had practiced, they sat down to rest. Yemilyan approached them and asked:—

"Do you know, my brethren, where I must go, not knowing where, to get something, not knowing what?"

The bowmen listened to what he had to say, and they were filled with wonder.

"Who sent you to find out?" they inquired.

"The governor," said he.

"No," said they, "we cannot help you."

After Yemilyan had sat a little while, he proceeded on his way.

He went and he went, and at last he came to a forest. In the forest lived the old grandmother.

The old woman was sitting in a cottage—the ancient peasant mother—she was spinning flax—and she was weeping. When the old woman saw Yemilyan, she cried out to him:—

"What have you come for?"

Yemilyan gave her the distaff, and told her his wife had sent it to her. And Yemilyan began to tell her all about his life, how he had married the girl, how he had gone to the city to live, how he had been taken as a handyman, how he had served the governor, how he had built the cathedral and made the river with the ships, and how now the governor had commanded him to go somewhere, not knowing where, to get something, he knew not what.

The old woman listened to him and ceased to weep. She began to mutter to herself.

"That is very good," said she, "but sit down, little son, and eat."

Yemilyan ate his fill, and the old woman began to talk with him.

"Here is a little ball," said she, "roll it before you and follow it, wherever it may roll. You will find there a great city. When you enter the city, ask for a night's lodging at the last house. There you will find what you need."

"But how shall I know it, grandmother?"

"Well, when you see what men obey sooner than father and mother, that is what you want; seize on it and take it with you." You will take it to the governor, but he will say to you that you have not brought the thing that was required, and then do you say to him: 'Well, if it is not what is wanted it must be broken'; then hit the thing a blow and take it down to the river, break it, and fling it into the water, and then you will recover your wife."

Yemilyan bade the old woman good-by, rolled the little ball ahead of him; it rolled and it rolled, and it took him to the sea, and by the sea was a great city. At the border of the city was a large house. Yemilyan there demanded hospitality for the night; it was granted, and he went to bed. He woke up early in the morning and listened; the father was getting up, he called his son and sent him to split kindlings. But the son would not heed; "It is too early as yet," said he, "I shall have time enough." Yemilyan heard the mother get down from the oven and say:—

"Go, little son, your father's bones pain him; would you make him go?"

"There's plenty of time."

The son made a smacking noise with his lips, and dropped off to sleep again. As soon as he had fallen asleep there was a noise like thunder, and a loud crash in the street. The son leaped down, put on his clothes, and ran down into the street. Yemilyan also jumped down and followed him to see what the son obeyed better than his parents. Yemilyan ran down and saw a man going along the street, carrying a round object and beating on it with  sticks, and it rumbled, and the son listened to it. Yemilyan ran closer and examined the object, and saw that it was round like a small tub, and both ends were covered with skin. And he insisted on knowing what it was called.

"A drum," they told him.

Yemilyan was amazed, and asked them to give it to him. They refused to give it to him. So Yemilyan ceased to ask for it, but he walked along following it. He walked all that day, and when the man that had it lay it down to sleep, Yemilyan seized his drum and ran off with it.

He ran and he ran, and at last came back to his own city. He expected to see his wife at home, but she was not there.

On the next day they had brought her to the governor. Yemilyan went to the governor's, and bade them announce him in these words:—

"Here! The man who went he knew not where, has come back, bringing he knows not what."

The governor bade Yemilyan to return the next day.

Yemilyan then ordered them to say to the governor:—

"I," said he, "have come to-day. I have brought what he bade me bring; let the governor come to me or I will come to him."

The governor replied:—

"Where did you go?" he asked.

"I don't know," said he.

"And what did you bring with you?"

Yemilyan was about to show it to him, but the governor refused to look at it:—

"It's nothing," said he.

"Yes, it's nothing," said Yemilyan; "but then one must beat on it, and the devil is in it."

Yemilyan came with the drum and beat on it.

As soon as he began to beat on it, all the governor's army came and joined Yemilyan. They saluted him and waited till he should give word of command.

The governor began to shout to his bowmen from the window of his palace, forbidding them to follow Yemilyan. They refused to obey him, and followed Yemilyan. The governor perceived this, and ordered them to restore his wife to Yemilyan, and then asked him to give him the drum.

"I cannot," said Yemilyan. "I must beat it," said he, "and throw the scrapings into the river."

Yemilyan went with the drum to the river, and the bowmen followed him. Yemilyan beat the drum by the river, broke it into pieces, and flung them into the river. And all the bowmen scattered in all directions. But Yemilyan took his wife and brought her home. And from that time forth the governor ceased to bother him, and he lived long and happily ever after.

Magic circle of Mephistophiles.

DEVILS, DEMONS, AND OTHER CREATURES THAT MIGHT BE INVOLVED IN SEX MAGIC

Naturally, I suggest that you look at the other books in my *The Complete Book of*—series, but they are by no means the only ones on *Devils and Demons* or the *Devil's Disciples*, let alone *Vampires* and *Werewolves* and the rest of my subjects. Have a look at histories of magic and witchcraft by Montague Summers, Henry Lea and others, perhaps with special attention to feminist approaches to *Reading Witchcraft* (Marion Gibson) or the examination of *The Witch in History* (Diane Purkiss) and *Malevolent Nurture* (Deborah Willis). Of course do not bypass the handbooks of Wiccary, of which *Drawing Down the Moon* is my favorite.

Check out Carol & Dinah Mack's *Field Guide to Demons, Fairies, Fallen Angels and Other Subversive Spirits* that might be encountered in sex magic, from Pan of the forest to the Yukki-Onna (not Yoko Ono) of Japan, the Chinese White Lady or the British one. There are a great many (but not all great) books on fairies, leprechauns, the Little People in general, and some of these Good Companions thought to be helpful in matters sexual; they don't just cobble shoes. The fairy books are easier to read than the tomes on demonology. From ecclesiastical history and the *furor Satanæ* to the flimsy *1,001 Things You Always Wanted to Know About Angels, Demons, and the Afterlife*, there is plenty to keep you reading at any level you choose. Get online and see, or ask your reference librarian for help.

SEX MAGIC IN SHORT FICTION

A world of wonder and delight awaits those who want to read short stories on the subject of this book. Jealous witches make potions (think of *Snow White*'s poisoned apple) and men and women manipulate each other in sexual games. Even people in portraits get into the act. Consider Edgar Allen Poe's lady in an oval frame or a mysterious count in M. R. James.

There is, however, as in science fiction and the detective story, a great deal of junk to wade through. If you can get recommendations from friends or librarians, or annotated bibliographies so much the better because then you will be on your way to a masterpiece of a short-short by John Collier or long-winded tales from much earlier eras in which attention spans were longer and there was no TV or movies. Speaking of movies, film buffs will find a number of fine films in which sex magic spins the plot.

Guides to short fiction by subject are available in libraries. One difficulty arises from good stuff hidden away in anthologies of short fiction; if you know the names of such experts as Peter Haining, it helps. He has edited good anthologies such as *The Witchcraft Reader* (8 stories), *The Necromancers* (10 stories), and *A Circle of Witches* (11 stories). Here are some collections from other hands with fairly relevant stories you might otherwise miss:

By the Light of the Silvery Moon (ed. R. Petrie): Fiona Cooper, "Love Finds Shirley Tempest"
Cthulhu 2000 (ed. J. Turner): Poppy Z. Brite, "His Mouth Will Taste of Wormwood"
Devil's Children (ed. M. Parry): John Collier, "The Possession of Angela Bradshaw"
Ellery Queen's 16th Mystery Annual: Avram Davidson, "Where Do You Live, Queen Esther?"
Great Short Stories of the World (ed. B. H. Clark & M. Lieber): Anon., "The Fickle Widow"
Love Kills (ed. E. Gorman & M. H. Greenberg): Barbara Collins, "Obeah, My Love"
Magic in Ithkar 1 (ed. A. Norton & R. Adams): Roger C. Schlobin, "For Lovers Only"
Magic in Ithkar 3 (ed. A. Norton & R. Adams): T. S. Huff, "What Are Little Girls Made Of?"
Mammoth Book of Comic Fantasy (ed. M. Ashley): Anthony Armstrong, "The Warlock's Daughter"
Sisters of Sorcery (ed. S. Manley & G. Lewis): Lady Gregory, "Herb Healing"
Supernatural Omnibus (ed. M. Summers): W. B. Sealock, "Toussel's Pale Bride"
The Ultimate Witch (ed. B. Preiss & J. Betancourt): Tim Sullivan, "Mother and Child Reunion"
Warrior Enchantresses (ed. K. M. Massie-Ferch & M. H. Greenberg): William F. Wu, "The Ginseng Potion"
World's Great Romances (ed. W. J. Black): La Motte-Fouqué, Friedrich Heinrich Karl, Freiherr de, "The Abduction of Agnes"

If you look up individual authors, from Lord Dunsany to Woody Allen, Robert Boch and Stephen King you will find they occasionally touch on sex magic. Lesser-known writers' sex magic tales appear in periodicals or collections of short stories, such as the following:

Bradley, Mary Higgins. "Love Magic" in *The Five-Minute Girl*
Davis, Mary Evelyn Moore. "The Love-stranche" in *Elephant's Track and Other Stories*
Finney, Jack. "Love, Your Magic Spell is Everywhere" in *I Love Galesburg in the Springtime*
Grendon, Stephen. "Miss Eperson" in *Mr. George and Other Odd Persons*
Irwin, Margaret Emma Faith. "Monsieur Seeks a Wife" in *Bloodstock and Other Stories*
McConkey, James. "Witches of Love" in *Night Stand*
Sabatini, Rafael. "Night of Witchcraft: Louis XVI and Madame de Montespan" in *Historical Nights' Entertainments* (First Series)

Schwob, Marcel. "The Strigae" in *The King in the Golden Mask and Other Writings*
Tolney, Thomas. "The Magic Whorehouse" in *The Magic Whorehouse*

TRUE STORIES OF WITCHES

Harriet Martineau wrote *Witch Stories* (1883, reprinted 1972) about women accused of witchcraft in England and Scotland. She makes an important point when she says:

> To be skilful in healing was just as dangerous as to be powerful in sickening . . . and the testimony of a healed friend was the strongest strand in the hangman's cord. . . . This was the saddest feature of the whole matter—the total want [lack] of gratitude, reliance, trustiness, or affection between a "witch" and her friends.

You must know that authorities often regarded good (white) and bad (black) sex magic as equally blasphemous and equally deserving of punishment. Wise women who meant well and hateful creatures who were negative and malicious were lumped together.

A more recent feminist look at the persecution of witches in the sixteenth and seventeenth centuries has come from Françoise Mallet-Joris in *The Witches* (1968). She tells the stories of three women: two burned as witches and the third a contested case of possession by demons. True, she writes about a few examples from the past, but the significance for everybody here and now is inescapable.

Other books by women address the *Witchcraze: A New History of the European Witch Hunts* (Anne Llewellyn Barstow) and women and witchcraft in America, *Spellbound* (an anthology edited by Elizabeth Reiss, &c.).

Witches occur in a number of novels by women (as well as by men) such as Sigrid Unset's *Kristin Lavransdatter* (3 volumes, 1920–1926). Ms. Unset, who won the Nobel Prize for Literature (1928), naturally had to have witches as well as nuns and other women in her picture of daily life in fourteenth-century Norway.

Now that the biography of God has been written by Jack Miles it seems only fair that J. B. Russell and others write that of Satan. An important new *History of the Devil* was written in French by Gerald Messadie and is available in English translation by Marc Romano (1997). Messadie traces the personification of evil back six centuries before Christ to the time when Persian priests of Zoroaster decided to demonize their adversaries and invented "The Adversary," which is what *Satan* means.

Later, Jews, Christians and Muslims took up the idea. While eastern cultures often do not so personify the negative forces, western culture certainly does. At some times and places Satan has been regarded as equal to God and locked in battle with Him. As The Prince of This World, in fact, Satan has sometimes been perceived to be winning and some have committed to him, or what he represents. So long as we need to identify a force opposing light and truth and good, a force of darkness will be named.

In order for you to grasp the scope of the scholarly *History of the Devil*, its sometimes revolutionary concepts, and the varieties of religious experience, permit me to list the section titles: The Ambiguous Demons of Oceania; India: Spared from Evil; China and Japan: Exorcism through Writing; Zoroaster, the First Ayatollahs, and the True Birth of the Devil; Mesopotamia: The Appearance of Sin; The Celts: Thirty-five Centuries without the Devil; Greece: The Devil Driven Out by Democracy; Rome: The Devil Banned; Egypt: Unthinkable Damnation; Africa; The Cradle of Religious Ecology; The North American Indians: Land and Fatherland; The Enigma of Quetzalcoatl, the Feathered Serpent, and the God-Who-Weeps; Israel: Devils as the Heavenly Servants of the Modern Devil; The Devil in the Early Church: The Confusions of Cause and Effect; The Great Night of the West: From the Middle Ages to the French Revolution; Islam: The Devil as State Functionary; and Modern Times and the God of Laziness, Hatred, and Nihilism.

Any research university library will have this book and maybe some large civic library where you live will also have it or get it for you on interlibrary loan. It is very expensive to buy.

To see demonology, witchcraft and all kinds of magic in context, consult Messadie and get your *yin* and *yang* straightened out. Do not forget that in the East the two are fitted equally into a circle, with a bit of the "bad" in the "good" and a bit of the "good" in the "bad," which seems like a sophisticated way to look at Dualism, I believe.

What could be more interesting, I ask you, than reaching some sensible conclusions for yourself about how good people turn bad and why bad things happen to good people? I think Dr. Johnson was right when he observed that anything that makes you think about the past, the present, and the future is celebrating the greatest gift that we have, the gift that raises us above the brutes. Don't you agree?

W. W. SKEAT IN *MALAY MAGIC* ON THE
LANGSUIR OF FOLKLORE

There is a popular superstition about the Langsuir [a kind of vampire] thus described by Sir William Maxwell:

"If a woman dies in childbirth, either before delivery or after the birth of a child, and before the forty days of uncleanness have expired, she is popularly supposed to become a *langsuyar*, a flying demon of the nature of the "white lady" or "banshee." To prevent this a quantity of glass beads are put in the mouth of the corpse, a hen's egg is put under each armpit, and needles are placed in the palms of the hands. It is believed that if this is done the dead woman cannot become a *langsuyar*, as she cannot open her mouth to shriek or wave her arms as wings, or open and shut her hands to assist her flight."

The superstitions about the Langsuir (whose embodiment is supposed to be a kind of night-owl) describe a woman of dazzling beauty who died from the shock of hearing that her child was stillborn. On hearing this terrible news, she "clapped her hands," and without further warning "flew whinnying away to a tree, upon which she perched." She may be identified by her robe of green, by her tapering nails of extraordinary length (a mark of beauty), and by the long jet-black tresses, which she allows to fall down to her ankles—only, alas! in order to conceal the hole in the back of her neck through which she sucks the blood of children! These vampire-like proclivities of hers may, however, be successfully combated if the right means are adopted, for if you are able to catch her, cut short her nails and luxuriant tresses, and stuff them into the hole in her neck, she will become tame and indistinguishable from an ordinary woman, remaining so for years. Cases have been known, indeed, in which she has become a wife and a mother, until she was allowed to dance at a village merry-making, when she at once reverted to her ghostly form, and flew off into the dark and gloomy forest from whence she came.

GOING IT ALONE

You do not need to have a partner to be able to play the sex magic game (as the title of J. G. Hughes' *Celtic Sex Magic for Couples, Groups, and Solitary Practitioners* makes clear). In fact, people without partners seem to be the most likely to turn to sex magic. Figures.

READING ABOUT IT

Garland Publishers always offer well-researched books and one of their recent titles is *Witchcraft, Magic, and Demonology*. Also see Weiser Books' *The Well-Read Witch*, Routledge's *Witchcraft Reader*, university press books such as *Hopi Stories of Witchcraft, Shamanism, and Magic* (from Nebraska), and Omnigraphics' reprint of Thomas Wright's *Narratives of Sorcery and Magic, from the Most Authentic Authors*. Online and print bibliographies can keep you current in this department and you will be enlightened if you can keep clear of trashy "erotic" stuff about vampires and other sleazy wastes of time.

FOREIGN LANGUAGE BOOKS

Anand, Margo. *O Arte da magia sexual* [The Art of Sex Magic] (1996, Portuguese translation)
Ashley, Leonard R. N. *Die Welt der Magie* [The World of Magic] (1988, German translation)
Bulit, Faik. *Islam'da cinsel büyüler* [Islamic Spirit Witches] (1998, Turkish)
Del Río, Martin Antoine. *La magía demoniaca* [Demonic Magic] (reprinted 1978)
King, Francis. *Ésoterisme et sexualité* [The Esoteric and Sexuality] (1974, French translation)
Lignières, Jean. *Les messes noir* [Black Masses] (1928)
——— & Guilliermo Hipkiss. *La mágia sexual . . . missas negras . . . y el satanismo* [Sex Magic . . . Black Masses. and Satanism] (1929?)
Magali, Adriana. *Magia amatoria* [Love Magic] (2000)
McCormack, Kathleen. *Los astros y el amor* [The Stars and Love] (1990)
Quezada, Noemi. *Amor y mágia amotoso entre los aztecas* [Love and Sex Magic Among The Aztecs] (1984)
Rubenstein, Jacques. *Mes recettes magiques . . .* [My Magic Recipes] (1976)
Sperandio, Eric Pier & Marc-André Ricard. *La Magie blanche* [White Magic] (2001)
Torres, Jorge. *Mágia y santería* [Magic and Santería] (1975)
Verbeek, Yves. *La sexualité dans la magie* [Sex in Magic] (1978)

SOME RECENT STUDIES

The following contain material you will be interested in:

Ashley, Leonard R. N. *The Complete Book of Devils and Demons* (Barricade Books, 1996)
———. *The Complete Book of the Devil's Disciples* (Barricade Books, 1996)
———. *The Complete Book of Spells, Curses, and Magical Recipes* (Barricade Books, 1997)
———. *The Complete Book of Vampires* (Barricade Books, 1998)
———. *The Complete Book of Werewolves* (Barricade Books, 2001)
Clark, Stuart. *The Language of Witchcraft* (St. Martin's Press, 2000)
Craven, Amanda. *Sex Magic* (2000)
Eason, Cassandra. *A Magical Guide to Love & Sex* (Crossing Press, 2001)
Gardner, Athena. *Witchcraft Dictionary of Craft Terms* (Star Rising Publications, 2000)
Gray, Deborah. *How to Turn Your Boyfriend into a Love Slave* (HarperSanFrancisco, 2001)

Hughes, John G. *Celtic Sex Magic* (2001)
Hurwood, B. J. *Passport to the Supernatural: An Occult Compendium from All Ages and Many Lands* (Taplinger Publishers, 1972—there are many later books but this is mentioned to remind you that some old anthologies, encyclopedias, etc., contain materials that are not repeated even in this highly incestuous genre)
Pickering, David. *Cassell's Dictionary of Witchcraft* (Continuum International Publishing Group, 1998)
Random House Value Publications Staff, *Illustrated Guide to Witchcraft* (Random House, 1998)
Roséan, Lexa. *The Supermarket Sorceress's Sexy Hexes* (St. Martin's Press, 1997)
Shual, Keton. *Sexual Magick* (Mandrake of Oxford Books, 1995)
Tyson, Donald. *Sexual Alchemy* (Llewellyn Publications, 2000)

ON THE WORLDWIDE WEB

If you try "sex and magic" on *Google* you will get a great many pages of information. You will have to weed out the Red Hot Chili Peppers' album, and comments on the sex life of Magic Johnson, the ads for sex toys and such, the discussions of "the magic of sex" (which is by no means the same thing as "sex magic"), the information on sex shops in such unlikely places as Manaus, Brazil, not to mention the kooks. But if you persist you will find dozens of sites in sex magic, a couple on Crowley, at least one each for Jack Parsons and for "Dion Fortune," chat rooms, sample bits from books someone is anxious to peddle, this guy's serious lecture on the topic and that guy's off-the-top-of-his-head ramblings ("back when I was a freshman"), Omphalos and much, much more. You can also *Yahoo!* Check other search facilities as well. You probably will find some gold among the dross.

Books are more effectively searched under amazon.com or other on-line bookstores, but on The Web you can get in touch with fellow enthusiasts for anything at all—even sex magic. Some are sensible and some are off the wall. Topics range from black magic(k) to Tantric sex, the *Kama Sutra*, and numerology (at least one site deals with choosing sexual partners because of the numerology of their names). There is the history of sex magic as well as people devoted to it today (or tonight). Look for the oddball kind of thing space has prevented me from getting to in this book, Pan, for example.

On The Web you also will run into tacky toys (Hitachi "Magic Wand," read: dildo) and at the other extreme (*logosresourcepages.org*): "Sex magic is filthy and gross beyond words and involves child abuse, bestiality, sodomy, etc. You will never have a normal satisfying sex life once you. . . ." Click!

INDEX